THE BOOK OF SYNONYMS

THE BOOK OF SYNONYMS

Oliver Stonor

CITADEL PRESS SECAUCUS, N.J.

Second American printing, 1982

Published by Citadel Press
A division of Lyle Stuart Inc.
120 Enterprise Ave., Secaucus, N.J. 07094
Manufactured in the United States of America
ISBN 0-8065-0820-5 — *hardcover*
ISBN 0-8065-0191-X — *paperbound*

To

ERIC PARTRIDGE

Master of Words

and friend to all who study them,

in affection and admiration

CONTENTS

INTRODUCTION

> 'When *I* use a word,' Humpty Dumpty said in rather a scornful tone, 'it means just what I choose it to mean – neither more nor less.'
>
> 'The question is,' said Alice, 'whether you *can* make words mean different things.'
>
> 'The question is,' said Humpty Dumpty, 'which is to be master – that's all.'

TWO WORDS that have exactly the same meaning and can, in fact, be substituted for each other without altering in any way the sense of the passage in which they occur, are perfect synonyms, and there are very few of them in English. Indeed, H. W. Fowler, in his *Modern English Usage*, goes so far as to list only *gorse* and *furze* in this category; and even then it seems probable that this is a case where the district you hail from decides the word you use. There is, however, another pair of perfect synonyms which illustrates much better the nature of the problem that a book of this kind is designed to solve: and those are the words *china* and *porcelain* – words meaning precisely the same, interchangeable without any alteration of the sense, and yet possessing functions that are totally distinct, since *china* is the everyday term and *porcelain* that which is used by the specialist – the connoisseur, the auctioneer. If we keep this instance constantly in mind, we shall have gone some little way towards understanding the true nature of synonymy, which, as well as dealing with fine distinctions of meaning, is also very often concerned with appropriateness, with using the right word in a particular context.

Since, however, perfect synonyms are few, it is inevitable that a book of this kind should chiefly be concerned with the very much larger number of imperfect or loose synonyms which can, rather roughly, be defined as words that may be substituted for one another in certain contexts, but not in others. When, for instance, we say of a certain word that it has two *meanings* or two *senses*, *meaning* and *sense* are, in this context, synonymous. It is obvious, however, that if we alter our context and say that so-and-so is a man of *sense*, it is not at all the same as saying he is a man of *meaning*, which, in fact, is a phrase without meaning. Imperfect synonyms, then, are of this nature: depending upon how they are used, upon the contexts in which they are employed, they can range from complete equivalence, through loose approximation, to total differentiation. In this circumstance lies both their fascination and the need for handling them with caution and circumspection.

There are three other technical terms with which it is as well that the student of synonymy should be familiar: words which are alike in spelling but different in their meanings (*e.g. pole* equalling a stick, and the *pole* of a magnet) are called homonyms; those which are pronounced the same but are differently spelt and have different meanings (*e.g. gauge* and *gage*) are called homophones; and those pairs of words which are so precisely opposed in their meanings as completely to nullify or cancel out one another (*e.g. loss : gain*) are called antonyms. It is the purpose of this little book to provide a selection, with definitions, of the commonest English synonyms (which, usually, are imperfect ones) and, where such exist, of the proper antonyms to them. Homonyms and homophones are excluded.

It is, on the whole, a matter for self-congratulation that our English language should be richer than almost any other in synonyms, or rather in partial synonyms; and the reason for this is, of course, not far to seek. It resides in the peculiarly hybrid nature of our language to which, to its original basis of Germanic or Anglo-Saxon, were added, after the Norman Conquest, the Latin or Norman-French elements of our conquerors. And, on top of this, the English, as a seafaring people, have always been great adepts at picking up and naturalizing such alien words as they encountered on their travels. The result of all this was that, for a very long time, there were two if not three parallel streams of language flowing, as it were, side by side and it depended largely upon the social position and education of the speaker which of the streams he would employ. If, for example, he wanted to comment upon a bit of shady dealing, he could use the words *trick*, *device*, *finesse*, *artifice*, or *stratagem*, drawing respectively on the resources of the Dutch (or, as some think, the Old French), the Italian, the French, the Latin, and the Greek tongues. Again, if he wanted to characterize a particular juvenile action, he could call it either *boyish* (which is Germanic) or *puerile* (which is Latin);

expressions which, so far as derivation goes, are precisely equivalent, though in modern use they mean entirely different things, the first having taken over the idea of juvenility in the good sense, the other of juvenility in the bad one.

This existence, over so long a period, of two or more words meaning exactly the same was, naturally enough, a challenge to thoughtful speakers and writers; in the first place, it invited ambiguity, and in the second, it was wasteful. A tendency arose, therefore, among people with a sensitive ear and a superior sense of fitness, to separate, or as we now say to differentiate or discriminate, the meanings of these duplicated terms – quite arbitrary in the beginning, and depending upon the known practice of the best writers and speakers, but crystallizing eventually to accepted and customary use. This tendency was known as desynonymization (a term that we owe to Samuel Taylor Coleridge), and it simply meant that words which, at one time, were identical in meaning were given separate jobs by assigning to them partial though precise shades of significance that were not inherent in their origins. Words once completely interchangeable were thus rendered non-interchangeable, and the language was enriched by a great number of new terms which ensured that it should be at once more accommodating, more flexible, and more precise. This process, which continued with unabated vigour for a very long while, was a practical, unselfconscious and unsystematic one, based upon precedent and example, and it was largely unrecorded save in the pages of our early dictionaries. It was not until the middle of the eighteenth century that the English, inspired by the publication in 1718 of a work on French synonyms by the Abbé Girard, woke up to what was happening, and produced the first of all the many works on English synonymy. It was entitled *The Difference between Words Esteemed Synonymous*; its author was the Rev. John Trusler; and its date 1766.

After this publication similar volumes came thick and fast from the press; a new science, possibly a new art, had been born. In 1794 a somewhat unexpected Richmond entered the field – Mrs Thrale, the friend of Dr Johnson, with her *British Synonymy*; in 1805 came the work of William Perry; in 1813, William Taylor's *English Synonymes Discriminated* (a book that greatly interested Coleridge); and in 1816 appeared the fullest and the most complete of these early studies of the subject – George Crabb's *English Synonymes Explained* – which, under the slightly modified title of *Crabb's English Synonyms* and after numerous revisions, is still in print today.

Throughout the nineteenth century the flood of synonym books did not slacken, to reach at last its present culmination with Webster's great *Dictionary of Synonyms*, a volume of almost a thousand large double-column pages, published in the United States in 1942. This is, as it were, the Everest of the subject; he would be a bold man who could hope to climb higher.

Fortunately, however, the conquest of Everest has not put an end to the pleasures of mountaineering. Though it is obvious that a little book of this kind must be heavily indebted to all its larger and more comprehensive predecessors, it may still perhaps lay claim to a special use and function of its own, which is that it provides a simple guide to all who stand upon the lower slopes of the subject and who, when confronted by one of the commoner groups of synonyms, are uncertain which out of them it is best to use. It is with a reader of this sort in mind that the following pages have been composed, and it is to a reader of this sort that I should wish to present the two vital considerations that here follow:

(1) It is a great mistake to think that a reference-book of this nature can act as an automatic substitute for thought. In order to use the right word in the right place, a sense of the language, a knowledge of derivations, a feeling for fitness, for euphony, are of the utmost importance. In nine cases out of ten, a practised writer of English will use the correct word because of his ear and because of use and wont; it is only in the tenth case that recourse to a reference-book may preserve him from falling into a trap and using the wrong one. It follows then that the best way in which to learn to use words correctly is to study constantly the way in which the best writers have used them. Unintelligent use of aids to writing can lead to nothing but bad writing; in the last resort a man has to consult his own judgment and good sense.

(2) Further, because I have tried to get as many groups as possible of the commoner synonyms into this short book, I have often been obliged to cut the discriminatory definitions to the bone; and brevity in a matter of this kind tends to detract from absolute precision. Therefore, in any case where the reader is doubtful whether he understands my distinctions, I should strongly advise him to follow up the point in either Crabb or Webster, where he will find it made (sometimes though not always) at a very much greater length, though this does not invariably mean with a greater clarity.

A word or so may be required here as to the way in which to use this book. I have tried to include in the alphabetical sequence the commonest, most usual term in each particular group of synonyms, and I have refrained from overloading the text with a host of cross-references to the secondary words in each group. At the end of the book, however, will be found a full Index in which each of these secondary terms is listed in alphabetical order, with an indication of the parent-word in the alphabetical sequence under which it may be found. The parent-words themselves are also included in this Index in a bolder type, but with no reference following them. So, for example, should a synonym be sought for the word *wish*, recourse to the Index will show that it may be found in the alphabetical sequence under the heading *Desire*. The few abbreviations that I have employed may also be found, alphabetically listed and explained, on the page that follows this Introduction.

There remains now only the need to say a little upon synonyms in general, to explain why, though this book is primarily intended as a tool for those who aspire to write precisely, it has also a secondary though no less important function, which is to furnish its user with a fuller understanding of the richness and beauty of that incomparable instrument, the English language. Directly we begin to think of words, as words, which we do the moment we realize that one of them does its job better, in a certain context, than another, we become interested in them and aspire to discover their exact meaning. This, which naturally throws us back upon etymology, the study of the derivations or origins of words, is quite literally a life-work, since we can never hope to learn all there is to be known on the subject. We do, nevertheless, soon begin to develop the faculty of looking at a word quite differently, of trying to track down its former uses, components, connotations; and this, in itself, helps us to be more careful and precise in our own writing, and more discriminating in our enjoyment of the writing of others. It is evident that, when we understand the full meaning and the early history of a term, we are more likely to use it correctly and effectively than if we are only vague about it.

The pages that follow will give us many examples of this. Let us consider, almost at random, the entry under *Forerunner*, where both this word and its synonym, *precursor*, each have exactly the same root-meaning – that of one who runs before. It so happened, however, that the latter word, *precursor*, had early acquired a specialized connection with John the Baptist, the *forerunner* of Jesus, and had consequently added to itself, before anyone had noticed it, the idea of one who prepares the way for a greater than himself; whereas *forerunner* had kept the simpler significance of anything which announces or presages what is to come. *Harbinger*, likewise, deriving from the Old French term for one who precedes his master to secure lodging and shelter for him, is a word that carries within itself suggestions of pomp and colour and joyfulness, so that when Milton writes of 'the bright morning star, day's *harbinger*' we at once feel the fitness of his choice; whereas *herald*, with its linked associations of tabards and trumpets, suggests a proclamation of future happenings still more colourful and stirring.

Or again; reflect upon the word *fool*, with its two distinct significances of a stupid person and of a professed clown. Think of the distance the world has travelled since an *imbecile* was, in Latin, *imbaculum*, one too foolish, weak, or imprudent to grasp a staff in his hand; or when *idiotes*, in Greek, meant a private person, that is one not holding office, consequently an ignoramus, hence what we call an *idiot*. Think of the lift and colour that Shakespeare's sublime Fools have given to the word *fool*, in its dramatic sense; of how *clown* once meant any rustic (Keats still employed it so in

> The voice I hear this passing night was heard
> In ancient days by emperor and *clown*),

and has now come to mean only the gaping and bedizened buffoon of the circus or the pantomime; of how *harlequin*, coming from the Italian *arlecchino*, links up with the Early French *herlekin*, a demon or goblin, perhaps from *hellekin*, a devil, or, as we now colloquially say, a *heller*; of how, finally, *zany* derives straight from Zanni, the Venetian-dialect diminutive of Giovanni, John; John being, it would appear, the Venetian equivalent of a merry-andrew.

So one could go on. There are endless instances of the same fine shifts and gradations of meaning, instances which cause both writer and reader alike of books such as these to become passionately aware of the living significance of words, which (to adapt Milton's great pronouncement upon books – themselves no more than vast aggregations of words) 'are not absolutely dead things, but do contain a potency of life in them to be as active as that soul whose progeny they are; nay, they do preserve as in a vial the purest efficacy and extraction of that living intellect that bred them . . . They are as lively, and as vigorously productive, as those fabulous dragons' teeth; and being sown up and down, may chance to spring up armed men'.

Fowler, writing of synonymy-books in general, says, with what one cannot but fear is partial truth, that 'engrossing as they may have been to the active party, the analyst, [they] offer to the passive party, nothing but boredom'. It is in the hope of avoiding this imputation that I have ventured to invoke Milton's great dictum; because it seems to me that, if these pages are studied in the light of what he there says, something of this charge of tedium may be repelled. If my readers, in addition to using this book as a practical aid to composition, will from time to time dip into it in a spirit of disinterested curiosity, I hope they may find herein evidences of the truth of the saying that words 'are not absolutely dead things' and will so come to appreciate better the strength, the beauty, and the illimitable resources of our ancient tongue.

It is said that with a vocabulary of some fifteen hundred words a man can get through life in England pretty well, and this is perfectly true, as far as it goes. It is equally true, however, that a larger knowledge of words, of their shades and gradations of meaning, is a faculty which enriches a man beyond all others. Not only does it make him free of the greatest literature in the world, it makes him also the fellow of the immortals, for it ensures that he shall see, looming everywhere through the veil of the present, the mighty shadows of his predecessors. If this book helps a little to achieve such an end, my 'engrossing' labours (see Fowler) will not have been wholly in vain.

ABBREVIATIONS

adj.	adjective	*cf.*	compare
adv.	adverb	*ety.*	etymology, or etymologically
Amer.	American	*Lat.*	Latin
ant.	antonym	*n.*	noun
Br.	British	*v.*	verb

N.B. The antonyms supplied on the pages that follow are antonyms only of the parent-word in each group. They are not necessarily antonyms of the various synonyms that follow the parent-word.

A

ABANDON, DESERT, FORSAKE, RELINQUISH, though not precise synonyms, all imply the separation of self from something external to self. A man *abandons* his wife; *deserts* his post; *forsakes* his religion; *relinquishes* his appointment: examples which illustrate the relative strengths of the various terms.
ANT. **Reclaim.**

ABASE, DEGRADE, DISGRACE, HUMBLE, HUMILIATE. One *abases* one's self before God; *humbles* one's self before one's fellow-men; both actions not necessarily devoid of merit. On the other hand, one is *degraded* by improper conduct, which often leads to one's being *disgraced* in the eyes of others. To *humiliate* a person is to lower him in his own esteem and is seldom regarded as a meritorious action.
ANT. **Exalt.**

ABATE, DECREASE, DIMINISH, LESSEN. Whereas *abate* suggests the idea of a progressive dying down of a powerful force, such as a storm, *lessen* and *diminish* are more precisely quantitative, the former being seldom used intransitively, the latter suggesting a more elevated context. A *decrease* implies a process the result of which is a *diminution*: *decrease* the taxes and revenue *diminishes.*
ANT. **Augment; Intensify.**

ABILITY, CAPABILITY, CAPACITY. *Ability* is the undifferentiated power of doing; *capacity,* a special sort of *ability*: the *ability* to pay means one has the money; the *capacity* to do so, that one has the earning-power. *Capability* implies the possession of those qualities necessary to perform a particular action.
ANT. **Inability.**

ABJURE, RECANT, RETRACT, REVOKE. One *abjures* one's solemnly professed beliefs; *recants* them because of threats or pressure; *retracts* a promise; *revokes* a decree or an ordinance.
ANT. **Pledge.**

ABOLISH, ABROGATE, ANNUL, REPEAL. To *abolish* is to put a final end to something; but laws are *abrogated* or *repealed*: *repeal* implies constitutional action, *abrogation* often, though not invariably, despotic force. To *annul* is to render invalid by legal process that which has once existed, as a marriage or a statute.
ANT. **Establish.**

ABOVE, OVER, UPON. *Over* is that which is vertically *above*; and that which is *upon* rests on that which is beneath.
ANT. **Below.**

ABSOLUTE, ARBITRARY, DESPOTIC, TYRANNICAL. *Absolute* signifies absolved from all restraint; a monarch is said to be *absolute* in his own nature; he behaves *despotically* in relation to his subjects. *Arbitrary* is similar to *absolute* but adds a suggestion of caprice; and *tyrannical* implies an oppressive exercise of *despotic* power.
ANT. **Limited.**

ABSORB, ENGROSS, ENGULF, IMBIBE. Blotting-paper *absorbs*; earthquakes *engulf*; more abstract matters *engross*, as when one speaker *engrosses* the conversation. *Imbibe*, which commonly means to drink, can also, in a more trivial sense, carry the common swallowing-up connotation of all these words.
ANT. **Exude.**

ABUSE, MISUSE. A thing *abused* is injured thereby; if *misused* it is used for the wrong reasons or not used at all.
ANT. **Use.**

ABUSE, INVECTIVE. By transference, the use of harsh words, likely to cause injury, is called *abuse*; *invective* is more generally used of written *abuse*, and there is, moreover, some suggestion that it may be justified. It is also stronger.
ANT. **Adulation.**

ACCIDENTAL, ADVENTITIOUS, CASUAL, CONTINGENT, FORTUITOUS, INCIDENTAL. The *accidental* is what happens by chance; the *casual*, without pre-arrangement; the *fortuitous*, without a cause or apparent cause; and the *contingent* is the unpredictable. The *incidental* is the non-essential and is thus synonymous with the secondary meaning of *accidental* as opposed to *essential*; the *adventitious* is also something lacking in essential connection that has been added as an afterthought.
ANT. **Planned; Essential.**

ACCOMPANY, ATTEND, CONDUCT, CONVOY, ESCORT. *Accompany* suggests companionship; *attend*, accompaniment by a subordinate; but *conduct* implies guiding or leading. To *escort* is to protect as one *conducts*; to *convoy* was originally to *escort* by sea, though the use has now been extended to military escorts on land.

ACCOUNT (1), BILL, STATEMENT. An *account* in this sense is a periodic or running reckoning of money owed; a *statement* is the record of it; and a *bill* is a demand for its payment.

ACCOUNT (2), CHRONICLE, REPORT, STORY. An *account* in this sense is a verbal or written statement of events; a *report* is such *account* transmitted by one or more persons to others; a *chronicle* is a lengthy and detailed *account* or *report*, especially of historical events; a *story* is a statement of events which may or may not be true.

ACCUSE, ARRAIGN, **CHARGE**, IMPEACH, INCRIMINATE, INDICT. *Accuse* is the common and comprehensive term; to *charge* is to *accuse* formally of a serious offence; to *indict* is to *charge* before a jury or persons acting as such; to *incriminate* is to *charge* with a crime; to *impeach* is, technically, to bring a criminal charge against a public official; to *arraign* is to *charge* formally in a court of law.
ANT. **Exculpate.**

ACKNOWLEDGE, ADMIT, CONFESS, OWN. To *acknowledge*, in this sense, is to disclose something contrary to one's own advantage; to *admit* is to make such disclosure under pressure; to *own* is a weaker form of to *acknowledge*: *e.g.* He *owned* he was wrong. To *confess* is, properly, to *admit* formally that one has done wrong or held erroneous moral views.
ANT. **Deny.**

ACRIMONY, ACERBITY, ASPERITY, all agree in suggesting irritation and resentment in word and deed. *Acrimony* implies bitterness; *acerbity*, sourness added to bitterness; *asperity*, harshness or roughness.
ANT. **Suavity.**

ACT *v*. (1), BEHAVE, FUNCTION, OPERATE, REACT, WORK, all relate to the way in which a thing or person responds to circumstances. *Act* is the most general; *behave* applies to persons and their conduct; *work*, *operate* and *function* all mean to *act* in a way that is right and reasonable. *Work*, however, in this sense, suggests total effectiveness; *operate*, efficiency rather than absolute effectiveness; and *function*, accomplishment of the purpose for which the thing was made. *React*, properly to recoil or rebound, is now often used as though it were a full synonym of *act* or *behave*.

ACT *v*. (2), IMPERSONATE, PLAY. To *act*, in this grouping, usually implies playing a part on the stage; to *play* has generally the same meaning, though it can also be used figuratively, as when one '*plays* a part'. To *impersonate* is to imitate someone else, whether on the stage or off it, the latter often illegally.

ACTION, ACT, DEED. An *act* is a single exercise of power; *action*, a continued one. A *deed* refers to an *act* that is completed, and whereas *act* relates more closely to the power exerted, *deed* stresses the operation performed.

ACTIVE, DYNAMIC, LIVE, OPERATIVE, all mean in effective action, but *active* is the general term, and *operative* is confined to such abstractions as principles or laws. *Dynamic* stresses the potential qualities which belong to the *active* body; *live*, in this connotation, stresses vitality and modernity – *cf.* 'a *live* wire'.
ANT. **Inactive.**

ADD (1), CAST, SUM, TOTAL. *Add* is the usual term; *sum* refers more to the result than to the process of addition; *total* does so exclusively. To *cast*, or *cast up*, is a colloquial version of to *add*.

ADD (2), ANNEX, APPEND, SUBJOIN. *Add* is again the common term; to *append* is to *add* something that is not an integral part of the

principal thing involved; to *annex* is to *add* a subsidiary item; to *subjoin* is to *add* an afterthought, a postscript.
ANT. **Subtract; Deduct.**

ADDRESS, ACCOST, GREET, HAIL, SALUTE. *Address* suggests a formal approach; *accost*, a bold and sometimes impudent one. *Greet* is friendly; *salute*, ceremonious; *hail* implies a certain ebullience, as when one *hails* an acquaintance or a cab.

ADJACENT, ABUTTING, ADJOINING, CONTIGUOUS, JUXTAPOSED, all mean in close proximity. *Adjacent* things are near one another though they need not touch; *adjoining* ones must touch at some point; *contiguous* ones touch over a considerable portion of their perimeter. If one thing is *abutting* another it borders it along at least one edge; things which are *juxtaposed* are placed alongside one another for purposes of comparison.
ANT. **Non-adjacent.**

ADMISSION, ADMITTANCE. *Admission* is the more general term; *admittance* is now confined to the sense of letting in: 'no *admittance*'. On the other hand, one 'pays for *admission*'.

ADORN, BEAUTIFY, DECK, DECORATE, EMBELLISH, ORNAMENT. To *adorn* is to add a final touch to what is already well-looking; to *decorate* is to add adornment to what is plain; to *ornament* is to add small detailed decorations with a view to enhancing the effect; to *embellish* is to add ornament, sometimes to an excessive degree; to *beautify* may involve either gilding the lily or disguising the ugly; to *deck* usually implies more than a trace of ostentation.
ANT. **Disfigure.**

ADVANCE *v.*, FORWARD, FURTHER, PROMOTE, all mean to move, or cause to move, ahead; but whereas *advance* is the common term, *promote* emphasizes more strongly the idea of assistance than of the effect produced. *Forward* is used in connection with things rather than persons; and *further* is generally applied to such abstractions as aims and desires, and stresses the removal of obstacles rather than the idea of positive progress.
ANT. **Retard; Check.**

ADVENTUROUS, DARING, FOOLHARDY, RASH, RECKLESS, TEMERARIOUS, VENTURESOME. Adventures, as d'Israeli says, are to the *adventurous*; *venturesome* suggests an excessive tendency in the same direction. *Daring* implies fearlessness; *rash*, imprudence; *reckless*, heedlessness. The *temerarious* is reckless to the point of undertaking forlorn hopes; the *foolhardy* is foolishly daring.
ANT. **Unadventurous; Cautious.**

ADVERSE, ANTAGONISTIC, AVERSE, COUNTER. The *adverse* is the contrary; the *antagonistic*, the hostile; *counter* suggests moving in the opposite direction though without the idea of hostility. *Averse*, on the other hand, is not a synonym for the other words in this group; it implies

repugnance and so brings in the notion of feeling, which is absent from the term *adverse*.
ANT. **Propitious.**

ADVICE, COUNSEL. The latter is stronger than the former, and suggests that the person giving it really knows his subject.

AFFAIR, BUSINESS, CONCERN, MATTER, THING are all vague terms meaning something done or dealt with. *Affair* suggests action; we speak of a 'man of *affairs*'. *Business* relates to duty or office; *concern*, to a personal interest. *Matter* is vaguer still; *thing*, vaguest of all: *e.g.* 'The *matter* shall be attended to; *things* will soon be better'.

AFFECT, IMPRESS, INFLUENCE, STRIKE, SWAY, TOUCH, all mean to exert an effect, but *affect* implies a more or less powerful stimulus, and *influence* a weaker one. *Touch* suggests an emotional reaction; *impress*, a vigorous one; *strike* is a colloquial version of *impress*; and *sway* suggests vacillation produced by the given stimulus.

AFFLICT, TORMENT, TORTURE, TRY. A small infliction *tries* us; a greater *afflicts* us; a greater still *torments* us. *Torture* in this grouping is stronger than *torment*.
ANT. **Comfort.**

AFTER, BEHIND. *After* refers to order, *behind* to position; and whereas *after* may be used literally or figuratively, *behind* can only be used literally.
ANT. **Before.**

ALL, EACH, EVERY. *All* is collective: *all* men are mortal. *Every* refers to each separate member of the collective group: *every* man is mortal. *Each* resembles *every* except that it refers to every member of the group as a separate entity: *each* of us is aware of his mortality.
ANT. **No.**

ALLIANCE, COALITION, CONFEDERATION, FUSION, UNION, LEAGUE, all suggest combination for political ends. *Union*, the most general term, implies creating a single entity out of several diverse bodies; a *confederation* is a *union* in which each of the participants surrenders some of his individual rights to a central authority, while yet retaining his separate identity. An *alliance* is a combination for mutual benefit of two or more sovereign states or other units; a *league* suggests a more formal combination; a *coalition* is usually a temporary *alliance* of states, or of opposed parties within a state, formed to deal with some specific emergency. A *fusion*, in this grouping, is the merging together of two or more political parties with the loss of individual identity.

ALLOT, ALLOCATE, APPORTION, ASSIGN. To *allot* is to share out haphazard; to *assign*, to do so according to some rational principles; to *apportion*, to do so upon an equitable basis; and to *allocate* is to earmark a definite share for some special person or purpose.

ALONE, DESOLATE, FORLORN, LONELY, SOLITARY. *Alone* means simply that one is unaccompanied; *solitary* adds the sense of isolation and remoteness; *lonely*, that one is unhappy in that condition;

forlorn, that one is cast down because of it. *Desolate* is the strongest term of all and implies a high degree of unhappiness.
ANT. **Accompanied.**

ALSO, BESIDES, FURTHERMORE, LIKEWISE, MOREOVER, TOO are all used when adding one proposition to another. *Too* is the least formal; *also* joins propositions of equal weight; *likewise* is both more formal and more explicit than *also*. *Besides* usually adds a statement which strengthens what has gone before; *moreover* is more emphatic than *besides*; *furthermore* introduces the pinnacle, as it were, of a chain of such cumulative propositions.

AMBASSADOR, ENVOY, LEGATE, MINISTER, NUNCIO. An *ambassador* is a diplomatic officer of the highest rank, resident in a foreign country; a *minister* is a similar officer of lower rank; an *envoy* is much the same in status as a *minister*, but the term is usually confined to a *minister* employed on a special occasion and non-resident. A *legate* is a papal *envoy*; a *nuncio* is a papal *ambassador*.

AMIABLE, COMPLAISANT, GOOD-NATURED, OBLIGING. *Amiable* implies the desire to please; *good-natured*, to please and be pleased; *obliging* stresses a readiness to help; *complaisant* (not to be confused with *complacent*), a disposition to be agreeable, sometimes to save trouble.
ANT. **Unamiable; Surly.**

AMUSE, DIVERT, ENTERTAIN, RECREATE. To *amuse* is to engage the attention with anything it deems pleasing; to *divert* is to distract the attention so that one forgets graver issues; to *entertain* is to *amuse* or *divert* others; to *recreate* is to *amuse* by a change of occupation.
ANT. **Bore.**

ANGER *n.*, FURY, INDIGNATION, RAGE, WRATH. *Anger* is the general term; *rage* adds to *anger* the suggestion of loss of self-control; *fury* is violent *rage*. *Indignation* suggests righteous *rage*; *wrath* is an altogether loftier term: we speak of the *wrath* of God, or of nature; *wrath* in humans adds to *rage* the suggestion of desiring to punish.
ANT. **Forbearance.**

ANGER *v.*, ENRAGE, INCENSE, INFURIATE, MADDEN. *Anger* is again the common term; *incense* implies a hot, quick burst of *anger*; *enrage*, a violent display of fury; *infuriate*, exasperation beyond endurance; *madden* is loosely used to mean anything from the infuriating to the merely vexatious.
ANT. **Please; Pacify.**

ANGRY, ACRIMONIOUS, INDIGNANT, IRATE, WRATHFUL. *Angry* is the general term; *irate* is applied only to persons and rather suggests constitutional testiness; *indignant* implies justifiable or righteous anger; *wrathful* is stronger than *indignant* and has loftier connotations (see **ANGER** *n.*). *Acrimonious* adds to *angry* the idea of protracted contention and mutual bitterness.
ANT. **Good-tempered.**

ANIMADVERSION, ASPERSION, REFLECTION, STRICTURE, all, in this grouping, imply adverse criticism. A *stricture* is one which may or may not be justified; an *animadversion* is one grounded in malice; an *aspersion* is one that verges upon slander; a *reflection*, in this sense, is usually an *aspersion* indirectly or covertly made.
ANT. **Commendation.**

ANIMAL, BEAST, BRUTE are synonyms when used to mean creatures other than man: *animal* has the fewest overtones; *beast* emphasizes the kinship between man and animals; *brute*, the difference between them.

ANNUAL, ANNIVERSARY, YEARLY are synonymous when they refer to things occurring once a year; but whereas *anniversary* is linked to one special day in the year, *annual* and *yearly* can also take in the year as a whole, as when we speak of *yearly* or *annual* income. *Annual*, however, can differ from *yearly* by defining things that last for one year only: *e.g. annual* plants, or parliaments.
ANT. **Perennial.**

ANSWER, REJOINDER, REPLY, RESPONSE, RETORT, all imply that a question has been asked. *Answer* is the general term; a *response* is a willing *answer*; a *reply* is a complete and efficacious one; a *rejoinder* is, strictly, an *answer* to an *answer*; a *retort* is a swift and militant *answer*, as when one rebuts an accusation.

APOLOGY, EXCUSE, PLEA, PRETEXT. We make an *apology* when we think we are at fault; an *excuse* when we wish to escape the consequences of our fault. A *plea* is an appeal for sympathy and understanding; a *pretext* suggests the substitution of a false for the true reason for our conduct.

APPARENT, ILLUSORY, OSTENSIBLE, SEEMING. *Apparent* is used when the senses tell us one story and the intellect another; *illusory*, when a false impression of this kind derives from our imperfect vision; the *seeming* is that which so much resembles the real thing that we mistake the one for the other; *ostensible* is used when the true reason for a thing is different from that which is professed or proclaimed.
ANT. **Real.**

APPEARANCE, ASPECT, LOOK, SEMBLANCE. *Appearance* applies more usually to abstract things; *look* or *looks* only to concrete ones. *Aspect* alludes literally to facial expressions, and figuratively to superficial *appearances*; *semblance*, a seeming, applies to false or illusory *appearances*.

APPRECIATE, CHERISH, PRIZE, TREASURE, VALUE. To *appreciate* is to esteem with discrimination; to *value* is to esteem highly; to *prize*, as one's own personal possession; to *treasure* is to regard as singularly precious. To *cherish* suggests a more emotional attachment, akin to love.
ANT. **Despise.**

APPREHEND, COMPREHEND. To *apprehend* is to grasp or understand partially; to *comprehend*, fully: a child *apprehends* many things which, in later life, after reflection, he *comprehends*.

APPROBATION, APPROVAL. *Approval* is a weaker thing than *approbation*: if we *approve* a plan we sanction its execution; if we give it our *approbation* we regard it enthusiastically.
ANT. **Disapprobation.**

APT, LIABLE, LIKELY are words subject to confusion when followed by *to* and an infinitive. *Apt* implies tendency and predisposition; *likely*, probability in the future; and *liable*, possible exposure to some risk or undesirable thing. So, if we are *apt* to oversleep, we are *likely* some day to lose our train, and become *liable* to get into hot water when we meet our employer.

ARGUMENT, CONTROVERSY, DISPUTE. *Argument* stresses the use of reason in a discussion; *dispute*, the contentiousness of the parties engaged in it. A *controversy* is usually an *argument* over a specific question carried on at a fairly high level.

ART, ARTIFICE, CRAFT, CUNNING, SKILL. *Art*, in this grouping, implies technical knowledge and mastery; *skill* stresses the manual dexterity necessary for such activity; *cunning*, as here considered, though now inclined to be archaic, adds to *skill* a suggestion of intellectual power. *Artifice* suggests technical ability without much creative power; *craft* refers to a lower level of technical achievement than *art*.

ASK (1), REQUEST, both precede the hoped-for granting of favours, but *request* is more formal and courteous than *ask*.

ASK (2), CATECHIZE, ENQUIRE, EXAMINE, INTERROGATE, QUESTION, all precede the hoped-for giving of information. *Ask* is the general, most neutral, term; *question* suggests the asking of a series of questions; and *interrogate*, a formal questioning. *Catechize* adds to *interrogate* the ideas of repetition and of requiring a specific answer; *enquire*, of wanting a true answer; *examine* suggests prolonged interrogation for the purpose of evaluating the person questioned.

ASSENT *v.*, ACCEDE, ACQUIESCE, AGREE, CONSENT, SUBSCRIBE, all embody the idea of concurrence with the views of another: one *assents* to intellectual propositions; *consents* in everyday matters; in neither case does the word necessarily imply approval. To *accede* is to grant one's *assent* under pressure; to *acquiesce* stresses doing so without opposition; to *agree* is to do so after discussion; to *subscribe* is to agree wholeheartedly.
ANT. **Dissent.**

ASSERT, AFFIRM, AVOW, DECLARE, PROTEST, WARRANT, all mean to state positively. To *assert* is to do so without advancing any proof of the fact stated; to *declare* is to *assert* publicly; to *affirm* is to base one's assertions upon one's own private convictions; to *protest* is to state emphatically despite contradiction; to *avow* is to state upon one's personal responsibility. To *warrant*, in this sense, equals 'to guarantee'.
ANT. **Deny.**

ASSUME, AFFECT, COUNTERFEIT, FEIGN, PRETEND, SIMULATE, all mean to put on a false appearance. To *assume* is to take on a character not really one's own; to *affect* is to *assume* a certain air to produce a certain effect; to *pretend* is to profess what is untrue; to *feign* is to enhance such pretences with physical imitations; to *simulate* is to carry *feigning* to its highest point. To *counterfeit* is to attempt exact imitation, as false coins *counterfeit* true ones.

ATTACK, ASSAIL, ASSAULT. *Attack* is the general term; to *assail* (literally to jump on) nowadays suggests *attack* by repeated minor blows; *assault*, by brute strength and extreme violence.

ATTEMPT *v.*, ENDEAVOUR, ESSAY, STRIVE, STRUGGLE, TRY. To *attempt* is to begin something one hopes to achieve; to *try* is to experiment whether such achievement is possible. To *endeavour* suggests repeated and energetic *attempts*; to *essay* is to *try* something especially difficult; and to *strive* and *struggle* both imply *attempts* made in the face of much opposition: we *strive*, roughly speaking, against that caused by our own deficiencies, and *struggle* against that coming from outside ourselves.
ANT. **Succeed.**

ATTENTION, APPLICATION, CONCENTRATION, STUDY. *Attention* is the power of focussing the mind; continuous and close *attention* is *study*; the centring of the *attention* upon one thing to the exclusion of others is *concentration*; general diligence in controlling the *attention* is *application.*
ANT. **Inattention.**

ATTRACT, ALLURE, BEWITCH, CAPTIVATE, CHARM, ENCHANT, FASCINATE. *Attract* implies a physical drawing, as by a magnet; *allure*, drawing by visual attraction, which, for some reason, gives the word a derogatory connotation. *Charm* suggests the casting of a spell; *fascinate*, that the spell is virtually irresistible; *bewitch* and *enchant* mean much the same, but in certain contexts may not mean much more than that a strong attraction exists. *Captivate* is a weaker but more reasonable expression for the same sort of thing.
ANT. **Repel.**

AUTHENTIC, GENUINE, VERITABLE. The *authentic* carries the idea of authority; the *genuine*, of truth: an *authentic* picture is one painted from the life; a *genuine* one is the indubitable work of its alleged creator. *Veritable* implies a strong assertion of belief, but has generally fallen upon evil days, in the sense that (in English, at any rate) it now seems to protest a little too fervently.
ANT. **Spurious.**

AUXILIARY, ACCESSORY, ANCILLARY, CONTRIBUTORY, SUBSIDIARY, all mean supplying help; but, unlike the *auxiliary*, the *subsidiary* and the *ancillary* suggest subordinate or inferior status in the helper. *Subsidiary* derives from the Latin word for reserve troops, *ancillary* from the Latin word for a handmaid, and these origins are still reflected in the proper use of each term. *Contributory*, on the other hand, stresses the assistance given rather than the status of the giver; and in *accessory* the suggestion of association is so strong that the notion of helping is somewhat obscured.

AVENGE, REVENGE. Generally speaking, one *revenges* the wrongs supposed to have been done to oneself; and *avenges* those supposed to have been done to others.

AWARE, ALIVE, COGNIZANT, CONSCIOUS, SENSIBLE, all mean to have knowledge of. We are *aware* of what we observe; *cognizant* of what we know; *conscious* of what we apprehend; *sensible* of what we feel. We are *alive* to that of which we are acutely *sensible*.
ANT. **Unaware.**

AWKWARD, CLUMSY, GAUCHE, INEPT. The *awkward* is that which it is difficult to handle; the *clumsy*, that which is ponderously constructed; the *inept* is the inappropriate, the wrong thing for the given time. *Gauche* (*ety.* left-handed) suggests a lack of social grace, leading both to *clumsiness* and *ineptitude*.
ANT. **Handy; Deft.**

B

BAD (1), EVIL, ILL, WICKED. *Bad* is the common term, *evil* implies greater moral obliquity and has sinister implications, *e.g.* 'the *evil* eye'. *Ill* as a synonym of *evil* occurs chiefly in such idioms as *ill* temper, *ill* nature; *wicked* in its true sense implies the breach of some specific moral law.
ANT. **Good.**

BAD (2), POOR, WRONG are, in this grouping, roughly equivalent to unsatisfactory. We speak of a *bad* workman; a *poor* crop; something *wrong*. The right word here depends largely upon the context.
ANT. **Good.**

BANISH, DEPORT, EXILE, EXPATRIATE, EXTRADITE, OSTRACIZE, TRANSPORT, all originally meant to remove a person, by an act of authority, from where he is. To *banish* is to compel him to leave a country (not necessarily his own) for ever, or for a certain time; to *exile* is to *banish* him from his own country; to *expatriate* is to cause such exile to lose his citizenship, a thing which, however, a man may sometimes choose to do of his own volition. To *ostracize* is nowadays to exclude a person from the society in which he lives, formerly it involved banishment; to *deport* is to send him from a foreign country back to his own; to *transport* is to *banish* him to a penal settlement; to *extradite* is to despatch a suspected criminal back to the country in which he has committed his alleged misdeeds.

BARE, BALD, NAKED, NUDE, all imply the absence of appropriate covering: *bare* suggests the removal of added or superfluous covering; *naked*, of all and every covering; *nude* refers only or chiefly to the *naked* human body; *bald*, to the *naked* or hairless human head, or figuratively to matters that resemble it, *e.g.* 'a *bald* statement'.
ANT. **Covered.**

BASE, BASIS, FOUNDATION, GROUND, GROUNDWORK, all mean that upon which another thing is built or fixed. *Base* is the concrete term; *basis*, the abstract. A *foundation* is a solid, reliable *base*; a *ground* is a substance or surface upon which a second substance is displayed or laid; *groundwork* differs from *foundation* in that it is principally used in the figurative sense, to mean something preparatory to the real work in hand.
ANT. **Top.**

BE, EXIST, LIVE, SUBSIST are synonyms when they mean to have substantial reality. *E.g.* 'When I have fears that I shall cease to *be*'. *Exist* adds to *be* the idea of continuance; *live*, the idea of organized life, the opposite of death, *e.g.* 'Man cannot *live* by bread alone'. *Subsist*, properly, is a species of *existing* which involves the idea of dependence upon something outside oneself (*cf.* the word 'subsistence').

BEAR *v.* (1), PRODUCE, YIELD. *Bear* in this grouping conveys the idea that the fruit or crop is actually carried by that which *bears* it; *produce* is much wider in application, and the fruit of anything, whether actual or figurative, is said to be *produced* by it. *Yield*, on the other hand, means a giving out and so throws the stress more upon the *product* itself than on the *producer*.

BEAR *v.* (2), ABIDE, ENDURE, STAND, SUFFER, TOLERATE, all mean to put up with something unpleasant. *Bear* stresses the ability to put up with it, *e.g.* 'grin and *bear* it'; *suffer*, the acceptance of the unpleasantness, *e.g.* '*suffering* fools gladly'. *Endure* and *abide* relate to protracted trials of this nature, but *abide* emphasizes the patience required, and *endure*, the fortitude. *Tolerate* and *stand* stress the need of overcoming one's own resistance to such trials, but *tolerate* is dignified usage, *stand*, colloquial.

BEAT *v.*, BELABOUR, BUFFET, POUND, THRASH, THRESH. *Beat* is the common term in this group; to *pound* is to *beat* to a pulp, as in a mortar; to *thrash* and *thresh* originally meant to *beat* out the grain from the chaff, a use now confined to the latter, while the former has taken over the meaning of flogging a person. To *buffet* is to *beat* with, or as if with, the open hand; to *belabour* is to heap blows on a person.

BEAUTIFUL, COMELY, FAIR, HANDSOME, LOVELY, PRETTY, PULCHRITUDINOUS. *Beautiful* is the strongest, most abstract, most comprehensive of these terms; *lovely* suggests emotional rather than spiritual appreciation; *handsome*, that the object is viewed with emotional and spiritual detachment; *pretty*, that it pleases by small graces rather than by loftier ones. *Comely* nowadays means little more than wholesome and agreeable; *fair*, in this connection, is now verging upon the archaic; *pulchritudinous* suggests that, though a great deal of obvious charm is present, the spectator is on the whole not impressed: the term, though erudite, has been debased by the higher – especially American – journalism.
ANT. **Ugly.**

BEG, ADJURE, BESEECH, ENTREAT, IMPLORE, IMPORTUNE, SUPPLICATE, all mean to request urgently. *Beg* implies earnestness; *entreat* implies the desire to overcome resistance; *beseech* suggests anxiety; *implore*, great anxiety. *Supplicate* adds to *entreat* the suggestion of prayer; *adjure*, of peremptoriness; and *importune*, of continuous and irritating pertinacity.

BEGIN, COMMENCE, INAUGURATE, INITIATE, START. To *begin* is opposed to *to end*; to *commence*, to *to conclude*; to *start*, to *to stop*. *Begin* is thus the simplest, most straightforward term, and *commence* is dedicated to more formal uses. To *start* implies a sudden beginning, as when one *starts* a race or a motor; to *initiate* suggests taking the first step

in a process; to *inaugurate* is, in this connection, a more grandiose way of saying to *begin* and contains the idea of ushering in.
ANT. **End.**

BEHAVIOUR, CONDUCT, DEPORTMENT. *Behaviour* has the widest implications; *conduct* applies to human beings and carries a suggestion of moral responsibility. *Deportment* relates to more or less conventional standards of *behaviour.*

BELIEF, CREDIT, CREDENCE, FAITH. *Belief* is the most comprehensive of these terms; *credence* suggests merely intellectual assent, and *credit* is a weaker sort of *credence. Faith,* on the other hand, is *belief* of the most implicit kind which transcends any purely intellectual criteria.
ANT. **Unbelief** (*passive*); **Disbelief** (*active*).

BELOW, BENEATH, UNDER, UNDERNEATH. *Below* is the opposite of *above*; *under,* of *over*; that is, *under* suggests an almost vertically lower position, and *below,* a lower position generally. *Beneath* can mean either *below* or *under,* and also has a special derogatory connotation, as when we speak of a man 'marrying *beneath* him'. *Underneath* adds to *under* or *beneath* the idea of almost complete concealment.
ANT. **Above.**

BENEFIT, AVAIL, PROFIT, all mean to derive advantage, but *benefit* is the widest in its implications, and *profit* stresses gain, often of a material sort. *Avail* suggests efficacy: *of no avail* equals 'of no use'.
ANT. **Harm.**

BLAME *n.*, CULPABILITY, FAULT, GUILT, all imply responsibility for wrongdoing. *Fault* and *culpability* refer to small misdeeds, the former being the term more appropriate to simple contexts. *Blame* has graver associations; and *guilt,* graver still, since it adds to *blame* the idea of a definite infraction of moral law.

BLEMISH, DEFECT, FLAW. A *blemish* is an external disfigurement; a *defect,* an imperfection either external or internal; a *flaw,* a *defect* likely to lead to the ultimate destruction of the thing under consideration.
ANT. **Immaculacy** (*Br.*) or **Immaculateness** (*Amer.*).

BLOOM, BLOSSOM. A *bloom* is the flower itself; a *blossom,* the flower considered as the precursor of the fruit. The distinction is, however, not always preserved.

BOAT, CRAFT, SHIP, VESSEL. A *boat* is properly a small open floating construction used for passage over water; a *ship* is a large ocean-going *boat. Vessel* stresses the idea that the *ship* contains and carries freight; and *craft* is a general term that covers all kinds of *boats* or *ships.*

BODY, CADAVER, CARCASE, CORPSE. *Body* is the comprehensive term; a *corpse* is the dead *body* of a human being; a *carcase,* the dead *body* of an animal; a *cadaver,* a *corpse* used for medical research.

BORDER, BRIM, BRINK, EDGE, MARGIN, RIM, VERGE. The *border* of anything is its boundary or that part of its surface which is just inside that boundary; a *margin* is a *border* that has definite width or some other specific or recognizable peculiarity; an *edge* is a boundary made by two converging lines; and *verge* usually implies the ultimate extremity of an *edge*. A *rim* is normally the *edge* of something curved; a *brim*, the inner or outer side of a cylindrical body, such as a pot or a hat, and also, by extension, the top or danger level of a body of water. *Brink* denotes the *edge* of something steep.

BRAVE, AUDACIOUS, BOLD, COURAGEOUS, DAUNTLESS, INTREPID, VALIANT. *Brave* is the simple, comprehensive term; *courageous* suggests a natural aptitude to behave *bravely*; *bold* adds to *courageous* a spice of recklessness, which *audacious* carries to the point of foolhardiness. *Dauntless* suggests an inability to fear; *intrepid* etymologically implies a complete absence of fear, though the word now, in practice, suggests a combination of dauntlessness and fortitude. *Valiant* has higher associations than any of the foregoing and suggests the perfection of knightly courage and endurance.
ANT. **Craven.**

BREACH, CONTRAVENTION, INFRACTION, INFRINGEMENT, TRANSGRESSION, TRESPASS, VIOLATION, all relate to failures to keep the law. A *breach* simply means breaking it; an *infraction* is a more grandiose version of the same; and a *violation* is a flagrant *breach*. *Transgression* is usually applied to breaches of the moral law, as also is *trespass*, except when it has the specialized legal meaning of illegally entering someone else's property. An *infringement* is an encroachment upon a right (such as copyright) protected by law; a *contravention* is an act done in defiance of what is lawful.
ANT. **Observance.**

BRIGHT, BEAMING, BRILLIANT, LAMBENT, LUMINOUS, LUSTROUS, RADIANT, REFULGENT. *Bright* is the reverse of dim or dull; *brilliant* suggests intense brightness; *radiant*, brightness caused by the emission of rays; *luminous*, a self-originating brightness or one caused by reflected light. *Lustrous*, however, applies only to such things as owe their brightness to reflection; *refulgent* suggests extreme lustrousness; *beaming*, a brightness caused by beams of light; *lambent*, a brightness which plays gently over a thing without making it either too *brilliant* or *lustrous*.
ANT. **Dull; Dim.**

BRING, FETCH, TAKE, though not synonyms, are subject to confusion. To *bring* is to convey something from elsewhere to the person using the word; to *take* is to convey something from the person using the word to some other place; to *fetch* involves going from the person using the word to another place and conveying from there to him the object required.
ANT. **Withdraw; Remove.**

BROAD, DEEP, WIDE are all applied to horizontal measurements. *Broad* and *wide* are very closely related, the difference being that *wide* refers dispassionately to the distance that separates the limits, and *broad*, with some approval, to the amplitude of what connects them. So shoulders are *broad*, but sleeves are *wide*. *Deep*, in this grouping, refers to the front-to-back dimension of certain plane surfaces, such as a building-plot, which

we describe as being 50 feet *wide* and 80 feet *deep* (*wide* in this use having been employed for what otherwise would be the *length*).
ANT. **Narrow.**

BUY, PURCHASE. *Buy* is the simpler term; *purchase*, the more inflated. It is, however, reasonable enough to talk of *buying* a loaf; and *purchasing* a mansion.

C

CALCULATE, COMPUTE, ESTIMATE, RECKON. Which of these words is used depends, broadly, upon the complexity of the operation involved. We *reckon* simple sums in our heads; *compute* with exactitude more elaborate ones from given data. To *calculate*, on the other hand, suggests a process of greater intricacy in which some of the factors may be tentative or doubtful. To *estimate* still further involves the element of the unknown, and suggests that the result must necessarily be approximate.

CALL *v.*, CONVENE, CONVOKE, MUSTER, SUMMON. *Call* is the common colloquial term in this group; *summon* is more formal and official. *Convoke* implies a *summons* to assemble and is applied to public bodies, parliaments and the like. To *convene* is a weaker version of to *convoke* and so can be used when the assemblage in question is not a specially august one. To *muster* is, properly, to *call* or *summon* a body of fighting-men, but it can also be used figuratively in such phrases as '*mustering* up one's courage'.

CALM, PEACEFUL, PLACID, SERENE, TRANQUIL. *Calm* is simply the opposite of stormy; *tranquil* suggests a more inherent and native quietude; *serene*, tranquillity of the loftiest kind. *Placid*, on the other hand, is opposed to *ruffled* and can sometimes suggest a complacent *calm*. *Peaceful*, in this grouping, implies a gentle and undisturbed quietude of a more homely sort than is suggested by *tranquil*.
ANT. **Stormy; Agitated.**

CAN, MAY. Though liable to be confused, *can* should express ability, and *may*, possibility, depending upon permission. It is therefore incorrect to say, '*Can* I have that book?'; correct to say, 'I *can* spell', and '*May* I have that book?'

CAPRICE, FREAK, VAGARY, WHIM (or WHIMSY), all suggest arbitrary behaviour, but whereas *caprice* implies lack of any apparent motive, *freak* suggests an impulsive and seemingly wanton change of course. *Whim* suggests a sort of capricious freakishness; *whimsy*, a fanciful and humorous one. *Vagary* stresses the extravagance and irresponsibility of the course pursued.

CARE, ANXIETY, CONCERN, SOLICITUDE, WORRY. *Care* suggests preoccupation because of responsibilities, apprehensions and so forth; *concern*, interest, an absence of indifference, and can therefore, according to circumstances, be either stronger or weaker than *care*. *Solicitude* is a deep *concern*, usually for others; *anxiety* is the *care* we feel in the face of possible misfortune; *worry* suggests that the *cares* besetting us are such as cause intense mental activity, usually of a fruitless order.

CARELESS, HEEDLESS, INADVERTENT, THOUGHTLESS. Whereas *careless*, in this grouping, suggests a failure to take reasonable pains, *heedless* adds the idea of a certain innate frivolity, and *thoughtless* stresses the total absence of any prior reflection. *Inadvertent*, on the other hand, implies an accidental *carelessness* often arising from thinking of other things.
ANT. **Careful.**

CARICATURE, BURLESQUE, PARODY, TRAVESTY. A *caricature* is a ludicrous exaggeration; a *burlesque*, a ludicrous and exaggerated imitation. A *parody* involves the *burlesquing* of stylistic mannerisms; a *travesty*, the treating of a subject (usually a lofty one) in an absurd or inappropriate manner.

CASE, EXAMPLE, ILLUSTRATION, INSTANCE, SAMPLE, SPECIMEN, all relate to such things as are typical manifestations of the particular group to which they belong. *Case* is the common comprehensive term, *e.g.* 'Hard *cases* make bad law'. An *instance* is a *case* adduced in proof or disproof of a general statement; an *illustration* is a *case* cited to illustrate a particular point of view; an *example* is a typical *case*; a *sample* is an actual part of the thing in question, exhibited to represent the quality or nature of the whole of it; a *specimen* is a representative *sample* of a special class of things.

CAUSE, ANTECEDENT, OCCASION, REASON, all denote that which produces an effect. *Cause* is the common, most neutral, term; *reason* implies an explicable *cause*; *antecedent* stresses the priority in time of the *cause*; an *occasion* (in this grouping) is an incident or situation which sets in motion a train of events, and so, to that extent, is the *cause* of them.

CAUTIOUS, CALCULATING, CHARY, CIRCUMSPECT, WARY, all suggest prudent behaviour in the face of possible risk or danger, but *cautious* puts fear as the principal motive-force, and *circumspect*, carefulness. To be *wary* stresses suspicion; *chary*, extreme discretion; and *calculating*, great deliberation of approach.
ANT. **Adventurous; Temerarious.**

CERTAIN, INEVITABLE, NECESSARY. That which is *certain* cannot be disputed; that which is *inevitable* cannot be escaped; that which is *necessary*, in this grouping, is the logical outcome of what has gone before.
ANT. **Probable; Supposed.**

CHANCE, ACCIDENT, FORTUNE, HAZARD, LUCK, all relate to that which happens without an apparent cause, but *chance* is the general term, and *accident* adds to *chance* an emphasis on lack of intention which renders the word the exact opposite of *design*. *Fortune* has supernatural overtones, and so has *luck*, the latter being the colloquial version of the former. *Hazard* brings in the idea of casting a die, and so is similar to *accident*, though it embodies a stronger suggestion of arbitrariness.
ANT. **Law.**

CHANGE *v.*, ALTER, MODIFY, VARY. *Change* is the strongest term, implying essential difference; *alter* implies difference in some respects but not in all. *Vary* suggests more gradual, fluctuating *change*; *modify*, a *change* that limits or restricts and is often of minor importance.

CHASTE, DECENT, MODEST, PURE. *Chaste* stresses restraint; *pure*, the absence of unchaste thoughts; *modest*, the absence of bold or unchaste behaviour; *decent*, a concern for what is fitting and seemly.
ANT. **Lewd; Wanton; Immoral.**

CHEAT *v.*, DEFRAUD, OVERREACH, SWINDLE. To *cheat* implies trickery; to *defraud*, lying; to *swindle*, both one and the other. To *overreach* is to get the better of a person, often, though not invariably, by one or all of the three preceding activities.

CHIEF *adj.*, CAPITAL, FOREMOST, LEADING, MAIN, PRINCIPAL, all suggest priority. The *chief* is the head of its particular category; the *principal* is that which precedes all others; *main* refers to that which excels others of its sort in size and importance; *leading* resembles *principal*, but adds the idea of peculiar fitness for the position; *foremost* adds to *leading* the idea of eagerness to assume such a situation; and *capital*, that the thing in question comes first because of its natural importance or significance. We thus speak of a *chief* magistrate; a *principal* boy; *main* line trains; *leading* seamen; the *foremost* in the fray; *capital* offences.
ANT. **Subordinate.**

CHOICE *n.*, ALTERNATIVE, ELECTION, OPTION, PREFERENCE, SELECTION. *Choice* involves the right to pick freely from among a number of possibilities; *option*, that the choice is offered us by some external authority. An *alternative* is the *choice* between two things; a *preference* stresses that one's *choice* is determined by personal feelings; *selection* suggests a wide range of *choice*, and discrimination in making it; *election* adds to *selection* the idea of an ultimate purpose which renders necessary the act of selection.

CHOOSE, ELECT, OPT, PICK, PREFER, SELECT. *Choose* is the common term; *select* implies a wide range of choice and discrimination in making it; *elect* underlines the idea of the rejection of what is not chosen; *opt* is a choice between alternatives; *pick*, a careful selection; *prefer* indicates a choice dictated by personal feeling.
ANT. **Refuse; Eschew.**

CIRCUMSTANCE, EPISODE, EVENT, INCIDENT, OCCURRENCE, all relate to happenings. *Occurrence* is the general and comprehensive term; an *event* is a notable *occurrence*; an *incident*, a trifling one; an *episode*, a small, distinct and separate one. *Circumstance*, in this grouping, can mean either *incident* or *event*, but being less precise than either is best suited to neutral contexts.

CIVIL *adj.*, CHIVALROUS, COURTEOUS, COURTLY, GALLANT, POLISHED, POLITE, REFINED. To be *civil* is to fulfil the minimum requirements of good-breeding; to be *polite* is altogether more positive and implies conformity to the recognized good manners of one's time.

Courteous blends politeness with dignity and consideration; *courtly*, with stateliness and ceremony. *Chivalrous* implies a *courteous* attentiveness to women; *gallant*, a spirited but often spurious attentiveness to them. *Polished* behaviour comes from art and study; *refined* behaviour from inherent good-breeding.
ANT. **Uncivil; Rude.**

CLAIM *n.*, PRETENCE, PRETENSION, TITLE, all relate to the right to demand something as one's own. *Claim* carries the strongest suggestion of vigorous demand; *title*, that the *claim* is just and reasonable; *pretension*, in modern usage, that the *claim* is not well-founded. *Pretence*, as in the phrase *false pretences*, suggests simple and unsupported assertion.

CLEAR, LIMPID, LUCID, PELLUCID, TRANSLUCENT, TRANSPARENT. *Clear* is the common term; *transparent* is that which is so clear that it may be seen through. The *translucent* permits the passage of light but does not allow a clear view of what is beyond; the *lucid* is both transparent and luminous; the *pellucid* is crystal-clear and does not distort images seen through it; the *limpid* has the clearness of pure water.
ANT. **Turbid** (of physical things); **Confused** (of mental ones).

CLEVER, ADROIT, CUNNING, INGENIOUS. *Clever* suggests quickness and resourcefulness; *adroit*, astuteness and adaptability; *cunning* (here used in the good sense), a high degree of skill and craftsmanship. *Ingenious* adds to *clever* the idea of brilliance, sometimes of the more erratic sort.

CLOSE *adj.* and *adv.*, NEAR, NIGH. *Close* suggests a much higher degree of adjacency than does *near*; *nigh* is the poetical or archaic equivalent of *near*.
ANT. **Remote.**

CLOSE *v.* (1), SHUT. To *close* is to put *close* together; *shut* is much stronger, deriving from the Saxon word to fasten with a bolt (*cf.* '*shoot* the bolt'). Yet to *close* also implies a higher degree of permanence: 'the theatre is *closed* (for the summer); is *shut* (on Mondays)'.
ANT. **Open.**

CLOSE *v.* (2), COMPLETE, CONCLUDE, END, FINISH, TERMINATE, all mean to bring to a stop. *Close* suggests action upon something formerly regarded as open, *e.g.* one *closes* an account. *End* carries a stronger sense of finality; *conclude* is a more formal version of *end*; *finish* implies the completion of what one has set out to do; *complete*, the perfection of what one has attempted. *Terminate*, to the idea of *ending*, adds that of setting up a limit.

COARSE, GROSS, OBSCENE, RIBALD, VULGAR. The *coarse* is opposed to the *fine*; the *vulgar* is boorish and ill-bred; the *gross* is opposed to the spiritual; the *obscene* is indecent; the *ribald* is jolly and on the whole harmless vulgarity.
ANT. **Fine; Refined.**

COAX, BLANDISH, CAJOLE, WHEEDLE. To *coax* is to persuade gently and persistently; to *cajole* is to beguile or allure; to *wheedle* is to

cajole with unctuous flattery; to *blandish* is to win over by the exercise of charm.
ANT. **Bully.**

COLD, ARCTIC, CHILLY, COOL, FREEZING, FRIGID, FROSTY, GELID, ICY are all used to denote temperatures below the normal. *Cold*, the general term, merely implies the absence of heat; *cool*, a moderate *coldness*; *chilly*, the *coldness* that causes shivering; *frosty*, that frost is about. *Frigid* and *freezing* imply temperatures below freezing-point, but *frigid* stresses the intensity of the *cold*; and *freezing*, the effects of it. *Gelid* is that which produces ice; *icy* suggests great *coldness*; *arctic*, *coldness* in the highest degree.
ANT. **Hot.**

COLOUR *n.*, HUE, SHADE, TINGE, TINT. *Colour* is the general term; *hue* is less specific and often applies to colour-changes, *e.g.* 'his face assumed a darker *hue*'. *Shade* relates to the gradations of a particular colour, actually by adding black to it; *tint* to similar gradations, actually produced by adding white and so producing pale or pastel colours; *tinge* suggests a stained effect as when one colour interfuses another.

COMBINATION, CABAL, COMBINE, FACTION, JUNTO, PARTY, RING, all suggest a union of persons directed towards a common end. *Combination* is the most comprehensive term, and *combine*, the colloquial version of it; a *party* is, usually, a political *combination*; a *faction* is a *party* within a *party*; a *ring* is a more or less secret *combination* with corrupt intentions; a *cabal* is a small group of intriguers; a *junto* is similar, but is a more modern use.

COME, ARRIVE. *Come* is less explicit than *arrive* (which etymologically implies landing). One says, 'I shall *come* on Thursday', but 'I shall *arrive* at 3 o'clock'.
ANT. **Go.**

COMFORT *v.*, CONSOLE, SOLACE. *Comfort* is the most intimate word in this group; *console* is more formal: we *comfort* a child, *console* adults. *Solace* suggests relief by distraction, and is provided more often by things than persons.
ANT. **Afflict.**

COMMAND *v.*, BID, CHARGE, DIRECT, ENJOIN, INSTRUCT, ORDER. In *command* and *order* we hear the voice of authority; but *order* is more peremptory than *command*. *Bid*, in this grouping, suggests rather more than a request and rather less than an *order*. *Enjoin*, *direct* and *instruct* are all less imperative than *command* but still suggest that compliance is expected; *enjoin* implies urgent admonition; *direct* and *instruct*, some official relationship, *direct*, however, being stronger than *instruct*. *Charge* adds to *enjoin* the definite idea of duty. So we *command* a soldier; *order* off a trespasser; *bid* our child behave; are *enjoined* by the clergy; *direct* our servants; *instruct* our solicitor; while bishops *charge* their clergy.
ANT. **Comply; Obey.**

COMMIT, CONFIDE, CONSIGN, ENTRUST, RELEGATE, all mean to assign a thing to some person or place for a definite object, such as safekeeping. *Commit* is the most general term; to *entrust* is to *commit* with confidence; to *confide*, with complete assurance. To *consign* is to do the thing formally and often suggests transporting the object in question; to *relegate* is to *consign* in such a way that the thing involved is set aside or lost sight of.

COMMON, FAMILIAR, ORDINARY, POPULAR, VULGAR. The *common* is the unexceptional everyday article; the *ordinary*, that which accords with the general run of the mill, and when used in derogatory contexts is less severe than *common*. The *familiar* is that which is generally known; the *popular*, that which is accepted by or prevalent among the great mass of the people; the *vulgar*, in this grouping, is similar but has more uncomplimentary implications: we speak of *popular* songs, but of *vulgar* curiosity.
ANT. **Uncommon; Exceptional.**

COMMONPLACE, CLICHÉ, PLATITUDE, TRUISM. A *commonplace* is an unoriginal observation; a *platitude* is a *commonplace* enunciated *con brio*, with an air of profundity; a *truism* is a self-evident truth; a *cliché* is an expression which, though once original, has become worn out through excessive employment.

COMMUNICATE, IMPART. To *communicate* is to render something common to all parties involved; to *impart* is to share with others what is properly one's own: so, we *communicate* our thoughts; but *impart* information.

COMPARISON, ANTITHESIS, COLLATION, CONTRAST, PARALLEL, all imply the setting of things side by side to reveal their resemblances and differences. *Comparison* is the comprehensive term; *contrast* is used when one wishes to stress the differences rather than the resemblances; an *antithesis* is when the two things compared are diametrically opposed to one another. A *collation* is a *comparison* made with a view to discovering what differences (if any) exist; a *parallel* is an elaborate and detailed *comparison* to discover correspondences and discrepancies.

COMPENSATE, BALANCE, COUNTERBALANCE, OFFSET. One thing *compensates* for another when it makes up for what the other has lost, on the swings-and-roundabouts principle; one *balances* another when each of the things concerned is of equal weight and importance; one *offsets* another when the former neutralizes the latter; and one *counterbalances* the other when perfect equilibrium is arrived at because of the adjustment between the two things in question.

COMPOSE, COMPRISE, CONSIST OF, CONSTITUTE, all convey the idea of making up a whole out of its parts. *Compose* is the general term; *consist of* corresponds to the passive of *compose*: we can say 'all matter *consists of* atoms', or 'atoms *compose* all matter'. *Comprise* stresses inclusiveness, *e.g.* 'The book *comprises* all that he wrote before 1900'. *Constitute*, in this grouping, refers to the constituents which make up a given entity, *e.g.* 'Bread and water do not *constitute* a banquet'.

CONCEIT, EGOISM, EGOTISM, SELF-ESTEEM. *Conceit* leads one to believe oneself superior to others; *egotism*, to believe that all the

world is interested in one's doings; but *egoism* is a form of extreme self-absorption which does not necessarily lead to *egotistic* behaviour in public. *Self-esteem,* on the other hand, can, and often does, mean no more than a proper pride in oneself and one's activities.
ANT. **Humility.**

CONCLUSIVE, DECISIVE, DEFINITIVE, all suggest that which brings to an end. We speak of *conclusive* evidence; a *decisive* battle; a *definitive* edition of a classic. There is nothing to say after the first has been produced; nothing to hope after the second has been fought; and the *definitive* ousts for ever the tentative and the provisional.
ANT. **Inconclusive.**

CONFER, ADVISE, CONSULT, NEGOTIATE, PARLEY, TREAT, all suggest discussion tending towards a decision. To *confer* implies equality of status in those discussing; to *consult* adds the idea of taking counsel together; to *advise*, in this grouping, suggests *consultation* over less lofty or personal matters. To *parley* is simply to talk about terms; to *treat* adds the idea that one wishes to reach a settlement; to *negotiate,* that in order to do this one is willing to bargain and compromise.

CONFIRM, AUTHENTICATE, CORROBORATE, SUBSTANTIATE, VERIFY, all mean to attest the truth of something. To *confirm* is definite, suggesting an authoritative statement; to *corroborate* is to back up testimony already given; to *substantiate* suggests the providing of proof or evidence; to *verify*, that pains have been taken to check the correctness of the thing asserted; to *authenticate*, that the genuineness of the thing under consideration has been demonstrated by someone speaking with authority.
ANT. **Deny; Contradict.**

CONFUSION, CHAOS, DISORDER, JUMBLE, MUDDLE, all relate to things being in their wrong places, but *confusion* suggests a total absence of order, and *disorder*, the derangement of an order that has once presumably existed. *Chaos* is total *confusion*; a *jumble* is a crowded mixture of many incongruous items; a *muddle* suggests *disorder* of an unintelligent and rather squalid kind. Both *jumble* and *muddle* are terms of much less dignity than the others.

CONJECTURE, GUESS, SURMISE. To *conjecture* is to form an opinion on slight evidence; to *surmise,* on evidence still less adequate; to *guess* is to arrive at a solution at random, often on no evidence at all. The same distinctions apply to the nouns related to these verbs.
ANT. **Fact.**

CONQUER, BEAT, DEFEAT, OVERCOME, REDUCE, ROUT, SUBDUE, SURMOUNT, VANQUISH, all mean to get the better of someone or something. *Conquer* stresses gain on the part of the conqueror, as when we *conquer* our difficulties or our desires; but *vanquish* stresses the plight of the person or thing *conquered. Defeat* lacks the finality of *vanquish*: one can be *defeated* in a battle without being *vanquished* in the war. *Beat,* which is somewhat colloquial, is sometimes the equivalent of *vanquish* but more often of *defeat*; *subdue* adds to the idea of *defeat* that of submission;

reduce implies bringing a fortress or other entity to a state of capitulation, usually by gradual means. *Overcome* and *surmount* suggest the *conquering* of something very difficult; *rout* implies flight and dispersion following upon total military defeat.

CONSIDER (1), CONTEMPLATE, EXCOGITATE, STUDY, WEIGH. To *consider* is to apply the mind to a problem; to *study* is to apply it deeply; to *contemplate* is to focus one's attention keenly upon the matter in question; to *weigh*, in this connection, is to evaluate the relevant points of the given problem; to *excogitate* is to think out the matter in all its implications.

CONSIDER (2), ACCOUNT, DEEM, RECKON, REGARD, all, in this grouping, are roughly the equivalent of 'to have an opinion'. *Consider* implies an opinion attained after reflection; *regard*, a judgment based upon appearances; *account* and *reckon* are most properly used when they imply calculation or evaluation; *deem* emphasizes the use of the judgment rather than of simple reflection.

CONSONANT, COMPATIBLE, CONGENIAL, CONGRUOUS, CONSISTENT, SYMPATHETIC, all suggest agreement of one thing with another. *Consonant* stresses the absence of discord between them; *compatible*, a capacity for existing together without disagreement; *congruous*, an exact mutual fitness; *consistent*, uniformity; *congenial*, similarity in taste; *sympathetic*, in this grouping, implies a capacity for feeling in the same way.
ANT. **Inconsonant.**

CONSUMMATE, ACCOMPLISHED, FINISHED, all imply a state of high attainment. The *finished* needs nothing to complete it; the *accomplished* exhibits genuine mastery; the *consummate* is that which has attained the topmost pinnacle of perfection.
ANT. **Crude.**

CONTAIN, ACCOMMODATE, HOLD. A thing *contains* what is actually inside it; it may be able to *hold* twice as much. On the other hand, it *accommodates* as much as it can *hold* comfortably and without packing too tightly.

CONTEMPTIBLE, CHEAP, DESPICABLE, PITIABLE, SORRY, all imply scorn or disdain, but *despicable* is stronger than *contemptible*, and *pitiable* (in this grouping) adds the idea of pity to that of contempt. *Sorry* is similar to *pitiable* but has lower applications: we speak of *pitiable* attempts, but of *sorry* nags. *Cheap* suggests a petty contemptibleness, as in 'the *cheap* and nasty'.
ANT. **Admirable; Estimable.**

CONTEND, BATTLE, COPE, FIGHT, WAR. To *contend* with a thing is to struggle with it; to *cope* with it is to struggle successfully. *Fight* is stronger than *contend*; and *battle* and *war* are stronger and more picturesque, though the contexts in which they can be used fittingly need careful choice.

CONTENT, SATISFY. To *satisfy* means to have all one's desires granted; to *content*, a reasonable modicum of them. *Contentment* thus depends on our capacity to be *satisfied* easily.

CONTINUAL, CONSTANT, CONTINUOUS, INCESSANT, PERENNIAL, PERPETUAL. The *continual* recurs at close intervals; the *continuous*, without intermission; the *constant* (in this grouping) adds to the idea of close recurrence that of persistence and uniformity. *Incessant* stresses the uninterrupted quality of the thing; *perpetual*, its length of duration; *perennial*, its constant recurrence over the years.
ANT. **Intermittent.**

CONTINUATION, CONTINUANCE, CONTINUITY. A *continuation* is a prolongation; *continuance* involves duration, *e.g.* '*continuance* in well doing'; *continuity*, unbroken connection.
ANT. **Cessation.**

CONTINUE, ABIDE, ENDURE, LAST, PERSIST, all contain the idea of remaining in existence. To *continue* refers to the process and stresses its lack of termination; to *last* emphasizes the time-factor, *e.g.* 'These sheets have *lasted* well'. To *endure* adds to *to last* the idea of resistance to destruction; to *abide*, that of constancy, *e.g.* 'Here we have no *abiding* city'; while *persist* adds to *continue* the idea of exceeding the normal or customary time.

CONTRARY, ANTITHETICAL, ANTONYMOUS, CONTRADICTORY, OPPOSITE. The *opposite* of 'All men are mortal' is 'No men are mortal'; but the *contrary* to it is 'Not all men are mortal'. When two statements are so worded that both of them cannot be true (*e.g.* 'He is old: he is young') then we say they are *contradictory*. Things *antithetical* are diametrical opposites set in juxtaposition to reveal the essential nature of each, *e.g.* 'Mysticism is the *antithesis* of materialism'. *Antonymous* applies to words that are so opposed in meaning to one another as to have the effect of cancelling each other out, *e.g. gain : loss.*

CONVERSE *n.*, OBVERSE, REVERSE, though not synonyms, are exposed to confusion. The *converse* of a proposition is the proposition with its major terms transposed. The *converse* of 'It's a wise child that knows his own father' is 'It's a wise father that knows his own child'. The *obverse* and *reverse*, however, are the front and back faces of a coin or medal, the *obverse* being the principal face which usually carries the head.

COOL, COLLECTED, COMPOSED, IMPERTURBABLE, NONCHALANT, UNRUFFLED, all suggest calm behaviour. To be *cool* is to exhibit no *heat*; to be *composed* is to show no sign of excitement; to be *collected* suggests that the composure exhibited is the result of mental stability. The *unruffled* exhibit poise in the midst of distractions; the *imperturbable* seem incapable of being *ruffled*; the *nonchalant* are calm because, to all appearances, unconcerned.
ANT. **Ardent; Agitated.**

COPY *v.*, APE, IMITATE, MIMIC, MOCK. To *copy* is to duplicate exactly; to *imitate* is to take something as a model and to produce that which resembles the model. To *mimic* is to *copy* a person's mannerisms

and so on; to *ape* is to *mimic* emulously someone that one admires; to *mock* adds to *mimic* the idea of derisory impersonation or even of cruelty.
ANT. **Originate.**

CORRECT *adj.*, ACCURATE, EXACT, NICE, RIGHT. The *correct* is that which is free from error; the *accurate*, that which, after the exercise of care, has been demonstrated as true; the *exact* is that which neither exceeds nor falls short of the truth. *Nice*, as in the phrase 'a *nice* distinction', implies great precision; *right*, in this grouping, is the opposite to *wrong*; but whereas the *right* answer to a sum is the *correct* one, *correct* behaviour is not necessarily the same as *right* behaviour.
ANT. **Incorrect.**

COSTLY, DEAR, EXPENSIVE, INVALUABLE, PRECIOUS, PRICELESS, VALUABLE. *Costly* simply means costing a great deal; *expensive* adds the suggestion that the article in question is priced higher than it should be or, alternatively, is somewhat beyond the purchaser's means. *Dear* (here opposed to *cheap*) implies that the price is unreasonable; *valuable*, that the thing in question will sell for a good price, or is of great value if monetary considerations are not involved. *Precious* applies strictly to values hardly to be estimated in monetary terms; or, in such a phrase as '*precious* stones', implies the most *costly* of its particular class. *Invaluable* and *priceless* literally mean beyond monetary value, and apply to such things as can be obtained only by good fortune rather than purchase.
ANT. **Cheap.**

COUPLE, BRACE, PAIR, YOKE. A *couple* applies to two things of similar kind; a *pair* to two things one of which is useless or imperfect without the other, *e.g.* a *pair* of gloves. A *brace* is a specialized term referring to a *couple* of birds, pistols, etc.; a *yoke* is strictly a *couple* of animals linked together.

COURTESY, AMENITY, ATTENTION, COMITY, GALLANTRY. *Courtesy* suggests consideration, deference, well-bred politeness; *amenity*, the disposition to make social relations pleasant; *attention*, the bestowing of special *courtesies* upon a single person or group of persons. *Gallantry* implies *attentions* specially directed by a man to a woman; *comity* now refers to the exchange of courtesies between nations.
ANT. **Discourtesy.**

COVETOUS, ACQUISITIVE, AVARICIOUS, GRASPING, GREEDY. *Covetous* suggests an inordinate desire for material possessions, usually someone else's; *greedy*, a simple absence of restraint in one's desires: one can be *greedy* for gold, but also for knowledge. *Acquisitive* adds to the idea of *greedy* that of capacity for acquiring what is desired; *grasping* always suggests *greed* in its worst, most self-regarding, sense; *avaricious*, a miserly *greed* with which is linked the concomitant idea of stinginess.

COWARDLY, CRAVEN, DASTARDLY, PUSILLANIMOUS, RECREANT. *Cowardly* is the general term; *pusillanimous* is one shade lower in the scale of contempt; *craven* suggests an abject pusillanimity; *dastardly*,

a stabbing-in-the-back kind of cowardice. *Recreant* adds to cowardice the idea of faithlessness and betrayal.
ANT. **Bold.**

CRITICAL, CAPTIOUS, CARPING, CAVILLING, CENSORIOUS, FAULTFINDING. A *critical* approach to anything is one that attempts to find out its good and its bad qualities; a *faultfinding* one concentrates on its bad ones; and a *captious* one evinces a temperamental readiness to seize on such faults. A *cavilling* one is eager to raise trifling objections; a *carping* one adds to *captious* a suggestion of definite ill-will. *Censorious* suggests criticism of a highly severe and generally condemnatory kind.
ANT. **Uncritical.**

CRITICIZE, BLAME, CENSURE, CONDEMN, DENOUNCE, REPREHEND, REPROBATE. To *criticize* is, strictly, to have the *critical* approach (see above); to *reprehend* is to *criticize* adversely; to *blame* is to impute guilt of one sort or another; to *censure* is to *blame* strongly. To *reprobate* adds to disapproval the idea of total rejection; to *condemn* is to pass an irrevocably unfavourable judgment; to *denounce* is to *condemn* publicly.

CRY, BLUBBER, WAIL, WEEP, WHIMPER. To *cry* is the common and familiar term; to *weep*, the more formal and elevated. To *wail* is to *cry* piteously and unrestrainedly; to *whimper*, feebly, fretfully and intermittently; to *blubber*, noisily and without dignity.

CURE *v.*, HEAL, REMEDY. To *cure* applies generally to illnesses; to *heal*, to wounds. To *remedy* is to set right what is wrong, whether it be an illness or any other bad state of things.

CURIOUS, INQUISITIVE, PRYING. *Curious* simply implies the desire to know; *inquisitive* suggests an impertinent and inopportune *curiosity*; *prying*, an officious and meddling *inquisitiveness*.
ANT. **Incurious; Uninterested.**

D

DANGER, HAZARD, JEOPARDY, PERIL, RISK. *Danger* is the general term, but is less strong than *peril* which suggests more imminent and acute *danger*. *Jeopardy* implies exposure to great potential *danger*; *hazard*, that the danger which threatens comes by chance: it is not so strong a term as *jeopardy*. *Risk* suggests a possibility, not unduly strong, of *danger*.
ANT. **Security.**

DARK, DIM, DUSKY, GLOOMY, MURKY, OBSCURE, OPAQUE. *Dark* is the common term; *dim* implies a partial *darkness* in which outlines may be descried; *dusky*, a twilight *darkness*, unilluminated; *obscure* (in this grouping), a partial *darkness* caused by shadows and the like. *Murky* is now usually applied to a foggy *darkness*; *opaque* is the opposite to *transparent*: we call a thing *opaque* when it obstructs the passage of light. *Gloomy* applies to that semi-darkness which is caused by heavy clouds or much shade.
ANT. **Light.**

DEAD, DECEASED, DEFUNCT, DEPARTED, INANIMATE, LATE, LIFELESS. *Dead* is the common, comprehensive term; *defunct* is more pompous and is best applied to such things as institutions which have failed to stay alive. *Deceased* is a legal and somewhat euphemistic way of referring to a dead person; *departed* is confined to religious occasions and usages; and *late* is used formally to indicate recent decease: 'the *late* Mr So-and-so' is often used to distinguish the person so styled from a living one of the same name. *Lifeless* and *inanimate* differ from the preceding terms in that in order to be *dead* one must have had life, but the *lifeless* and the *inanimate* need not have done so: *inanimate* is, however, the more precise of these terms if one is describing matter that has not lived, since, in such a phrase as 'a *lifeless* corpse', *lifeless* approximately equals *dead*.
ANT. **Alive.**

DEADLY, FATAL, LETHAL, MORTAL. The *deadly* is that which is very likely to cause death; the *mortal* always produces it. *Fatal* brings in the concept of destiny, but is otherwise indistinguishable in strength from *mortal*. *Lethal* means that which in its own nature is certain to cause death: we speak of a *lethal* dose.

DEATH, DECEASE, DEMISE, PASSING. *Death* is the general and dignified term; *decease* and *demise* are applied only to humans, the former being a legal usage, the latter an inflated one sometimes appropriate when

applied to the great. *Passing* is a generally rather undesirable euphemism for *death*.
ANT. **Life.**

DECAY *v.*, CRUMBLE, DECOMPOSE, DISINTEGRATE, PUTREFY, ROT. *Decay* involves a general breaking-down from the perfect to the less perfect; *decompose*, a specific chemical breaking-down of matter into its constituents; *rot*, the *decomposing* of animal or vegetable matter; *putrefy*, the *rotting* of animal matter with its offensive concomitants. *Disintegrate* suggests the complete breaking-down of anything into its components; *crumble*, the disintegration of a solid substance into fine particles.

DECEIT, CUNNING, DISSIMULATION, DUPLICITY, GUILE. *Deceit* is the most comprehensive of these terms and implies an intention to mislead; *duplicity* properly suggests *deceit* by way of double dealing and insincerity; *dissimulation*, by way of concealment of the truth; *cunning*, by way of trickery; *guile*, by way of treachery: though *guile*, in modern use, has weakened almost to the extent of becoming the equivalent of *artfulness*.

DECEIVE, BEGUILE, BETRAY, DELUDE, MISLEAD. To *deceive* is the most general of these terms, and to *betray* is much the strongest since it suggests that the victim of the *betrayal* has been put into actual jeopardy. To *mislead* is no more than to lead astray, which a false signpost can do; to *delude* is literally to cause *delusions*, actually to make a fool of one's victim; to *beguile* is to *deceive* by fair words and false promises.
ANT. **Undeceive; Enlighten.**

DECIDE, DETERMINE, RESOLVE, RULE, SETTLE. To *decide* is to make up one's mind; to *determine* is to come to a fixed decision; to *settle* is to come to a decision that puts an end to all discussion. To *rule*, in this connection, implies a decision backed by authority, as when a judge makes a *ruling*; and to *resolve* is to come to a decision which will bear fruit in the future.

DECIDED, DECISIVE. The *decided* is unquestionable; the *decisive* goes a long way towards helping on the process of *decision*. There seems a tendency nowadays to elevate *decisive* at the expense of *decided*, as when we speak of a *decisive* victory as if it were a stronger expression than a *decided* one.

DECLARE, ADVERTISE, ANNOUNCE, PROCLAIM, PROMULGATE, PUBLISH. To *declare* is to make something known, usually in a formal manner; to *announce* is to do so for the first time; to *publish* is to do so in print; to *advertise* is to do so by repeated (and now usually printed) statements. To *proclaim* is to *announce* publicly, originally by word of mouth, but now by any suitable means; to *promulgate* is formally to make known to all concerned either some doctrine or general principle likely to affect them, or a law certain to do so.

DECOROUS, DECENT, DEMURE, NICE, PROPER, SEEMLY. The *decorous* observes the proprieties; the *decent* adds to propriety the idea of good-taste and breeding; the *seemly* is pleasing as well as *decorous*;

the *proper* is that which is appropriate to the milieu in which it exists; the *nice*, in this grouping, is that which satisfies the fastidious; the *demure* has nowadays almost degenerated to the suggestion of an artfully assumed and spurious decorum.
ANT. **Indecorous.**

DEDUCTION, ABATEMENT, DISCOUNT, REBATE. A *deduction* is an amount subtracted; an *abatement* is a *deduction* from a tax or duty; a *rebate* is a *deduction* that is returned after the payment of the full amount due; a *discount* is a *deduction* from a sum owed, given in consideration for prompt payment or for some other agreed reason.

DEFECTION, APOSTASY, DESERTION, all imply a breaking away from some cause or organization with which one is morally or legally involved; but whereas *defection* carries only a minor hint of reproach, *desertion* is much more forthright and may even suggest a base or dubious motive. *Apostasy* is still stronger in condemnation, and is usually applied to those who abandon their religious beliefs, especially by those who retain such beliefs.

DEFER, INTERMIT, POSTPONE, STAY, SUSPEND. To *defer* is to put off until later; to *postpone* is to put off until some specified later time; to *intermit* is to break off for a short time prior to eventual resumption; to *suspend* is to *intermit* indefinitely for a definite reason, *e.g.* one *suspends* judgment until one has better evidence. To *stay*, in this connection, is to impede, either completely or partially, something that is proceeding and is mostly a legal use, except in the phrase 'to *stay* one's hand'.

DEFICIENT, DEFECTIVE. *Defective* implies a defect; *deficient*, a deficit: the former a fault, the latter a lack.
ANT. **Sufficient; Adequate.**

DELAY (1), DETAIN, RETARD, SLACKEN, SLOW. To *delay* is to keep back or impede; to *retard* is to cause something in motion to reduce its speed; to *slow* and to *slacken* are colloquial versions of to *retard*: one *slows* down a car, *slackens* one's pace. To *detain* is to hold back beyond an appointed time: the train was *delayed* at Crewe (for an unspecified time); was *detained* for an hour at Rugby.
ANT. **Expedite; Hasten.**

DELAY (2), DALLY, DAWDLE, LAG, LOITER, PROCRASTINATE. To *delay*, in this use, is to put off; to *procrastinate* is to do so culpably: '*Procrastination* is the thief of time'. To *lag* is to *delay* by falling short of the pace set by others; to *loiter* is to proceed slowly and aimlessly; to *dawdle* is still stronger than to *loiter*; to *dally* adds to *dawdling* the idea of hesitation and vacillation, or of frivolity.
ANT. **Hasten; Hurry.**

DELIGHTFUL, DELECTABLE, DELICIOUS, LUSCIOUS. The *delightful* is anything that affords delight; the *delicious* confines the delight to the pleasures of the senses; the *delectable* suggests a more refined and discriminating enjoyment. *Luscious* adds to *delicious* the idea of peculiar fineness and richness in the thing enjoyed.
ANT. **Distressing.**

DELIVERANCE, DELIVERY. *Deliverance* is the state of being *delivered*; *delivery*, the act of *delivering*.

DELUSION, HALLUCINATION, ILLUSION, MIRAGE. A *delusion* commonly implies either self-deception or wilful deception by others; an *illusion* is a deceptive appearance or belief the falsity of which is, or can be, rationally apprehended by the person experiencing it; a *hallucination* is a false appearance which has no ground in reality; a *mirage* is an optical *illusion* visible in certain conditions.

DEMAND *v.*, CLAIM, EXACT, REQUIRE. To *demand* is to request peremptorily; to *claim* is to *demand* as of right; to *require* is to *demand* because of need, *e.g.* 'I shall *require* a firm guarantee'. To *exact* is not only to *demand* but to get what is demanded.

DEMUR, BALK (or BAULK), BOGGLE, SCRUPLE, STICK, STRAIN. To *demur* at anything is to raise objections to doing it; to *scruple* is to do so on grounds of conscience. To *balk* at something is to refuse to do it, as a horse refuses a fence; to *boggle* is to fuss and dither over a decision; to *stick* is a colloquialism similar to *scruple*, as when one says, 'He will *stick* at nothing'. *To strain* at something is to emulate the blind guides in the New Testament, who *strain* at the gnat and swallow the camel. *Baulk* equals *balk*, but the former is the preferred spelling in the game of billiards.
ANT. **Accede.**

DENOTE, CONNOTE are complementary, not synonymous terms. A word *denotes* that which is expressed in its definition and no more; but it *connotes* all the rich, subjective and emotional overtones which are added to it by experience, personal association and so on. Thus the word 'England' *denotes* one country of many; but it *connotes*, for an Englishman, patriotic feelings, 'this precious jewel set in a silver sea', etc. etc.

DENY, CONTRADICT, GAINSAY, IMPUGN, NEGATIVE. To *deny* is to say no, to refuse; to *gainsay* is to dispute the truth of what others assert; to *contradict* is not only to *deny* flatly the truth of an assertion but often also carries the implication that the very reverse is true. To *negative* is to refuse assent to a proposal or proposition; to *impugn* is to attack the veracity of a statement or a person.
ANT. **Confirm; Concede.**

DEPLORE, BEMOAN, BEWAIL, LAMENT. To *deplore* is to express strong regret; to *lament* implies a demonstrative exhibition of sorrow; to *bewail* is literally to *lament* with wailing, and to *bemoan* with moans, though in neither case need such sounds be uttered for the words to be suitably employed, in the proper context.

DESIRE *v.*, COVET, CRAVE, WANT, WISH. To *desire* is to long ardently for something; to *wish* is less vehement and applies to *desires* rather less likely to be gratified. To *want* is now almost the colloquial form of to *wish*, though it formerly carried a much stronger implication of *need*. To *crave* is to *desire* passionately, even physically; to *covet* is to *desire* immoderately, and applies usually to that which is the property of others.

DESPISE, CONTEMN, DISDAIN, SCORN, SCOUT. To *despise* is to look down upon a thing; to *contemn* it is to condemn it vigorously; to *scorn* it suggests a fiery and indignant contempt; to *disdain*, a lofty aversion to that which is deemed base; to *scout* suggests not only derision but total rejection.
ANT. **Appreciate.**

DESPONDENT, DESPAIRING, DESPERATE, FORLORN, HOPELESS. *Despondent* implies deep dejection; *despairing*, the loss of hope; *desperate*, a sort of reckless and active despair. *Hopeless*, though it involves loss of hope, differs from *despairing* in that it may also contain the idea of resignation. *Forlorn*, in this grouping, carries overtones of the phrase 'forlorn hope', and so adds to hopelessness the idea of action which is almost certainly foredoomed to failure.
ANT. **Lighthearted.**

DESTROY, DEMOLISH, RAZE. To *destroy* is the opposite of to *construct*, and may be applied to anything destructible; to *demolish* is to reduce any structure, whether literal or figurative, to ruins; to *raze* is to level to the ground, and is applied literally to buildings, or figuratively to anything susceptible of complete obliteration.

DIALECT, ARGOT, CANT, JARGON, PATOIS, SLANG, VERNACULAR, all relate to non-standard forms of speech or language. *Dialect* is that which is used by the inhabitants of a certain locality; the *vernacular* is that which is employed by the common people in contrast to the learned. A *patois* is, commonly, a hybrid *dialect*; *jargon* is nowadays mostly technical speech, 'shop' or any other ugly-sounding lingo; *cant*, as here used, is the specialized secret speech of thieves and beggars; *argot* nowadays is the language used by a clique or set; *slang* is the racy, recently-coined speech of the common people, which either becomes soon outmoded or else, in its happier manifestations, adds permanent enrichment to the language.

DICTIONARY, GAZETTEER, GLOSSARY, LEXICON. A *dictionary* has come nowadays to mean almost any work of reference which is arranged in alphabetical order; a *gazetteer* is a geographical *dictionary*; a *lexicon* is, properly, a book which interprets the words of one language into those of another; a *glossary* is a list of unfamiliar words together with their glosses or definitions.

DIFFERENT, DISPARATE, DIVERGENT, DIVERSE, VARIOUS. The *different* implies distinction and separation; the *diverse* is stronger and adds the idea of contrast; the *divergent* stresses that the *difference* is increasing and that the chance of reconcilement has vanished. The *disparate* implies absolute *difference*, as between incompatibles; *various* stresses the number of *differences* available, *e.g.* '*various* flavours'.
ANT. **Identical; Alike; Same.**

DIRTY, FILTHY, FOUL, NASTY, SQUALID. *Dirty* is the general term; *filthy* is much stronger; *foul* adds the idea of loathsomeness. *Nasty* has now fallen upon evil days and commonly means not much more than

unpleasant; it was once as strong as *foul*. *Squalid* adds to the idea of dirtiness that of abject sordidness.
ANT. **Clean.**

DISAPPROVE, DEPRECATE. If we *disapprove* of something, we object to it and often roundly condemn it; if we *deprecate* it, we do so diffidently and with regret.
ANT. **Approve.**

DISASTER, CALAMITY, CATACLYSM, CATASTROPHE. A *disaster* is a physical mischance of magnitude; a *calamity* is a misfortune producing far-reaching distress. So a railway-accident is a *disaster*; the death of one man may be a *calamity* if, because of it, civil disorders ensue. A *catastrophe* is the disastrous conclusion to a process, and carries with it the idea of finality; a *cataclysm*, which is literally an earthquake, is figuratively used of an event by which the social order is turned upside down.

DISCERNMENT, ACUMEN, DISCRIMINATION, DIVINATION, INSIGHT, PENETRATION, PERCEPTION. *Discernment* gives a clear vision of things and requires accuracy and understanding; *discrimination* emphasizes the ability to distinguish the false from the true; *perception* adds to quickness of *discernment* a sureness of feeling. *Penetration* implies depth; *insight* is *penetration* plus sympathy; *divination* is natural *insight*; and *acumen* adds to *penetration* the idea of judgment.

DISCOVER, ASCERTAIN, DETERMINE, LEARN. To *discover* is to find out that which already exists; to *ascertain* is to *discover* facts of which one was previously ignorant; to *determine* (in this grouping) is similar to *ascertaining*, but is stronger and suggests that weightier matters are at stake. To *learn*, in this sense, is simply to find out something, as it were in passing. We say, 'I *learnt* by chance that he was Portuguese'.

DISCUSS, AGITATE, ARGUE, DEBATE. To *discuss* is to exchange opinions honestly for the sake of settling something; to *argue* is to *discuss* matters upon which the minds of those discussing them are already made up; to *debate* is to *argue* formally, or it may also mean to *discuss* silently with oneself. To *agitate* is to *argue* with a practical, and usually a political, end in view.

DISEASE, AFFECTION, AILMENT, COMPLAINT, DISTEMPER, MALADY. A *disease* is a physical disorder of a specific kind; the word *affection* implies that some particular organ is *affected*, as when we speak of 'an *affection* of the liver'. An *ailment* is usually a minor illness and, like *malady*, is applied chiefly to humans; *malady*, however, though much looser, can mean something as serious as *disease*. *Complaint* looks at the thing from the sufferer's point of view, and is not commonly a serious matter; *distemper*, once applied to human *ailments*, is now chiefly applied to those of animals.

DISHONEST, DECEITFUL, LYING, MENDACIOUS, UNTRUTHFUL. That which is not honest is *dishonest*, whether it involves lying, stealing or cheating; that which is *deceitful* implies the intention to mislead in order to gain one's ends. *Lying* applies merely to one who tells untruths; *mendacious*, to one who is an habitual liar. *Untruthful* is a kind of euphemism for *lying*, but is properly applied to such things as false statements: we say, 'He gives an *untruthful* account of so-and-so' rather than 'a *lying* one'.

ANT. **Honest.**

DISMAY *v.*, APPAL, DAUNT, HORRIFY are all words that have partially lost their original force. To be *dismayed* now means not much more than to be at a loss; to be *appalled* is stronger and suggests feeling powerless in the face of the inevitable. *Horrify* still retains some of its former strength and implies very considerable shock; and *daunt*, not being a word much in current use, keeps something of its old meaning of being restrained by fear from doing a brave deed: we still use such phrases as 'Nothing can *daunt* him'.

ANT. **Cheer.**

DISMISS, CASHIER, DISCHARGE, SACK. To *dismiss* is to let go, to cease to employ; to *discharge* is stronger and suggests dismissal because of shortcomings and inadequacies. To *cashier* is to *discharge* ignominiously from a position of trust, especially from one of the combatant services; to *sack* is the colloquial version of to *dismiss* or *discharge*.

DISORDER, DERANGE, DISARRANGE, DISORGANIZE, DISTURB, UNSETTLE. To *disorder* is to put out of order that which, for its proper functioning, depends upon being in order; to *derange* is much stronger and implies the complete destruction of normal conditions. To *disarrange* is to create a minor *disorder*; to *disorganize* is to destroy the order throughout a whole organized system; to *unsettle* is, as it were, to loosen the components of an organization so that it functions imperfectly; to *disturb*, in this grouping, is to *unsettle* or interfere with the settled order of things.

ANT. **Order.**

DISPOSAL, DISPOSITION. *Disposal* is a personal act, depending on the will of the individual; *disposition* is an act of judgment, depending on the nature of the things concerned. We thus speak of the *disposal* of rubbish; but of the *disposition* of troops in a battle.

DISPOSITION, CHARACTER, INDIVIDUALITY, PERSONALITY, TEMPERAMENT, all refer to the prevailing qualities which distinguish a person or group. *Disposition* stresses the predominant quality; *temperament*, the sum of the qualities; *character* augments *temperament* with moral overtones; and *personality* drops the idea of morality and stresses the unconscious as well as the conscious aspects of the *temperament*. *Individuality* underlines the uniqueness of the *personality* concerned.

DISTRESS, AGONY, MISERY, SUFFERING. *Distress* is remediable; *suffering* is personal and calls for endurance; *misery* stresses the mental aspects of *suffering*; *agony* is *suffering* in its highest degree.

DISTRIBUTE, DEAL, DISPENSE, DIVIDE, DOLE, all mean to share out. To *distribute* is to give promiscuously; to *dispense*, to give only to appropriate persons, as when one '*dispenses* alms'. To *divide* is to *distribute* with forethought to selected persons, often in equal shares. To *deal* is to give out one at a time, as when *dealing* cards; or, alternatively, is

simply to give, as when one *deals* a blow. To *dole* out is to give hesitatingly and frugally.
ANT. **Collect; Amass.**

DISTRUST, MISTRUST. *Distrust* is much the stronger and implies some measure of certitude concerning the person or thing *distrusted. Mistrust*, on the other hand, implies little more than suspicion and perhaps fear.

DOCTRINE, DOGMA, TENET. A *doctrine* is a principle accepted as authoritative by persons sharing the same belief; a *dogma* is a *doctrine* laid down as binding by a higher authority; a *tenet* stresses the factor of belief rather than that of authority: it is a principle held by a body of like-minded people.

DOUBTFUL, DUBIOUS, PROBLEMATICAL, QUESTIONABLE. *Doubtful* is stronger than *dubious*, the latter implying mere suspicion or mistrust, the former that one has grave reasons for doubting. *Problematical* suggests a nice balance of probability and is devoid of moral overtones; and *questionable* merely suggests that some slight dubiety exists. There is, however, a secondary use of *questionable*, now very common, which makes it a vague euphemism for any general impropriety, *e.g.* one speaks of '*questionable* activities'.
ANT. **Positive.**

DULL, BLUNT, OBTUSE are the reverse, respectively, of *sharp, keen, acute*. The *dull* lacks edge and intensity; the *blunt*, in its figurative usage, suggests lack of perception; the *obtuse*, a bluntness carried to the point of crass insensitiveness.
ANT. **Sharp; Poignant.**

E

EAGER, ANXIOUS, ATHIRST, AVID, KEEN. *Eager* suggests ardour and often impatience; *avid* adds to *eager* an implication of greed; *keen* suggests a quick, bright responsiveness; *anxious*, fear and apprehension; *athirst*, yearning and longing.
ANT. **Listless.**

EARTH, COSMOS, UNIVERSE, WORLD. The *earth* is this globe that we inhabit; the *world* is much less definite and commonly includes such of the space surrounding the earth as is visible to the ordinary man, together with its stars and planets. The *universe* is more strictly the entire system of creation; the *cosmos* is similar, but carries a far stronger implication of its being an ordered whole – the opposite, in fact, of *chaos*.

EASY, EFFORTLESS, FACILE, LIGHT, SIMPLE, SMOOTH. The *easy* makes few demands on one; the *facile* is now a somewhat derogatory term for that which comes with excessive *ease*; *simple*, in this grouping, stresses easiness of apprehension; *light*, the opposite of *heavy*, suggests the absence of burdensomeness. *Effortless* implies mastery of such a kind as makes something difficult seem *easy*; *smooth*, the easiness attained by the prior removal of all difficulties and obstacles.
ANT. **Hard.**

ECCENTRICITY, IDIOSYNCRASY. *Eccentricity* involves divergence from the normal or customary; *idiosyncrasy*, the following of one's own peculiar bent. The former therefore suggests strangeness; the latter, strongly individual action which, though it may result in strangeness, does not necessarily do so.

ECSTASY, RAPTURE, TRANSPORT. *Ecstasy* is a type of joy that exalts the mind and causes self-forgetfulness; *rapture* is a species of intense happiness: it is not, customarily, so strong a term as *ecstasy*. *Transport* may be applied to any violent emotion, not necessarily of happiness, that induces self-forgetfulness.

EFFECT, AFTERMATH, CONSEQUENCE, EVENT, ISSUE, OUTCOME, RESULT, SEQUEL. An *effect* follows a cause; a *consequence*, a chain of causes; a *result* is that which terminates a series of *effects* deriving from a single source. When *consequences* are beyond human control or foreknowledge, that which results is the *event*: 'We await (we say) the *event* with equanimity'. The *aftermath* is the (usually disastrous) belated *consequence* of past happenings; *issue* adds to *result* the idea of emergence, as from difficulties or troubles: 'A happy *issue* out of all our afflictions'. *Outcome* resembles *issue* but is less forceful; a *sequel* is a *result* that

follows as the logical *consequence*, though usually after an interval of time.
ANT. **Cause.**

EFFECTIVE, EFFECTUAL, EFFICACIOUS, EFFICIENT, all imply a capability to produce results. *Effective* stresses the production of, at least, the right effect, 'an *effective* speech'; *effectual*, the accomplishment of the desired result, '*effectual* measures'; *efficient* suggests personal capability and competence to produce what is required, 'an *efficient* officer'; *efficacious* implies the possession of the power that makes for effectiveness, '*efficacious* remedies'.
ANT. **Ineffective; Futile.**

EMBARRASS, ABASH, DISCOMFIT, DISCOMFORT, DISCONCERT. To *embarrass* is to cause uneasiness and constraint in another; to *discomfit* is figuratively to put him to flight; to *abash* is suddenly to *embarrass* the over-confident; to *disconcert* is so to upset someone as to cause him a temporary loss of self-confidence. To *discomfort*, not a true synonym of the foregoing, is to render physically or mentally uncomfortable.
ANT. **Relieve.**

EMPHASIS, ACCENT, ACCENTUATION, STRESS, all convey the idea of one thing being more conspicuous or prominent than another or others. *Emphasis* implies the bringing out of that which one deems most significant or important; *e.g.* 'He puts great *emphasis* on physical fitness'. *Stress* suggests pressure and strain, as when one *lays stress* on this or that. *Accent* always implies contrast, usually for the sake of effect and sharper definition; *accentuation* is a little stronger than *accent* and suggests a kind of magnified contrast.

EMPTY, BLANK, VACANT, VACUOUS, VOID. The *empty* has nothing inside it; the *vacant* is without an occupier: an *empty* house has no contents, a *vacant* one, no tenant. The *blank* is the unmarked, *e.g.* 'a *blank* page'; the *void* is *empty* in the highest degree, *e.g.* '*void* of understanding'; the *vacuous*, now generally used figuratively, implies the total emptiness of a vacuum.
ANT. **Full.**

ENCOMIUM, CITATION, EULOGY, PANEGYRIC, TRIBUTE. An *encomium* is a warm public expression of praise; a *eulogy* is more solemn and formal and is often posthumous; a *panegyric* suggests elaborate praise, often of eminent persons; a *tribute* is a more modest token of approval; a *citation* is the *eulogy* which accompanies and explains the presentation of some specific honour, civil or military.

ENEMY, FOE. An *enemy*, the opposite of a *friend*, is anyone for whom one nourishes hostile feelings; a *foe* is one with whom one indulges, either literally or figuratively, in active conflict. We say 'A man is his own worst *enemy*', not *foe*. There is, however, a tendency nowadays to replace *foe* with *enemy* in cases of national conflict, as the former is felt to have somewhat archaic connotations.

ENMITY, ANIMOSITY, ANTAGONISM, ANTIPATHY, HOSTILITY, RANCOUR. *Enmity* implies hatred whether open or concealed;

hostility is *enmity* in action. *Antipathy* and *antagonism* suggests instinctive causes for one's dislike: *antipathy* arises from aversion or repugnance, *antagonism* from the clash of opposed temperaments. *Animosity* suggests vindictiveness such as is likely to lead to open hostility; *rancour*, bitterness caused by a sense of grievance.
ANT. **Amity.**

ENORMOUS, COLOSSAL, GIGANTIC, HUGE, IMMENSE, VAST, all mean extremely large. *Enormous* suggests abnormality: we speak of *enormous* crimes. *Immense* is a little less strong, though it still suggests dimensions greatly exceeding the ordinary; *huge* implies *immensity* of bulk; *vast*, of extent; *gigantic*, literally, is giant-sized; *colossal*, though deriving from the not especially large Colossus of Rhodes, is now perhaps as strong as any of these terms, which are none of them, however, in their present uses, notable for their exactitude.

ENOUGH, ADEQUATE, COMPETENT, SUFFICIENT. We have *sufficient* when our wants are supplied; *enough* when our desires are satisfied. The *adequate* is a reasonable sufficiency; the *competent* is that which is *adequate* to the end in view.

ENTER (1), PENETRATE, PIERCE, PROBE. *Enter* is the general, comprehensive term; *penetrate* has a much stronger implication of violence; *pierce* is stronger still. To *probe* is to *penetrate* circumspectly, in an exploratory way.
ANT. **Issue from.**

ENTER (2), ADMIT, INTRODUCE. To *enter*, in this sense, is to make an entry, as in a ledger; to *introduce* is to insert what was not previously there, as, for example, rabbits into Australia; to *admit* is to cause to *enter*, to let in, *e.g.* 'one *admits* a ray of light'.

ENTHUSIAST, BIGOT, FANATIC, ZEALOT. *Enthusiast* has now largely lost its old sense of religious *fanatic* and means not much more than one who is keenly interested; *fanatic*, however, is still a word of power, and continues to imply monomania and determination to further the objects of that mania. A *zealot* is ardent and active in the service of that in which he believes, and resists all innovation; a *bigot* is obstinate and intolerant, a sort of soured *zealot*.

EQUAL, EQUIVALENT, IDENTICAL, SAME, TANTAMOUNT, VERY. Things are *equal* when there is no numerical difference between their properties; they are the *same* when there is no difference at all; they are *equivalent* when, though differing, they amount to the same thing, or set off one against another. *Identical* suggests the strongest possible form of *sameness*; *very*, in this use, *e.g.* 'That's the *very* thing I mean', is equivalent to *same*. *Tantamount* is to immaterial things what *equivalent* is to material ones.
ANT. **Unequal.**

ESCAPE *v.*, AVOID, ELUDE, ESCHEW, EVADE, SHUN, all mean to get away from that which one wishes not to encounter, as when one *escapes* the consequences of one's actions. *Avoid* here, in contrast to *escape*, suggests keeping clear of the menacing object; *evade*, dodging it;

elude, escaping it by guile or even shiftiness. To *shun* is to *avoid* because of a temperamental or reasoned aversion; to *eschew* is to avoid for reasons of prudence: a bilious person *eschews* rich dishes.

EVERLASTING, ENDLESS, INTERMINABLE, NEVER-ENDING, UNCEASING, all literally mean to go on for ever, but *everlasting* is a serious word with scriptural connotations, *e.g.* '*everlasting* felicity', and *endless* (which can apply to continuation both in time and in space) merely means that to which we can see no end, *e.g.* '*endless* discussions'. *Interminable* adds to *endless* the idea of tedium and loss of patience; *unceasing* and *never-ending* both imply excessive continuation, but the former stresses the idea of persistence, as in '*unceasing* efforts'; the latter, a certain unrelentingness, as in '*never-ending* torment'.
ANT. **Transitory.**

EVIDENT, APPARENT, CLEAR, DISTINCT, MANIFEST, OBVIOUS, PATENT, PLAIN, all mean readily apprehensible. *Evident* suggests visible signs that reveal the existence of the point in question; *manifest*, that the evidence for it speaks for itself; *patent*, in this grouping, that the evidence is visible on the face of the thing; *distinct*, that it can be seen with the utmost clarity; *obvious*, that it can be seen by practically anybody. *Apparent* here resembles *evident* except that it adds to the idea of visible evidence that of some reasoning from it; *plain* and *clear* are colloquial versions of the preceding terms, *plain* suggesting an absence of complexity and *clear* an absence of obscurity.

EXAMPLE, IDEAL, MODEL, PATTERN, STANDARD, all mean something that is set up for imitation. A *model* is often no more than something provided as a copy; an *example* has greater moral overtones, as when one 'sets an *example*'. *Ideal* has, nowadays, assumed the meaning of a perfect *example*: we speak of so-and-so providing our *ideal* of manhood. A *standard*, in this grouping, is an *ideal* imposed by external authority; a *pattern* may be no more than a detailed *model*, though it carries greater implications of perfection than *model*.

EXCEED, EXCEL, OUTDO, OUTSTRIP, SURPASS, TRANSCEND. To *exceed* is to go beyond a certain limit or measure; to *surpass* adds to *exceed* the idea of doing so because of skill or merit; to *transcend* suggests that the limit surpassed is not of human establishing. To *excel* implies pre-eminence; to *outdo* suggests that a previously established maximum has been exceeded; to *outstrip* adds to *surpass* the idea of competition and exertion.

EXCELLENCE, MERIT, PERFECTION, VIRTUE, all relate to that particular quality in a thing which renders it outstanding. Its *excellence* is that in which it excels others; its *merit*, in this connection, refers to its solid and inherent worth; its *virtue* suggests moral excellence, though this can also apply figuratively; its *perfection* suggests that the absolute ideal has been attained.
ANT. **Fault.**

EXCESSIVE, EXORBITANT, EXTRAVAGANT, EXTREME, IMMODERATE, INORDINATE, all suggest going beyond reasonable limits. The *excessive* is too large to be just and proper; the *immoderate* suggests positive lack of restraint; the *inordinate*, a transgressing of the bounds of authority and good judgment. *Extravagant* adds to *excessive* the moral idea of recklessness; *exorbitant*, an excessiveness quite beyond the established degree, hence it is generally applied to extortionate demands. The *extreme*, in this grouping, suggests an *extravagance* that knows no bounds.

EXCITE, GALVANIZE, PROVOKE, QUICKEN, STIMULATE. To *excite* is to rouse or stir up; to *provoke* is to *excite* to a lesser degree; to *stimulate* is to arouse from a state of inaction; to *quicken* is to *stimulate* with beneficial results; to *galvanize* is to *stimulate* strongly that which is moribund.

EXCUSE, CONDONE, FORGIVE, PARDON. To *excuse* is to overlook a fault; to *condone* is to overlook a graver offence; to *pardon* is to refrain from exacting punishment for an offence; to *forgive* is to refrain from harbouring feelings of resentment or any desire to punish.
ANT. **Punish.**

EXPEDIENT, ADVISABLE, POLITIC. The *expedient* is that from which definite and immediate advantage is thought likely to arise; the *politic* is that which it is judicious, in a practical way, to do; the *advisable* is a weaker term, but one free from the somewhat derogatory overtones which now tend to accompany the other two words.
ANT. **Inexpedient.**

EXPLAIN, CONSTRUE, ELUCIDATE, EXPOUND, INTERPRET. To *explain* is the general term; to *expound* is to *explain* elaborately; to *elucidate* is to *explain* by luminous expositions or illustrations. To *interpret* is to *explain* something which in its very nature is abstruse; to *construe* is to *interpret* when the difficulty of the thing interpreted lies in the actual words in which it is stated.

EXTEND, ELONGATE, LENGTHEN, PROLONG, PROTRACT, all mean to increase in length. To *lengthen* suggests extension in time and space; to *extend* has a similar meaning but can also apply, as *lengthen* cannot, to abstractions, such as a power or a privilege. To *elongate* is the opposite of to *abbreviate*; to *prolong* is to *extend* beyond the usual limits; to *protract* adds to *prolong* suggestions of needlessness and tedium.
ANT. **Abridge; Shorten.**

F

FABLE, ALLEGORY, APOLOGUE, MYTH, PARABLE are all short narratives that convey moral instruction. The characters in a *fable* are usually animals or inanimate objects, and the moral is stated at the end; an *apologue* is a more literary equivalent of the word *fable*. The characters in an *allegory* are usually human and the moral is implicit rather than stated; a very short *allegory* conveying a spiritual truth is called a *parable*; a *myth*, in this grouping, is a short *allegory* in which the characters are imaginary and the truth conveyed philosophical.

FACE *n*., COUNTENANCE, PHYSIOGNOMY, VISAGE. *Face* is the common term; *countenance* is properly applied to the *face* as it reveals, by its expression, mood, character, etc.; *visage* is more literary and often refers to the total and changing impression given by the *face*; *physiognomy* relates to the typical or racial character of the features.

FALLACY, CASUISTRY, SOPHISM, SOPHISTRY, all relate to faulty reasoning. A *fallacy* implies a logical flaw that vitiates the whole argument; a *sophism* is an equivocal argument intended to mislead; and *sophistry* is the species of argument that employs such devices. *Casuistry* suggests a sophistical way of arguing moral and theological problems.

FALSE, WRONG. *False* almost always implies the intent to deceive, *e.g.* 'To bear *false* witness'; *wrong* simply denotes error. There are, however, certain idiomatic exceptions, as when one speaks of a *false* note, which merely means a *wrong* note.
ANT. **True.**

FAME, CELEBRITY, GLORY, HONOUR, NOTORIETY, RENOWN, REPUTATION. *Fame* is the vaguest, least explicit, of these words; *renown* suggests solid *fame* because of high achievement; *honour* brings in the ideas of esteem and reverence; and *glory*, those of brilliance and achievement. *Celebrity*, on the other hand, suggests the acclamation of one's contemporaries; *reputation*, a reasonable measure of renown; *notoriety*, a meretricious *celebrity* as of a nine-days-wonder.
ANT. **Infamy; Obscurity.**

FAMOUS, CELEBRATED, DISTINGUISHED, EMINENT, ILLUSTRIOUS, NOTORIOUS, RENOWNED. The *famous* are such as enjoy fame in their own time or in the estimation of posterity; the *renowned*, a higher degree of the same sort of fame. *Celebrated* stresses the idea of being much in the public eye; *notorious*, in the public eye for the wrong reasons. *Distinguished* suggests that one is respected for one's superiority

to the common run of men; *eminent* carries the same idea to a higher degree; *illustrious*, still further, implying the highest kind of superiority.
ANT. **Obscure.**

FATE, DESTINY, DOOM, LOT, PORTION. *Fate* is inevitable and generally carries some suggestion of misfortune; *destiny*, though ineluctable, is freer from menacing connotations. *Lot* and *portion* contain the idea of distribution, but *lot* suggests a chance, and *portion*, an equitable, division. *Doom* implies a definitely unhappy and calamitous *fate*.

FAULT, FAILING, FOIBLE, FRAILTY, VICE. A *fault* is a falling away from virtue, not necessarily of a serious kind; a *failing* is a small *fault*; a *foible* is a harmless, and often an amiable, *failing*. *Frailty* suggests such weakness of character as makes one prone to faulty behaviour; a *vice* is a *fault* so serious that it infringes the moral code.
ANT. **Merit.**

FAVOURABLE, AUSPICIOUS, BENIGN, PROPITIOUS. *Favourable* implies that circumstances and conditions are on one's side; *benign* (which has astrological connotations) that they are well-disposed towards one; *auspicious*, that the omens are good; *propitious* that the powers-that-be are in compliant mood. The last is stronger than *favourable*, a little less strong than the two other words.
ANT. **Unfavourable; Antagonistic.**

FEAR *n.*, ALARM, CONSTERNATION, DISMAY, DREAD, FRIGHT, HORROR, PANIC, TERROR, TREPIDATION. *Fear* is the general term; *dread* is somewhat stronger and has a touch of the supernatural involved in it. A *fright* is a short-lived *fear*; *alarm*, a sudden *fright*. *Dismay* suggests a temporary loss of composure; *consternation*, a still stronger loss. A *panic* is a wild unreasoning *fear*; *terror* is violent *dread*; and *horror* brings in a sense of the loathsome and the unnatural. *Trepidation* adds to *fear* the idea of timidity and trembling.
ANT. **Fearlessness.**

FEARFUL (1), AFRAID, APPREHENSIVE. *Fearful*, in this grouping, means timorous; *apprehensive* implies the well-founded anticipation of some danger; *afraid*, weak or cowardly apprehension.
ANT. **Fearless; Intrepid.**

FEARFUL (2), APPALLING, AWFUL, DREADFUL, FRIGHTFUL, HORRIBLE, TERRIBLE, TERRIFIC. The *fearful* is frightening; the *awful*, impressive; the *dreadful*, loathsome and disagreeable. The *frightful* produces, at least momentarily, great alarm; the *terrible* excites extreme fear or distress; the *terrific* causes terror by its appearance or some other quality; the *horrible* adds to terror the idea of loathing and aversion; the *appalling* adds to the same the idea of dismay.

FEAT, ACHIEVEMENT, EXPLOIT. A *feat* is usually a single act of strength or dexterity; an *exploit*, an adventurous and heroic *feat*; an *achievement* is a distinguished action performed in the face of difficulties.

FELICITATE, CONGRATULATE. *Congratulate* is the common expression and stresses the idea that good fortune has come to the person congratulated; *felicitate* is more formal and carries a greater suggestion of wishing happiness to the person felicitated.

FEMALE *adj.*, EFFEMINATE, FEMININE, LADYLIKE, WOMANISH, WOMANLY. *Female* is the opposite of *male* and relates to the sex itself; *feminine* is the opposite of *masculine* and relates to the characteristics of the sex: we speak of '*female* children' but of '*feminine* graces'. *Womanly* suggests full womanhood, maternity, etc.; but *womanish* is a term of contempt usually applied to that which should be masculine. *Effeminate* also is usually applied to a non-virile man; and *ladylike* can mean anything from the behaviour of a lady to a false gentility.
ANT. **Male.**

FERTILE, FECUND, FRUITFUL, PROLIFIC. The *fertile* is, properly, that in which seeds take root and grow; the *fecund* is the opposite of the barren, and suggests that which bears fruit after its kind in abundance. *Fruitful* applies to anything that produces profitable results; *prolific* suggests an unusually high rate of reproduction.
ANT. **Infertile; Sterile.**

FICTION, FABLE, FABRICATION, FIGMENT. All these things are verbal inventions, but *fiction* is now chiefly applied to prose narratives, or novels. A *figment* is a derogatory term suggesting an unbridled feat of the imagination; a *fabrication* is a falsehood, a *fiction* intended to deceive; a *fable*, in this grouping, is an outrageous and incredible *fiction*.

FIDELITY, ALLEGIANCE, DEVOTION, FEALTY, LOYALTY, PIETY. *Fidelity* is keeping faith in a matter of obligation; *allegiance*, keeping faith with some superior authority. *Fealty* resembles *allegiance* but stresses the strength of the obligation. *Loyalty* suggests closer personal involvement than *fidelity*; *devotion*, an ardent attachment; *piety*, fidelity to natural and fundamental ties, such as those which link one to one's country or one's religion.
ANT. **Faithlessness; Perfidy.**

FIERCE, BARBAROUS, CRUEL, FEROCIOUS, INHUMAN, SAVAGE, TRUCULENT, all suggest an appearance of fury. The *fierce* inspires terror; the *truculent* wishes, with indifferent success, to do so; the *ferocious* adds to fierceness of mien fierceness of behaviour. *Barbarous* suggests a fierceness worthy of the uncivilized; *savage* is similar but stronger; *inhuman*, stronger still, implying all absence of human feeling. *Cruel*, in this grouping, suggests one that takes pleasure in his own ferocity.
ANT. **Tame; Mild.**

FIT *adj.*, APPROPRIATE, APT, FELICITOUS, HAPPY, MEET, PROPER, SUITABLE. The *fit* is adapted to the end in view; the *suitable* answers the requirements of the occasion; the *meet* is what is just and right; the *proper*, that which pertains by nature and reason to the thing in question. The *appropriate* is that which is so *suitable* that it seems the peculiar property of the thing concerned; the *apt* is that which is fitted by its own nature to the desired end; the *happy* is that which is singularly *appropriate*; the *felicitous*, that which is in the highest degree *happy*.
ANT. **Unfit.**

FLAGRANT, GLARING, GROSS, RANK. The *flagrant* is that which can be neither overlooked nor condoned; the *glaring*, that which is sadly evident to all; the *gross* has still more derogatory implications, and means so bad as to be unpardonable. *Rank*, in this grouping, is a very strong intensifier of the thing reprobated, *e.g.* '*rank* madness'.

FOLLOW (1), ENSUE, SUCCEED, SUPERVENE, all imply to come after in space or time. *Follow* is the loose, general term; *succeed* implies a prescribed order; *ensue*, a logical sequence; *supervene* often suggests that what *follows* is additional and of an unforeseen nature.

FOLLOW (2), CHASE, PURSUE, TRAIL, all mean to go after something. *Follow*, again, is the general term; to *pursue* is to *follow* with inveterate persistence; to *chase* is to *pursue* with speed; to *trail* is, literally, to *follow* by tracking.
ANT. **Precede.**

FOOD (1), COMESTIBLES, FODDER, FORAGE, PROVENDER, PROVISIONS, VIANDS, VICTUALS. *Food* is the general term; *victuals*, now somewhat archaic, are human foods, usually ready for consumption. *Viands* suggests rare and dainty *victuals*; *provisions* are *food* considered generally, in stock or bulk; *comestibles* stresses edibility, but is now largely facetious; *provender* is *food* of any kind, with a strong likelihood of its being animal-food. *Fodder* and *forage* are always animal-foods, but *fodder* is food for stall-feeding, and *forage*, food obtained by grazing.

FOOD (2), ALIMENT, NOURISHMENT, NUTRIMENT, SUSTENANCE, all relate to the abstract sustaining aspects of *food*, either literally or figuratively. Food is the common term, *e.g.* '*food* for thought'; *aliment* is that which promotes growth; *nutriment*, that part of the *food* which is assimilated; *nourishment* is *food* considered in its growth- and health-producing aspects; *sustenance* resembles *nutriment*, but stresses the idea of maintaining life rather than of building up.

FOOL (1), IMBECILE, IDIOT, SIMPLETON. A *fool* is stupid and thoughtless; an *idiot* is mentally deficient; an *imbecile*, in present use, is half-witted; a *simpleton* is silly but harmless.

FOOL (2), BUFFOON, CLOWN, HARLEQUIN, JESTER, ZANY. A *fool*, in this sense, is a *jester* or domestic entertainer, but the profound wisdom of Shakespeare's *fools* has given the word, in this usage, a seriousness much greater than that of *jester*. A *clown* was formerly the rustic who provided comic relief in a play, now he is the stock comic character of the pantomime; a *buffoon* is a low, slapstick *clown*, or an artificial *fool*; a *zany*, a rather pitiable laughing-stock; a *harlequin*, the lively and animated *jester* of the harlequinade.

FORBEARING, CLEMENT, INDULGENT, LENIENT, MERCIFUL, TOLERANT, all suggest the reverse of severe. *Forbearing* implies patience under provocation; *tolerant*, a liberal attitude towards opinions one does not oneself hold; *clement*, mildness and gentleness; *merciful*, a capacity for compassion and forgiveness. *Lenient* differs from *clement* in

suggesting softness rather than gentleness; *indulgent* implies an extreme leniency sometimes verging upon pampering.
ANT. **Unrelenting.**

FORBID, BAN, INHIBIT, INTERDICT, PROHIBIT. To *forbid* is the direct and familiar term; to *prohibit*, the official and formal, but *forbid* is a little stronger and carries a greater expectation of being obeyed, since *prohibit* nowadays suggests relations with an impersonal authority while *forbid* implies direct human relationship. To *interdict* is to *prohibit* authoritatively for a given time; to *inhibit* suggests restraints imposed either from outside or from within; *ban* adds to *prohibit* a sense of definite condemnation.
ANT. **Permit; Bid.**

FORCE, COERCION, COMPULSION, DURESS, RESTRAINT, VIOLENCE. *Force* is an exercise of physical power; *violence*, a vigorous and injurious exercise of it. *Compulsion* implies the exertion of physical force, moral pressure, or psychological conditioning to get one's way; *coercion*, a term of narrower application, sharpens the idea of physical or moral force. *Duress* means compelling or coercing by the threat of penalties; *restraint*, a forcible checking or holding back.

FORERUNNER, HARBINGER, HERALD, PRECURSOR. A *forerunner* is something or somebody serving as a sign or a presage of what is to come; a *precursor* (semantically the same word) is one who makes ready for a greater that is to come. A *harbinger* is one who announces something for which preparation needs to be made; a *herald*, one who proclaims the advent of something, *e.g.* 'the lark, the *herald* of the morn'.

FORESEE, ANTICIPATE, APPREHEND, DIVINE, FOREKNOW. To *foresee* is to know in advance that something will happen; to *foreknow* suggests a supernatural basis for such knowledge. To *divine* implies that such knowledge is due to one's own peculiar powers; to *apprehend*, that the knowledge is such as fills one with dread. To *anticipate* (literally, to take beforehand) suggests action taken in advance because of one's foresight, *e.g.* 'He *anticipated* my lightest wish'. To *anticipate* does not mean to *expect*; it can mean to *look forward to.*

FORETELL, AUGUR, FOREBODE, FORECAST, PORTEND, PREDICT, PRESAGE, PROGNOSTICATE, PROPHESY. To *foretell* is the common unqualified expression; to *predict* implies special knowledge and skill. To *forecast* is now, usually, to *predict* the weather; to *prophesy* supposes strong supernatural powers; to *prognosticate* is to base one's predictions (now usually medical) upon signs and symptoms. To *augur* is to foretell by omens; to *presage*, by occult powers – or else merely to adumbrate; to *portend* is similar to *to presage* but with the difference that only evil things are *portended*. *Forebode*, likewise, applies only to unfavourable happenings, predicted by dreams, presentiments and so on.

FORM, CEREMONIAL, CEREMONY, FORMALITY, LITURGY, RITE, RITUAL. *Form* is the comprehensive term in this grouping, meaning a recognized way of doing things; a *formality* is a *form* carried out perfunctorily. *Ceremony* is much more specific than *form*; and *ceremonial* implies either a succession or the practice of *ceremonies*. A *rite* is a *form* prescribed by an organization such as a church; a *ritual* is a collection of such *rites*; a *liturgy* is a strictly religious *rite* or *ritual*.

FOUND, ESTABLISH, INSTITUTE, ORGANIZE. To *found* is to take the initial steps in bringing something into being; to *establish* adds to the idea of *founding* that of maintaining. To *institute* resembles to *establish*, but is wider in application and can suggest the starting of something which does not have continuous or permanent existence. To *organize*, in this grouping, means so to direct a newly founded society that it functions properly.

FRANK, CANDID, OPEN, PLAIN. To be *frank* is to act and speak plainly and sincerely; to be *candid* is to be so *frank* that any other course is inconceivable. To be *open* is to be less conscientious than *candid*, more artless than *frank*; and to be *plain* suggests a candour that approaches bluntness.
ANT. **Reticent.**

FREE *v.*, DELIVER, DISCHARGE, EMANCIPATE, ENFRANCHISE, LIBERATE, RELEASE. *Free* is the common, general term; *release* carries a stronger implication of loosing from restraint; and *liberate* stresses the liberty which arises from the process of *releasing*. To *emancipate* is to *liberate* from that which dominates, often by one's own exertions; to *deliver* is to *liberate* by disburdening, whether the burden is a letter or a child; to *discharge* is to *liberate* with vigour, as when one *discharges* a gun, though it can also be only the equivalent of *release*, as when one *discharges* a prisoner. To *enfranchise* is to free from political disabilities.

FREE *adj.*, AUTONOMOUS, INDEPENDENT, SOVEREIGN, all convey the idea of not being subject to the rule of another. *Free* here stresses the absence of external compulsion; *independent*, the absence of relationship with any other body: with *independence* one stands alone. *Sovereign* emphasizes the absence of a superior power and the pre-eminence of the entity so described, *e.g.* 'a *sovereign* state'. *Autonomous* strictly implies independence coupled with freedom, in practice it usually refers to a self-governing body comprised within a greater unit.
ANT. **Bond.**

FREEDOM, LIBERTY, LICENCE (*Br.*) or LICENSE (*Amer.*). *Freedom* is the comprehensive term implying the absence of all restraint. *Liberty* has loftier political connotations and tends to suggest free power of choice within a conventional political framework: a wild animal enjoys *freedom*; a civilized man enjoys *liberty* of expression and so on. *Liberty* also, however, can simply mean release, as when a prisoner is given his *liberty*. *Licence* (or *license*) is *liberty* to break the customary rules: '*Licence* they mean when they cry *Liberty*', as Milton says of his contemporaries.
ANT. **Necessity.**

FRIGHTEN, ALARM, SCARE, STARTLE, TERRIFY, TERRORIZE. *Frighten* is the widest and loosest of these terms; *scare*, now mostly colloquial, means strictly to *frighten* so much as to cause flight, *e.g.* '*scarecrow*'. *Alarm* stresses anxiety and apprehension; *terrify*, extreme fear and agitation. To *terrorize*, on the other hand, suggests intention on the part of those *terrorizing*, usually with a view to coercion; to *startle* is to surprise suddenly and shock mildly.

FULL, COMPLETE, PLENARY, REPLETE, though not strict synonyms, all convey a similar idea. *Full* is the common term and suggests that nothing can be added; *complete* is synonymous with *full* when it implies perfection, *e.g.* 'a *complete* account of the revolution'. *Plenary* means *full* without any qualifications, but is restricted to certain uses, such as '*plenary* powers'. *Replete* is stronger than *full* in certain contexts where it suggests *full* to the brim, almost overflowing.
ANT. **Empty.**

FULSOME, OLEAGINOUS, OILY, UNCTUOUS. *Fulsome* means cloying and is applied to excessive praise, flattery, etc. *Oily* and *unctuous* both suggest the smoothness of oil, but whereas *oily* hints at an excessive ingratiatingness, *unctuous* often adds to it the idea of downright hypocrisy. *Oleaginous* is a somewhat pompous and facetious form of *oily*.

G

GAIN *n.*, EMOLUMENT, LUCRE, PROFIT are all words signifying increment, but the first is the general term, the others specific. *Profit* is the difference between the buying and selling price of an article; *emolument* is usually a salary or fee; *lucre*, often preceded by 'filthy', is used only in the pejorative sense, to imply immoderate *gains*.
ANT. **Loss.**

GATHER, ACCUMULATE, ASSEMBLE, COLLECT. *Gather* is the most general term; *collect* implies a certain specialization and discrimination, as when one *collects* stamps; *accumulate* suggests an indiscriminating heaping up; *assemble*, a more careful choice, as when one *assembles* the components of a machine.
ANT. **Disperse.**

GAY, ANIMATED, CHEERFUL, LIVELY, SPRIGHTLY, VIVACIOUS, all imply *animation*. The *gay* person is carefree; the *lively*, brisk and energetic; the *cheerful*, contented: but the *sprightly* one can be wearisome; the *vivacious* one may seem to overdo it.
ANT. **Grave.**

GENERATION, AGE. Contemporaries in point of birth-date constitute a *generation*; an *age* is a longer, though arbitrary, division of time, *e.g.* 'the Augustan, the Elizabethan *age*'.

GENEROUS, BOUNTIFUL, LIBERAL, MUNIFICENT. *Generous* implies a warm heart; *liberal*, an open hand; to be *bountiful* is to exhibit a lavish generosity; to be *munificent*, a splendid liberality.
ANT. **Mean.**

GERM, BACILLUS, BACTERIUM, MICROBE, VIRUS. *Germ* and *microbe* are non-scientific names for the minute organisms which, among other things, are responsible for many diseases; *bacteria*, the plural of *bacterium*, is the scientific name for a large group of single-celled micro-organisms of which the *bacillus*, or rod-shaped, is one species. A *virus* is a mysterious causer of disease, so minute that it can pass through a filter able to trap a *bacterium*.

GET, ACQUIRE, GAIN, OBTAIN, PROCURE are all words meaning to cause to possess; but *obtain* implies more effort, and *procure* more care, in the *getting* of the object desired. *Acquire* suggests that one is probably adding to what one has already *got*; *gain* implies the greatest effort of all, *e.g.* 'He has *gained* first prize'.

GHASTLY, GRIM, GRISLY, GRUESOME. *Ghastly* carries an implication of death (*ghostly*); *grim*, one of ferocity; *grisly*, of the supernatural. *Gruesome* may refer either to the supernatural or the merely physically horrible.

GIFT, DONATION, GRATUITY, PRESENT. A *gift* is the general term for what is given to an individual without payment; a *donation* is one publicly bestowed, usually upon an institution; a *present* is a complimentary or seasonal *gift*; a *gratuity* is one given in return for services rendered.

GIVE, BESTOW, DONATE, GRANT, PRESENT. For *give* and *donate* see the distinction made under **GIFT.** We *bestow* where there is necessity; and *grant* that for which a formal request has been made to us. To *present* implies a more formal giving, as when one '*presents* prizes'.

GLAD, CHEERFUL, HAPPY, JOYFUL, JOYOUS. Mark Tapley was *cheerful* in adversity; one is *glad* to hear pleasant news. To be *happy* suggests a much more positive condition of felicity, and to be *joyful* implies elation for some definite reason. The *joyous* is that which is in its own nature *joyful*: we speak of 'a *joyous* disposition'.
ANT. **Sad.**

GO, DEPART, LEAVE, QUIT, WITHDRAW are synonymous when they mean to move away from where one happens to be; but to *leave* implies separation, and to *depart* carries the same idea with more dignity: we say 'to *depart* this life'. To *quit*, on the other hand, often, though not always, suggests that the person concerned is glad to *go*; and *withdraw* suggests that the action is deliberate and often that it is dictated by prudence, as when one *withdraws* from an untenable position.
ANT. **Come.**

GOOD, MORAL, RIGHTEOUS, UPRIGHT. The *good* man is *moral* in his conduct, *upright* in his dealings; and, if others deem him so, they can call him *righteous*, though he had better not do so himself.
ANT. **Bad.**

GOODNESS, MORALITY, RECTITUDE, VIRTUE. *Goodness* may be innate, but *virtue* is acquired. *Rectitude* is a sterner quality, involving an undeviating adherence to what one believes to be right; *morality* implies a familiarity with ethical principles.
ANT. **Badness.**

GOODS, POSSESSIONS, PROPERTY. *Goods* are one's belongings, for which *possessions* is a more grandiloquent name; *property* has legal connotations. We endow with our worldly *goods*; enjoy our *possessions*; purchase *property*.

GOVERN, RULE. To *govern* implies a modicum of wisdom in the governor; not so, invariably, to *rule*. We *govern* our own passions; we *rule* other people.

GRACIOUS, CORDIAL, GENIAL, KIND. *Kindness* is the simple, domestic form of this quality; *graciousness*, usually, though not always, applies to *kindness* shown by superiors to inferiors. *Cordiality* implies especial warmth; and *geniality*, warmth exhibited between equals.
ANT. **Ungracious.**

GRAND, GRANDIOSE, IMPOSING, MAJESTIC, MAGNIFICENT are all words that imply importance, though *grand* contains the suggestion of true grandeur, and *grandiose*, of false. *Magnificent* usually hints at costliness; *imposing*, at impressiveness; and *majestic* adds to *imposing* the idea of solemnity and stateliness.

GRATEFUL, THANKFUL. One is *grateful* to men; *thankful* to higher entities, such as Providence; one is *thankful* also for small mercies.
ANT. **Ungrateful.**

GRAVE *adj.*, SEDATE, SERIOUS, SOBER, SOLEMN. The *serious* man eschews frivolity; the *solemn* makes it clear that he does so. The *sedate* person exhibits a surface gravity; the *sober* one (in this grouping), an absence of enthusiasm; the *grave* one is, in his own nature, *serious* through and through.
ANT. **Gay.**

GREAT, BIG, LARGE. While *large* refers only to physical magnitude, *great* can also apply to abstract matters, *e.g.* 'a *great* man; a *great* fool'. *Big* in contrast to *large* relates to volume rather than to area: a *big* house has a lot of room in it; a *large* one calls up a vision of an imposing façade.
ANT. **Little.**

GRIEVE, MOURN, SORROW. To *grieve* is to feel sorrow as an inward emotion; to *mourn* is to give outward expression to one's grief. To *sorrow*, now somewhat archaic, suggests a greater degree of feeling than to *grieve*.
ANT. **Rejoice.**

GUARD *v.*, DEFEND, PROTECT, SHIELD. One *protects* by measures taken beforehand; one *shields* on the spur of the moment. To *guard* implies a static defence; to *defend*, a formal mobilizing of forces.

GUIDE, LEAD, PILOT. To *guide* implies knowledge of the way, and so does to *pilot*; the first applies to the land, the other to the water. To *lead*, on the other hand, only means to go in front: the blind can *lead* the blind.
ANT. **Misguide.**

H

HABIT, CUSTOM, PRACTICE, USE, WONT. A *habit* is a way of behaving so often repeated as to have become unconscious, but a *practice* is a repeated act inspired by volition. *Custom* implies that such an act is done in conformity with communal practice; *use*, in conformity with the practice of a particular group, *e.g.* 'the *use* of Sarum'. *Wont* resembles *use*, but is narrower in application and generally applies only to individuals.

HAPPEN, BEFALL, BETIDE, CHANCE. *Happen* is the general term; *chance* suggests a greater absence of causation. *Befall*, on the other hand, suggests that Providence has a hand in the matter; and *betide*, which is largely archaic, is now confined to objurgations such as 'Woe *betide* you!'

HAPPINESS, BEATITUDE, BLISS, FELICITY. *Felicity* is a more elevated condition than *happiness*; *beatitude*, suggesting blessedness, is stronger than either. *Bliss* adds to *beatitude* a note of ecstasy, but the word has, nowadays, generally descended to trivial uses.
ANT. **Unhappiness.**

HARBOUR, HAVEN, PORT. A *haven* is a natural *harbour*; a *port* implies a *harbour* but also includes the town adjacent to it.

HARD (1), FIRM, SOLID. The *hard* is difficult to penetrate; the *solid* is opposed to the hollow; the *firm* is insusceptible to distortion.
ANT. **Soft.**

HARD (2), ARDUOUS, DIFFICULT. The *hard* is the reverse of the *easy*; the *difficult* presents obstacles that can be surmounted by skill and ingenuity; the *arduous*, by persistence and perseverance.
ANT. **Easy.**

HASTE, DESPATCH, HURRY, SPEED. 'More *haste*, less *speed*' shows that *haste* has overtones of recklessness. *Hurry* implies a certain bustle and disorder; *despatch*, a certain coolness and efficiency.
ANT. **Deliberation.**

HATE, ABHOR, DETEST, LOATHE. To *hate* is a personal feeling; to *detest*, an impersonal one; to *abhor* suggests a moral repugnance; to *loathe*, a physical disgust. So one may *hate* a man; *detest* his principles; *abhor* his vices; *loathe* his cruelties.
ANT. **Love.**

HAVE, ENJOY, OWN, POSSESS. *Have* is the general term, but *own* implies a legal right. *Possess* differs from *own* in being applicable to matters other than property, such as faculties and qualities. *Enjoy*, save in the strict legal use, means what it says – that one derives benefit from the thing possessed.

HEALTHY, SALUBRIOUS, SALUTARY, WHOLESOME. *Healthy* is the general term; *wholesome* usually refers to *healthy* diet, etc. *Salubrious* and *salutary* are more positive terms, the first meaning that which tends to improve the health, the other that which tends to correct some specific inadequacy.
ANT. **Unhealthy.**

HEAP, PILE. To *heap* is a random activity; to *pile*, an orderly one: we *heap* stones, but *pile* wood.

HEAR, LISTEN. To *hear* is to apprehend sounds through the ear; to *listen* is to do so consciously: one *hears* an explosion, *listens* to music.

HEAVY, CUMBROUS, PONDEROUS, WEIGHTY. The *heavy* is hard to lift; the *cumbrous*, awkward to handle; the *ponderous* is bulky as well as heavy. *Weighty* is generally used figuratively, as when we speak of '*weighty* reasons'.
ANT. **Light.**

HELP, AID, ASSIST, SUCCOUR. *Help* is the general term; *assist* implies a secondary or subordinate role; and *succour*, *help* given on the spur of the moment: 'first aid'. *Aid* itself implies *help* where it is badly needed.
ANT. **Hinder.**

HERETIC, SCHISMATIC, SECTARIAN. A *heretic* holds doctrines differing from those taught by the sect to which he belongs; a *schismatic* separates himself from his sect upon a point of doctrine; a *sectarian* is one who belongs to a heretical or schismatic body.

HESITATE, FALTER, VACILLATE, WAVER. To *waver* is to *hesitate* after having made up one's mind; to *vacillate* is to *hesitate* for a prolonged period; to *falter* is to *hesitate* to so great a degree that one fails to complete the action contemplated.

HETERODOX, HERETICAL. *Heterodox* beliefs are unorthodox or unaccustomed ones; *heretical* ones are condemned by authority.
ANT. **Orthodox.**

HIDE, CONCEAL, SECRETE. To *hide* is, etymologically, only to cover; to *conceal* usually implies the intent to *hide*. *Secrete* is stronger still and implies furtiveness and stealth.

HIGH, LOFTY, TALL. *High* is the general term; *tall* (with a few colloquial exceptions such as '*tall* stories') applies to human stature; *lofty* is reserved for poetic diction or for things of an impressive height.
ANT. **Low.**

HINDER, IMPEDE, OBSTRUCT, PREVENT. *Hinder* is applied, generally, to trifles; but *impede* and *obstruct*, both of which etymologically carry the sense of hindering physically, are much stronger terms: to *obstruct* implies the stopping of something that is desirous of moving; to

impede, the slowing down of its movement. To *prevent* is to stop completely the action contemplated.
ANT. **Further.**

HINT, IMPLY, INSINUATE, INTIMATE, SUGGEST. *Suggest* is the most direct of these words, while *imply* contains the idea that the person addressed must do some of the thinking himself. We *intimate* when we ourselves are uncertain; *insinuate* when we are being malicious; and *hint* when we are not being completely candid: 'Just *hint* a fault, and hesitate dislike'.

HOLINESS, SANCTITY. Though close synonyms, *holiness* is best applied to spiritual perfection, and *sanctity* to the quality of being sacred: *holiness* is more of the mind, *sanctity* of the conduct.

HOLY, DIVINE, RELIGIOUS, SACRED, SPIRITUAL. The *divine* is that which pertains to God; the *religious*, that which pertains to religion as opposed to the secular; the *spiritual* is that which is opposed to the material. *Holy* is a stronger term than *sacred*; what is *holy* is altogether *spiritual*, but what is *sacred* derives, to some degree, from human actions, such as blessing or consecration.
ANT. **Unholy.**

HONESTY, HONOUR, INTEGRITY, PROBITY. A sense of *honour* will cause a man to behave *honestly*: the greater includes the less. *Integrity* implies a soundness of principle which renders dishonesty impossible; *probity* is proven *honesty*.
ANT. **Dishonesty.**

HONOUR, DEFERENCE, RESPECT, REVERENCE. We show *honour* to great men; *respect* to our seniors; *reverence* to God; *deference* to those whom we deem, rightly or wrongly, our superiors.
ANT. **Dishonour.**

HOPE, EXPECT. Though we *hope* for better things, we *expect* the mixture of good and bad as before.
ANT. **Despair.**

HOT, ARDENT, BURNING, FIERY. *Hot* is the general term; *fiery* implies the actual presence of fire; *burning*, of actual combustion. All three may be used figuratively, and *ardent*, which likewise means *burning*, is seldom used in any other way, being roughly the equivalent of *fervent* (which, strictly, means *boiling*).
ANT. **Cold.**

HUMBLE, LOW, LOWLY, MEEK. Whereas *humble* implies humility, *lowly* implies lowness; yet rather strangely *humble* is more likely to be used in a depreciatory sense than *lowly*, *e.g.* '*humble* origins'. *Low*, on the other hand, is always used disparagingly: 'of *low* birth'. *Meek* implies a gentleness of demeanour not necessarily associated with humbleness.

HUMOUR *n.*, MOOD, TEMPER. *Humour* derives from the old doctrine that one's temperament is dependent upon one of the four *humours*, the hot, the cold, the wet, the dry, and characterizes a *mood* induced by one's physical condition. A man's *temper*, on the other hand, bears relation to his whole disposition; his *mood*, to his mental state.

HYPOCRISY, CANT, SANCTIMONIOUSNESS. While *sanctimoniousness* implies a cloaking of bad behaviour behind a mask of piety, *hypocrisy* is the capacity for self-deception which renders such behaviour possible. *Cant* is the verbal expression of *sanctimoniousness*.

HYPOTHESIS, THEORY. A *theory* is the explanation proposed for a set of circumstances; a *hypothesis* is a more tentative name for such explanation.

I

IDEA, CONCEPT, CONCEPTION, NOTION, THOUGHT. *Idea*, the general term, refers to an image seen in the mind; *concept* is the logical term for a generic *idea*, *e.g.* 'the *concept* of freedom'; *conception* carries much the same meaning outside logical usage, but adds the suggestion of mental activity in the *conceiving*. *Thought* suggests the idea of reasoning; *notion*, a certain whimsicality in the *conception*.

IDLE, INDOLENT, LAZY, SLOTHFUL. An *idle* person fritters his time away; a *lazy* one can only with difficulty be spurred to activity; an *indolent* one constitutionally lacks energy; *slothful* adds to *indolent* a strong spice of moral disapproval.
ANT. **Busy.**

IGNORANT, ILLITERATE, UNEDUCATED, UNLEARNED. *Uneducated* implies a lack of education; *unlearned*, a lack of higher education; *illiterate*, a scorn for education (or, literally, an inability to read); *ignorant*, a lack of knowledge, generally.
ANT. **Informed.**

IMAGINATION, FANCY, FANTASY. 'The *imagination*, or shaping or modifying power; the *fancy*, or the aggregative and associative power', in Coleridge's famous distinction. *Imagination* implies a lofty activity of mind; *fancy*, a trifling one. *Fantasy* is *fancy* unrestrained.

IMPERIOUS, DOMINEERING, MASTERFUL, OVERBEARING, PEREMPTORY. The *domineering* person is a bully; the *peremptory* will not take no for an answer; the *overbearing* beats down all opposition; the *masterful* is aware of his own superior position; the *imperious* behaves as if certain of it.
ANT. **Abject.**

IMPERTINENT, IMPUDENT, INSOLENT, RUDE. The *impertinent* man busies himself with other people's affairs; the *impudent* is shameless in his impertinence; *insolent* adds the idea of insult; *rude*, of a definite boorishness.
ANT. **Respectful.**

IMPLANT, INCULCATE, INSEMINATE, INSTIL. Usually all applied to the diffusion of knowledge, to *inseminate* is to sow the seed; to *instil* is to instruct gradually and gently; to *inculcate*, persistently; to *implant* implies successful *insemination*.

IMPORTANCE, CONSEQUENCE, MOMENT, SIGNIFICANCE, WEIGHT. *Consequence* is the *importance* a thing derives from its consequences; *moment* implies self-evident *consequence*; *weight* is the *import-*

ance a thing possesses intrinsically; *significance* is that within a thing which renders it important, whether recognized or not.
ANT. **Unimportance.**

INABILITY, DISABILITY, though often confused, are not synonymous. *Inability* arises from absence of power; *disability* from loss of power.
ANT. **Ability.**

INACTIVE, INERT, PASSIVE, SLUGGISH, SUPINE. To be *inactive* is simply not to be active, as in the case of an *inactive* volcano; *inert* implies an habitual indisposition to activity; *passive* adds the suggestion of reacting negatively to external force; *supine* adds to *passive* a moral suggestion of spinelessness; *sluggish* suggests slothful and heavy movement.
ANT. **Active.**

INCLINATION, LEANING, PRONENESS, PROPENSITY. An *inclination* is a *leaning* towards something, either good or bad; a *propensity* is a decided *leaning*; a *proneness*, an habitual one. Since the last two terms etymologically imply downward movement, they are applied chiefly to detrimental leanings. See also **TENDENCY.**
ANT. **Disinclination.**

INCONVENIENCE, ANNOY, DISCOMMODE, INCOMMODE, MOLEST, TROUBLE. To *inconvenience* is to subject to a slight annoyance; to *incommode* (still more to *discommode*), to one greater, though not yet grave. To be *annoyed* is to be troubled by something less serious than that which genuinely *troubles*; to be *molested* is to be gravely *troubled* or interfered with by persons definitely ill-disposed.

INCREASE, AUGMENT, ENLARGE, GROW. *Grow* is the general term; *increase* is progressive growth; *augment* implies growth by addition; *enlarge*, by expansion or extension.
ANT. **Decrease.**

INDIFFERENT, DETACHED, DISINTERESTED, UNCONCERNED, UNINTERESTED. *Indifferent* is the general term; *unconcerned* implies indifference arising from self-regarding motives. *Detached*, on the other hand, suggests indifference arising from unselfish motives; and *disinterested*, the complete *detachment* which scorns all thought of personal advantage. *Uninterested* does not belong to this group, but is included here because of the increasingly prevalent error of thinking that *disinterested* means *uninterested.*
ANT. **Avid.**

INFALLIBLE, UNERRING. To be *infallible* is to be incapable of error; to be *unerring* means, literally, the same; but in practice the latter does not mean much more than 'very accurate', as when we speak of 'an *unerring* aim'.
ANT. **Fallible.**

INFECTIOUS, CATCHING, CONTAGIOUS. *Catching*, in this grouping, means something, usually an illness, that can be transmitted from one person to another; *infectious*, something that can be so transmitted by proximity but without physical contact; *contagious*, by physical contact only.

INFINITE, BOUNDLESS, ILLIMITABLE, UNBOUNDED. The *boundless* knows no bounds (*e.g.* the ocean); the *unbounded* should have bounds but lacks them (*e.g.* egotism); the *illimitable*, though measureless to man, is yet thought of as finite; the *infinite* is that which by its own essential nature can know no limits.
ANT. **Finite.**

INFLUENCE, AUTHORITY, PRESTIGE. *Influence* is the power one man has over another; if the influencer has special qualifications of rank, mind, strength and so forth this power is called *authority*; if past achievement or reputation confers this power upon an entity, whether abstract or concrete, we speak of its *prestige* – a word which, oddly enough, by derivation, means illusion.

INFORM, ACQUAINT, APPRISE. *Inform* is the general term; to *acquaint* implies a greater measure of detail: *e.g.* 'He *informed* me of the matter; he *acquainted* me with the particulars'. *Apprise* is used more formally, to mean a communication of special interest or importance to the person concerned.

INHERENT, INGRAINED, INTRINSIC. The *inherent* refers to that which is permanent in a thing in contrast to that which is transitory; the *ingrained*, to that which is inseparable from it: the semantic base in the first instance is that of *adhering*, in the other of *dyeing*. *Intrinsic* means that which belongs to a thing by reason of its own nature, hence the *intrinsic* value of an article is what it will sell for as distinguished from its sentimental value.
ANT. **Adventitious.**

INJURY, DAMAGE, HARM, HURT, MISCHIEF. *Injury* is the comprehensive term; *hurt* applies literally to a physical *injury* or figuratively to an *injury* to the feelings; *damage* is an *injury* that involves loss, usually of a kind that can be computed; *harm* resembles *hurt* but is less strong; and *mischief* implies malice on the part of the person or thing committing the *injury*.

INJUSTICE, INJURY, TORT, WRONG. *Injustice* is the general term; *injury*, in this grouping, is a legal term, implying that compensation is obtainable for the *injustice* done; a *wrong* is a flagrant *injustice*; a *tort* is a legal term applicable to any *injury* except a breach of contract.

INSIPID, BANAL, FLAT, JEJUNE, VAPID. The *insipid* is naturally without flavour, literally and figuratively; the *vapid* is that which has lost its flavour; the *flat* is still more flavourless than the *vapid*. The *jejune* has no nourishing qualities; the *banal*, no originality.
ANT. **Sapid.**

INTENSE, VEHEMENT. Though both imply an extreme degree of vigour, *intense* carries a suggestion of greater depth, and *vehement*, of greater energy.
ANT. **Subdued.**

INTEREST, CONCERN. We have an *interest* in what touches our advantage; a *concern* with regard to our obligations.

INTERPOSE, INTERCEDE, INTERFERE, INTERVENE, MEDIATE. To *interpose* is the general term for the insertion of one thing between two others; to *interfere* is to *interpose* in a way likely to hinder; to *intervene* is to come between two things in space or time, or between two persons, in the latter case usually with a view to mediation or reconciliation. *Mediate* either means to reconcile in this sense, or may be abstractly used in the sense of providing a middle term between two others; to *intercede* is to *intervene* compassionately on someone else's behalf.

INVENT, CREATE, DISCOVER are not synonyms, though open to confusion. To *create* is to cause to exist what did not exist previously; to *discover* is to find something already existing, but unknown; to *invent* is to call into existence, by the exercise of one's ingenuity, something – usually of a practical nature – not thought of before.

INVINCIBLE, INSUPERABLE, INVULNERABLE, UNASSAILABLE, UNCONQUERABLE. *Invincible* carries the suggestion that the quality resides in the character of the person or thing so described, but *unconquerable* relates more precisely to practical fact: we speak of *invincible* ignorance, but of *unconquerable* armies. The *insuperable*, on the other hand, is that which cannot be surmounted or overcome (*insuperable* difficulties); the *unassailable*, that which has no weak point to be assailed; the *invulnerable*, that which it is impossible even to wound.

IRRATIONAL, UNREASONABLE. Whereas *irrational* suggests a total absence of control by the reason, *unreasonable* implies a measure of control by something other than the reason, such as the passions. We speak of *irrational* fears, but of *unreasonable* demands.
ANT. **Rational.**

IRREGULAR, ANOMALOUS, UNNATURAL. The *irregular* fails to conform to what is customary; the *anomalous*, to what is to be expected of the thing by reason of its inherent nature; the *unnatural* suggests a high degree of irregularity of a reprehensible kind.
ANT. **Regular.**

IRRELIGIOUS, GODLESS, UNGODLY. *Irreligious* implies a hostility to religion; *ungodly*, a still stronger hostility, plus disregard. *Godless* is a milder term suggesting a lack of interest in theology generally.
ANT. **Religious.**

J

JEALOUS, ENVIOUS. Though not synonyms, these words are subject to confusion. One is *envious* of that which belongs to someone else; *jealous* of what is, or what one regards as, one's own. So, authority is *jealous* of its privileges; men are *envious* of their superiors.

JEST, JOKE, WITTICISM. A *jest* carries a certain suggestion of lightness, triviality; a *joke* is broader, more likely to excite uproarious mirth; a *witticism*, by definition, should contain something resembling *wit*.

JOURNEY, EXCURSION, EXPEDITION, TOUR, TRIP, VOYAGE. *Journey* is the basic term; a *voyage* now implies a *journey* of some magnitude in a ship; a *tour* is a *journey* that returns to the place of its setting-forth; a *trip* is, strictly, a short *journey*, usually of only a day's duration; an *excursion* is, as it were, the 'official' word for a *trip*, as used by railway companies; an *expedition* is a *journey* undertaken to further a definite purpose, such as exploration.

JUDGE *n.*, ARBITER, ARBITRATOR, REFEREE, UMPIRE. *Judge* is the comprehensive term; an *arbiter* is a *judge* against whose ruling there is no appeal, though it is a word confined to matters of taste, not law. An *arbitrator* is one appointed to settle disputes, usually with the understanding that the parties concerned are bound by his decision; a *referee*, though the term can be used in law to mean someone very like an *arbitrator*, is more often the adjudicator of a game, such as football. *Umpire*, apart from certain legal usages, is in English almost confined to the adjudicators in the games of cricket and tennis.

JUDGE *v.*, ADJUDICATE, ARBITRATE. To *judge* means simply to form a judgment; to *adjudicate* is a more formal determination of an issue in a properly constituted court of law; to *arbitrate* is a similar determination on the part of a body not necessarily legally constituted but rather selected by the agreement of the parties to the issue.

JUSTICE, EQUITY. *Justice* is founded on the law; *equity*, on what is fair, right and reasonable. *Justice* is, however, a word of very high moral connotation implying that the law is infallible, otherwise *equity* would be the stronger term of the two, which it is not.
ANT. **Injustice.**

K

KEEP (1), CELEBRATE, OBSERVE. To *keep* (*e.g.* the peace) implies there is a possibility of not keeping it; to *observe* (*e.g.* the Sabbath) carries only a positive implication. To *celebrate* is usually to *keep* or *observe* a festival with suitable demonstrations and ceremonies.
ANT. **Break.**

KEEP (2), DETAIN, RESERVE, RETAIN, WITHHOLD. *Keep* is the general term; *retain* implies a continued keeping; *reserve*, a keeping back for future use. To *detain* is to hold back that which should not be present (*e.g.* a train); to *withhold* is to hold back that which, in other circumstances, might properly be given.
ANT. **Relinquish.**

KILL, ASSASSINATE, DISPATCH, EXECUTE, MURDER, SLAUGHTER, SLAY. *Kill* is the general term; to *slay* is to kill violently; to *murder*, violently and with criminal intent; to *assassinate* is to murder treacherously, the victim being usually a public figure, the murderer often an agent. To *dispatch* is to *kill* quickly, sometimes to end the victim's sufferings; to *execute*, to kill by judicial or quasi-judicial sanction; to *slaughter*, properly applicable to animals, is used on occasions when men are killed like animals.

KIND, BENIGN, BENIGNANT, KINDLY. Whereas *kind* suggests true sympathy and compassion, *kindly* implies a genial benevolence. *Benign* adds mildness and graciousness to *kind*, and so is often used of the kindness shown by superiors to inferiors. *Benignant*, though roughly equivalent to *benign*, is nowadays more often used as the antonym of *malignant*.
ANT. **Unkind.**

KNOWLEDGE, ERUDITION, INFORMATION, LEARNING, LORE, SCIENCE. *Knowledge* comprises everything that can be known; *learning* is *knowledge* acquired by study; *erudition* implies a deeper degree of *knowledge* than *learning*. *Information*, on the other hand, is indiscriminate, and often useless, *knowledge*; *lore* is a semi-poetical word only properly applied to certain branches of *knowledge* (*e.g.* folk-*lore*); and *science*, which was once a close synonym of *knowledge*, has now sunk to the specialized meaning of a *knowledge* of physical and chemical phenomena.
ANT. **Ignorance.**

L

LABYRINTH, MAZE. A *labyrinth* is a *maze* of a superior degree of complexity.

LANGUAGE, DIALECT, IDIOM, SPEECH, TONGUE. *Language* is the general term for every mode of expression: we speak of the *language* of flowers; *tongue* is confined to human *language*, and then generally to the spoken word; *speech* always implies the spoken word; a *dialect* is the technical name for a local peculiarity of *language*; an *idiom* is a turn of speech peculiar to a specific *language*.

LAST, CONCLUDING, FINAL, LATEST, ULTIMATE. *Last* and *ultimate* imply the end of a series, but whereas *last* means simply that no more will follow, *ultimate* carries the suggestion that the end is a consequence of what has preceded it, as when we speak of the *ultimate* collapse of an army. The *concluding* is that which brings anything to its conclusion; the *latest* relates to an end in point of time; *final* stresses the definiteness of the end attained.
ANT. **First.**

LAUGHABLE, COMIC, COMICAL, DROLL, FUNNY, LUDICROUS, RIDICULOUS. The first is the simplest, least emphasized term; the *ludicrous* is that which is *laughable* because of its preposterousness; the *ridiculous*, because of its foolishness: ridicule is unkindly merriment. The *comic*, properly, is the reverse of the *tragic* and applies to anything which awakens the spirit of comedy, but *comical* lacks this dignified connotation and implies a certain freakishness, though not foolishness. *Droll* suggests oddity; while *funny* is a colloquial term now loosely applied to anything laughable or peculiar.

LAW, ORDINANCE, PRECEPT, REGULATION, STATUTE. A *law* is an enactment of constituted authority; a *statute*, a written *law*; a *precept* is an individual's ruling concerning conduct; a *regulation* is a quasi-legal ruling laid down by a specific authority or organization; an *ordinance* is a *law* or *regulation* enacted by a body other than Parliament.

LAWFUL, LEGAL, LEGITIMATE, LICIT. *Lawful* is the comprehensive term; *legal* is that which is permitted by statute law; *legitimate* carries in addition the sense of customary, *e.g.* '*legitimate* trading'; and *licit* (permitted) embodies the moral idea of being contrary to that which is *illicit*.
ANT. **Unlawful.**

LEAN, GAUNT, LANK, SPARE. *Lean* suggests an absence of fat;

spare, the physical fitness of one who lacks it; *lank*, a certain tallness in addition. *Gaunt* is stronger than *lean* and verges upon cadaverousness.
ANT. **Fleshy.**

LET, ALLOW, LEAVE, PERMIT, SUFFER. *Let* is the simplest term, as when we *let* a person do something. To *allow* and to *permit* both imply the power to prohibit, but to *permit* is less passive than to *allow*. To *suffer*, in this sense, is slightly archaic ('*suffer* little children to come unto me'); to *leave* adds to *to let* the idea of deliberate non-interference.

LETTER, DESPATCH, EPISTLE, MISSIVE, NOTE. *Letter* is the ordinary term; *epistle* is either archaic or facetious; *missive* is pompous; *despatch* implies speed; and *note* (except when applied to diplomatic communications), brevity.

LIABLE, LIKELY, PRONE, SUBJECT, SUSCEPTIBLE. To say that one is *likely* to catch a cold is less strong than saying one is *subject* to doing so, and much less strong than saying one is *susceptible* to any sort of exterior risk. If, on the other hand, one is *prone* to any such thing, one is nearly certain, sooner or later, to experience it. *Liable* as the equivalent of *likely* in the example above is not standard English, but one can say 'he is *liable* (*i.e. subject*) to error'.
ANT. **Exempt; Immune.**

LIE *n.*, FALSEHOOD, MISREPRESENTATION, UNTRUTH. *Lie* is the direct term; *falsehood* is less forthright and opprobrious than *lie*; *untruth* is usually a euphemism although it can mean an unintentional *lie*; *misrepresentation* glosses over the moral implications of the matter and is especially suited to the *lies* of commerce.
ANT. **Truth.**

LIE *v.*, EQUIVOCATE, PREVARICATE. To *prevaricate* is to attempt to dodge the real issue; to *equivocate* is to hope you will pass off your *lie* by being misunderstood.

LIFT, ELEVATE, HEAVE, HOIST, RAISE. *Heave* and *hoist* carry with them the suggestion of effort, but *heave* implies an impulse from beneath, and *hoist*, the raising from above. To *elevate* has usually more abstract connotations than to *lift*, *e.g.* one *lifts* a stone, *elevates* one's taste; to *raise* suggests elevating from a horizontal to a vertical or upright position.
ANT. **Lower.**

LIGHT *v.*, IGNITE, INFLAME, KINDLE. *Light* is here the basic term; *kindle* suggests a slower and more laborious process; *ignite*, an almost instantaneous one; *inflame* is now usually confined to figurative uses.

LIGHTNESS, FLIGHTINESS, FLIPPANCY, FRIVOLITY, GIDDINESS, LEVITY. *Lightness* implies a lack of weight and seriousness; *levity*, an unseasonable gaiety; *frivolity*, a *levity* that eschews all seriousness. *Flippancy* is *levity* exhibited in the face of serious things; *flightiness* is characterized by extreme instability; *giddiness* is a sort of childish *flightiness*.
ANT. **Seriousness.**

LIKENESS, AFFINITY, ANALOGY, RESEMBLANCE, SIMILARITY. *Likeness* implies a correspondence less close than that of *similarity*; *resemblance*, that the *likeness* is visual. *Analogy*, on the other hand, is a *likeness* in relationship between things unlike in themselves; and *affinity* adds the idea that the *likeness* is due to a specific link or bond.
ANT. **Unlikeness.**

LIMIT *n.*, BOUND, CONFINE, TERM. Whereas *limit* can be applied to most things, *bound* and *confine* are applicable only to such *limits* as either literally or figuratively enclose something: *bound* tending to imply restriction, and *confine*, simple enclosure. *Term* is a *limit* in time, and sometimes in space; and it carries a suggestion of greater finality than is expressed by the other words.

LIMIT *v.*, CIRCUMSCRIBE, CONFINE, RESTRICT. *Restrict* suggests a boundary that encloses; *limit*, one that cuts short at a given point. *Circumscribe* still more than *restrict* insists on the enclosing boundary; and *confine* includes the sense that the boundary is one that cramps the thing enclosed by it.
ANT. **Widen.**

LIQUID, FLUID. *Liquid* is the more restricted term; anything that flows is *fluid*, but a *liquid* is, generally speaking, one of the *fluid* bodies that commonly exist in nature under normal circumstances. *Liquid* air seems to be an exception, perhaps it would be better termed *fluid* air.
ANT. **Solid.**

LIST, CATALOGUE, REGISTER, ROLL, SCHEDULE. *List* is the most general of these terms; a *catalogue* is a descriptive *list*; a *roll*, a *list* of names; a *register* suggests a *list* officially compiled; a *schedule* is a detailed statement of particulars, often appended to a larger document.

LITTLE, DIMINUTIVE, MINIATURE, SMALL, TINY. *Small* (the antonym of *large*) and *little* (the antonym of *big*) are often used interchangeably; but *small* is more purely quantitative than *little*, which often contains a trace of detraction, *e.g.* a *small* house is bigger than a *little* house. The *diminutive* is abnormally *small*; the *tiny*, smaller still; the *miniature* is an object complete in every detail but of a smallness not to be found in nature.
ANT. **Big.**

LIVING *n.*, LIVELIHOOD, MAINTENANCE, SUBSISTENCE, SUPPORT, SUSTENANCE. *Living* is now the general term, and *livelihood* applies to the means whereby one gains one's *living*. *Sustenance* emphasizes the aspect of nourishment; *subsistence* indicates a minimum standard of *living*; and *support* applies when the means of *living* come from an outside source. *Maintenance* is a term used chiefly by officials to describe that part of one's income which is spent on necessaries.

LONG, HANKER, HUNGER, THIRST, YEARN. *Hanker* suggests a trivial desire; *yearn*, a great one; *long* is the middle term. *Hunger* and *thirst*, although they may be used literally, are more often figurative terms, capable of being used in both good and bad senses: one can *hunger* and *thirst* after righteousness; one can also *thirst* for blood, or *hunger* for power.

LOOK, GLANCE, GLIMPSE, SIGHT, VIEW. A *glimpse* is what one sees in a *glance*, which is a quick *look*. *Sight* has reference to that which is seen, and *view* carries the suggestion of a *sight* worth looking at.

LOOSE, LAX, RELAXED, SLACK. *Loose* is the general expression; *relaxed* stresses absence of tension, and *slack*, absence of firmness or steadiness. *Lax* carries moral overtones implying undue relaxation.
ANT. **Tight.**

LOUD, CLAMOROUS, NOISY. We call a sound *noisy* when it annoys us; *loud*, when we merely note its magnitude. The *clamorous* is the *noisy* as produced by the human voice.
ANT. **Soft.**

LOVE, AFFECTION, ATTACHMENT. *Love* is much stronger than *affection*; *attachment*, implying little more than strong liking, can be lavished on non-sentient objects: one *loves* one's family; has *affection* for one's friends; an *attachment* to one's native town.
ANT. **Hate.**

LOW, BASE, VILE. The *low* is morally contemptible; the *base*, totally devoid of decency and nobility; the *vile* adds to the *base* a feeling of disgust and nausea.

LUXURIOUS, EPICUREAN, SENSUAL, SENSUOUS, VOLUPTUOUS. The *sensuous* is simply that which appeals to the senses; the *sensual*, that which appeals to them in a bad sense. *Epicurean* nowadays is nearer to *sensuous* than to *sensual*, and *luxurious* has come to mean little more than very comfortable or enjoyable. *Voluptuous*, on the other hand, still carries the idea of a certain abandonment to a not very reprehensible sensuality.
ANT. **Ascetic.**

M

MAKE, FABRICATE, FASHION, FORM, MANUFACTURE. *Make* is the general expression; *form* implies a shaping; *fashion*, a high degree of ingenuity in the making. *Fabricate* is more often used in a bad sense, as when one *fabricates* an excuse; *manufacture* stresses the idea of making objects in large numbers.

MALE, MANFUL, MANLIKE, MANLY, MANNISH, MASCULINE, VIRILE. *Male* is the opposite of *female* and relates to the sex itself; *masculine*, the opposite of *feminine*, relates to the characteristics of the sex; we speak of *male* children, but of *masculine* vigour. *Manly* stresses the laudable aspects of manhood; *manlike* can either mean *masculine* qualities and foibles, or the specific qualities which distinguish man from the animals; *mannish* is usually a term of contempt applied to that which should be feminine; *manful* stresses resolution and determination; *virile*, strength, masterfulness and vigour.
ANT. **Female.**

MALICE, GRUDGE, MALEVOLENCE, MALIGNITY, SPITE. *Malevolence*, the opposite of *benevolence*, is the will to do harm; *malice*, a love of evil for its own sake, vents itself in doing harm; *spite* is petty *malice*; *malignity*, *malice* of the strongest kind. *Grudge* is a homespun term that implies a grievance of long standing and the desire to get even.
ANT. **Charity.**

MANY, DIVERS, MULTIFARIOUS, NUMEROUS, SUNDRY, VARIOUS. *Many* is the common expression; *sundry* is mostly archaic or humorous; *divers* originally meant *many* of differing kinds; *multifarious* carries still further the idea of diversity and incongruity; *numerous* is both a little stronger and rather more explicit than *many*; *various* is vague and somewhat colloquial; as a rule it does not mean more than a fairly small number.
ANT. **Few.**

MARK, BADGE, NOTE, SIGN, SYMPTOM, TOKEN. A *mark* is a simple *sign*; a *badge* is a *sign* worn on the person; a *token* is an object that symbolizes something other than itself, usually something abstract, *e.g.* 'a *token* of friendship'. A *note*, in this grouping, is a distinguishing *mark* suggesting some peculiar property in a thing, *e.g.* 'the eternal *note* of sadness'; and a *symptom* is a *sign* which indicates a physical or mental change in the thing exhibiting it.

MARRIAGE, MATRIMONY, NUPTIALS, WEDDING, WEDLOCK. *Marriage* is the ordinary term; *matrimony*, the ecclesiastical; and *wedlock*, the legal. A *wedding* is the ceremony which solemnizes a *marriage*; an especially magnificent *wedding* ceremony may be referred to as *nuptials*.

MARTIAL, MILITARY, WARLIKE. *Warlike* suggests a natural bellicosity; *martial*, anything pertaining to war, such as *martial* music or *martial* law. *Military* (from *Lat. miles*, a soldier) is chiefly used to distinguish land forces from those that fight at sea (*naval*), though it may also loosely be applied to most activities that are executed by trained fighting-men.

MATTER, ARGUMENT, MOTIVE, SUBJECT, TEXT, THEME, TOPIC. *Subject* is now the most usual word with which to describe the principal idea in, *e.g.*, a work of the imagination; the somewhat archaic *matter* = subject-matter has much the same meaning, although it carries perhaps a greater suggestion of weightiness. An *argument* carefully defines a *subject*; a *text*, in this grouping, suggests that the *subject* is epitomized in a quotation; a *theme* is a selected *subject*; a *motive* implies that it has pattern and design. *Topic* is a less dignified word suggesting that the *subject* discussed is of a certain triviality.

MAXIM, ADAGE, APHORISM, APOPHTHEGM, PROVERB, SAW, SAYING. A *maxim* is a short moral observation; a *saying* is a somewhat sententious expression of a general truth; a *saw* is a homely and often-repeated *saying*. *Adage* is a more dignified version of *saw*; a *proverb* is an *adage* which has passed into the language; an *aphorism* has more of wit in it than a *saying*; an *apophthegm* is a very sharply pointed *aphorism*.

MEAN *n.*, AVERAGE, MEDIAN, MEDIUM. The *mean* is the mid-point between two extremes; the *median* is the mid-point in a mathematical series; *medium*, as the equivalent of *mean*, is best kept to adjectival uses. The *average* is a *mean* arrived at by mathematical calculation, and by extension is used as a synonym for the *ordinary* or the *typical*, *e.g.* 'the *average* man'.
ANT. **Maximum; Minimum.**

MEAN *v.*, DENOTE, IMPORT, SIGNIFY. *Mean* is the general term; *denote* relates to concrete things, and *signify* to those which are not concrete, *e.g.* + *denotes* plus, a look *signifies* interest. *Import*, on the other hand, follows its etymological meaning of 'carrying in', to give a sense of greater completeness: 'What does this *import*?' is stronger, more comprehensive, and more pompous than, 'What does this *mean*?'

MEAN *adj.*, ABJECT, IGNOBLE, SORDID. *Ignoble* implies the absence of all that is *noble*; *mean*, an inherent preference for the petty and trivial; *abject*, a relish for abasement and servility; *sordid*, the same for dullness, dinginess and dirt.

MELODY, AIR, TUNE. An *air* is the dominant *melody* in a simple musical composition, usually of a choral kind; a *tune* is the less technical name for an *air* of this nature.

MEMORY, RECOLLECTION, REMEMBRANCE, REMINISCENCE. *Memory* is the faculty by which one remembers; *remembrance* is the process of remembering; *recollection* suggests an intenser effort, a

deeper delving into the memory, than *remembrance*; *reminiscence* applies, strictly, to a more abstract or philosophical use of the *memory*, but it is now generally used as if interchangeable with *recollection*.
ANT. **Oblivion.**

MEND, AMEND, REPAIR, REMODEL. *Mend* is the general term; *amend* applies to the rectification of abstracter matters, such as Acts of Parliament, or printed texts. *Repair* implies a completely successful act of *mending*; *remodel*, a taking apart and putting together again of the thing concerned.

MENTAL, CEREBRAL, INTELLECTUAL, INTELLIGENT. *Mental* means anything that relates to the mind; *intellectual*, anything that relates to the intellect, which is the higher, more abstract power of the mind. *Intelligent* applies to any creature that exhibits the possession of an intellect; *cerebral* implies specific reference to the brain, though it is also sometimes used figuratively.

MERCY, CLEMENCY, GRACE, LENITY. *Clemency* and *lenity* both imply *mercy* exercised by constituted authority towards those who have offended it, but *lenity* carries an implication of a perhaps undue *clemency*. *Grace*, on the other hand, is now usually applied, in this grouping, to God's beneficence to man.

MIND *n*., BRAIN, INTELLECT, INTELLIGENCE, WITS. If *mind* is the part of man that thinks, *intellect* relates to the abstruser powers of that mind; and *intelligence* is distinguished from *intellect* by being the exhibiting in action of that *intellect*. *Brains* and *wits* are colloquial synonyms for *mind*: the former stressing slightly the power of comprehension, the latter quickness of apprehension.

MIRTH, GLEE, HILARITY, JOLLITY. *Mirth* is always good-humoured, but *glee* may have a smack of malice in it. *Jollity* is cruder than *mirth* and implies a number of people making merry together; *hilarity* suggests the kind of mirth that is produced, among gentlemen, by an adequate but not excessive amount of strong drink.

MISFORTUNE, ADVERSITY, MISCHANCE, MISHAP. A *mischance* or *mishap* is a trivial *misfortune*; *adversity* implies serious and continued *misfortune*.
ANT. **Prosperity.**

MISTAKE, BLUNDER, ERROR, LAPSE, SLIP. An *error* is a deviation from that which is correct, not necessarily caused by lack of care; a *mistake* arises from a fault in judgment, but is rarely as serious as an *error*. A *blunder* is caused by stupidity or gross carelessness; a *slip* by accident, generally in a matter of not much importance. A *lapse* resembles a *slip*, but one caused by forgetfulness or inattention, the fruits of which may be serious.

MIX, AMALGAMATE, BLEND, COALESCE, MERGE, MINGLE. *Mix* is the most general of these terms; *amalgamate* suggests the union of two or more entities without total loss of identity; *blend*, a mixing of commodities (such as tea) in such fashion that the product partakes of the qualities of each. *Coalesce* suggests a mixture in which the components produce an organic unity; *mingle*, one in which the items mixed together are still recognizable in the product; *merge*, one in which they are completely absorbed into one another.

MODERATE, QUALIFY, TEMPER. To *moderate* is to eschew excess; to *qualify*, to restrict by qualifications; to *temper* is to mitigate: one *moderates* one's language; *qualifies* one's praises; *tempers* justice with mercy.

MONEY, CASH, COIN, CURRENCY, SPECIE. *Money* is the general term; *cash*, in modern usage, is ready money, whether paper or metal; *coin* is minted money, and so is *specie*, though the latter word is used only in large transactions. *Currency* is the *money* that is in circulation, as distinguished from that which is not.

MONOPOLIZE, ABSORB, CONSUME, ENGROSS, all mean to take exclusive possession of something. *Monopolize* is the general term; *engross* is now applied chiefly to that which monopolizes the attention, and so is *absorb*, the difference being that the latter suggests a higher degree of monopolization. *Consume* carries greater moral overtones: one is *absorbed* in a book, but *consumed* by envy.

MOTION, LOCOMOTION, MOVE, MOVEMENT. *Movement* suggests a concrete object moving; *motion*, the abstract idea of moving. *Move* is restricted to special uses such as a *move* in chess or in such a phrase as, 'What will his next *move* be?' *Locomotion* is *movement* from one place to another, often by artificial means: a tree is capable of *movement*, but not of *locomotion*.
ANT. **Rest.**

MOVE *v.*, ACTUATE, DRIVE, IMPEL. *Move* means simply to set in motion; *actuate* applies chiefly to mechanical motion; *drive*, to motion in a forward direction; *impel* adds to *drive* a suggestion of more violent force.

MOVING, AFFECTING, PATHETIC, POIGNANT, TOUCHING. *Moving* is the general term for that which excites emotion; the *affecting* moves us to sympathetic tenderness; the *pathetic*, to pity, sometimes not unmixed with patronage; the *poignant*, to tears. *Touching* is now, as it were, a poor relation of *pathetic*.

MULTITUDE, ARMY, HOST, LEGION, SWARM. Each of these words suggests a great number of objects: '*Multitudes* in the valley of decision'; 'an *army* of locusts'; 'a *host* of angels'; 'a *legion* of devils'; 'a *swarm* of children'. Except that *swarm* (derived from bees) does not perhaps suggest quite such enormous numbers as the others, discretion and good sense should suggest which epithet to use in any particular case. *Multitude* is the most generally useful.

MYSTERIOUS, ARCANE, INSCRUTABLE, MYSTIC. The *mysterious* is that which defies all attempts at explanation; the *mystic*, in this grouping, suggests more that which is concealed by artificial and man-made obscurity. The *arcane* is that which is explicable only to those who are in the secret; the *inscrutable*, strictly, means that which cannot be discovered by reasoning, but is now in practice often degraded to something not much stronger than *baffling*.

N

NAME, APPELATION, COGNOMEN, DENOMINATION, DESIGNATION, STYLE, TITLE. *Name* is the inclusive term; a *designation* is a *name* distinguishing one thing from others of the same general description; a *denomination,* the name of a class, group, or category (*e.g.* coins of the same *denomination*). An *appelation* is a qualifying *name* given, usually to persons, by others (*e.g.* Charles the Bald); a *title* is a *name* referring to rank or office, and it also applies to such things as books and plays. *Style* is a formal *title* applicable to exalted personages or to such entities as corporations; a *cognomen* is a surname – a usage now either archaic or facetious.

NARROW *adj.,* STRAIT. Though *strait* is largely obsolete, it carries when used (*e.g.* '*strait* is the gate') a significance of extreme and even pinching *narrowness.*
ANT. **Broad.**

NATIVE, ABORIGINAL, AUTOCHTHONOUS, INDIGENOUS. He who is born in a certain place is a *native* of it; if he belongs to the earliest known race inhabiting that place, he is an *aboriginal.* That which has its origin in the place where it is found is *autochthonous,* a word applicable to other things than men. *Indigenous,* likewise, applies to persons or things that belong by nature to the place where they are found, but the word is applicable rather to species than to individuals, and relates more often to geographical than to national classifications.
ANT. **Alien; Foreign.**

NECESSARY, ESSENTIAL, INDISPENSABLE, NEEDFUL, REQUISITE. *Needful* is the weakest of these terms; *necessary* comes next; and *indispensable* implies very strong need. *Essential* is as strong as *indispensable,* but in a different way: you cannot complete a task without the *indispensable* materials, you cannot begin it without the *essential* ones. *Requisite,* on the other hand, implies that the thing needed is required by something or someone other than the actual agent: 'You cannot begin the task until you have filled in the *requisite* forms'.

NEED, EXIGENCY, NECESSITY. *Need* relates to the condition of the person who wants something; *necessity,* to the thing wanted: we *need* bread; bread is a *necessity. Exigency* is a *need* brought into being by special circumstances of emergency, and is a term even stronger than the others.

NEGLECT, DISREGARD, IGNORE, OMIT, OVERLOOK, SLIGHT. To *neglect* is to leave undone the things we ought to do; to *omit* is rather

to leave out a part of what we ought to have done. If we *disregard* anything, we do so deliberately; and if we *ignore* it we do so with still greater deliberation. To *overlook* is to *neglect* or *omit* by accident, though sometimes 'accidentally on purpose', as when we *overlook* an injury done to us. To *slight* is to *disregard* or *ignore* a person with deliberate intent to wound.
ANT. **Cherish.**

NEUTRAL, IMPARTIAL, INDIFFERENT. The *neutral* is colourless and does not take sides; the *indifferent* does not care which side it takes; the *impartial* says, in effect, 'a plague (or a blessing) on both your houses'.

NEW, CONTEMPORARY, FRESH, MODERN, NOVEL, ORIGINAL, RECENT. *New* is the inclusive term; *modern* usually implies a contrast with *ancient* and therefore a certain factitious modishness (the neologism *contemporary*, implying *modern*, is mere vicious jargon). *Fresh* is that which is so *new* that it has, as it were, the dew on it; *novel* is that of which the newness excites surprise, not invariably of a pleasing kind; the *recent* is only the relatively *new*; the *original* is that which not only is *new* but also differs completely from anything of its kind that has come before.
ANT. **Old.**

NEWS, ADVICE, INTELLIGENCE, TIDINGS. *Advice* has relation to the means by which information is communicated, such as letters or telegrams; *intelligence* stresses the practical value rather than the freshness of the *news*, *e.g.* 'Shipping *Intelligence*'. *Tidings*, though somewhat archaic, applies principally to *news* disseminated orally.

NICE, ACCURATE, DAINTY, EXACT, PRECISE. *Accurate* suggests careful faithfulness to the truth; *exact*, a strict and rigorous faithfulness; *precise*, a scrupulous exactness; and *nice*, a delicate, even over-delicate, *precision*. From this use, *nice* has come to mean finicking or *dainty*; and thence, because *daintiness* can suggest *prettiness*, it has become an indiscriminate term of approbation, culminating in such absurdities as 'a *nice* mince-pie'.

NIGHTLY, NOCTURNAL. *Nightly* is the simple term; *nocturnal*, the specialized and literary: *nocturnal* is properly used to define that which pertains only to the night; *nightly*, to define such things as are opposed to *daily*. We thus speak of *nocturnal* visions, but of *nightly* visits.
ANT. **Daily.**

NOBLE, ETHICAL, MORAL, VIRTUOUS. The *moral* man directs his life in accordance with a code of morals; an *ethical* system is one in which the morality does not necessarily derive from supernatural sanctions; a *virtuous* man is one who exhibits virtue in his actions, and this may often arise from an inherently *noble* disposition rather than from specific *moral* principles. To be *noble*, in short, is to be utterly opposed to the *ignoble*, in other words, disinterested.
ANT. **Ignoble.**

NOISE, CLAMOUR, SOUND. A *sound* is anything that is heard; a *noise* is a *sound* that attracts the attention, generally disagreeably; a *clamour* is a *noise* of human origin and always implies loudness.

NUMB, BENUMBED, TORPID. When a limb, or an animal, has become *benumbed* by cold, fright, etc., we say that it is *numb*. If the *numbness*, in the case of an animal, is continued, we say that it is *torpid*.

OBEDIENT, AMENABLE, DOCILE, SUBMISSIVE, TRACTABLE. The *obedient* person does as he is told; the *tractable* one is easy to manage; and the *amenable* one is *tractable* by disposition. The *docile* is, strictly, one who responds to teaching, but the word carries a further suggestion of mildness and meekness. To be *submissive* differs from to be *obedient* in that one is *submissive* to external power (*e.g.* to God's will) rather than to direct command; one may, moreover, be *submissive* in an unconvinced or hypocritical way, unlike *obedient*, which assumes that all orders are sensible orders.
ANT. **Disobedient; Contumacious.**

OBJECT *v.*, EXPOSTULATE, OPPOSE, PROTEST, REMONSTRATE. To *oppose* is the weakest of these terms; to *object* implies vigorous and vociferous opposition; to *protest*, opposition, either verbal or written, of a more or less formal kind. To *remonstrate* and to *expostulate* both suggest argued protestations, although *expostulation* is perhaps more fitted to the protestations of a friend, and *remonstration* to those of a stranger.
ANT. **Acquiesce.**

OBLIGATION, DUTY. An *obligation* is what one is obliged to do, or should do, out of common decency; a *duty* is what one is expected to do because of the ethical ambience in which one happens to live. So, to pay one's debts is a normal *obligation*; to die, if necessary, for one's country is the soldier's *duty*.

OBSCURE, AMBIGUOUS, CRYPTIC, DARK, ENIGMATIC, EQUIVOCAL, VAGUE. The *obscure*, in a matter of expression, arises from defective powers of communication ('inadequate thoughts embodied in inadequate language'); the *dark*, from an inherent tendency towards mystification; the *vague*, from indefiniteness; the *cryptic*, from intentional obscurity; the *equivocal*, from a desire to deceive; the *ambiguous*, from the propensity of certain words to possess double meanings. The *enigmatic* resembles the *cryptic* to the extent that an enigma resembles a cryptogram; the latter is perhaps a little stronger than the former.
ANT. **Distinct; Obvious.**

OBSERVANCE, OBSERVATION. *Observation* now means the act of observing objects; *observance*, the act of keeping them sacred. The first is based on the word *observe* used in the sense of *watching*; the other, on the word used in the sense of *keeping*; we speak of the *observation* of natural phenomena; of the *observance* of Sunday.
ANT. **Breach.**

OBSTINATE, CONTUMACIOUS, MULISH, PERTINACIOUS, STUBBORN. *Mulish* and *stubborn* imply a fixedness of purpose arising out of character; the former carries a slightly greater suggestion of unreasonableness than the latter. *Obstinate* suggests extreme stubbornness in the face of the well-meant advice of others, and lacks the suggestion of a possibly virtuous persistency such as may be contained in *stubborn*. The *contumacious* is characterized by an insolent or rebellious stubbornness; the *pertinacious*, by a persistent and usually irksome one.
ANT. **Pliant; Pliable.**

ODD, CURIOUS, OUTLANDISH, PECULIAR, QUAINT, QUEER, SINGULAR, STRANGE, UNEVEN. *Odd* originally meant that which lacked a fellow, *i.e. uneven*; *odd* man out. Thence, by transference, it came to mean something like *strange*, which, strictly, implies the alien, the unfamiliar. *Singular* suggests uniqueness; *peculiar*, conspicuous distinctiveness; *quaint*, an old-fashioned oddness. The *queer* is the twisted, the cross-grained, hence the eccentric; the *outlandish* is uncouth and bizarre; the *curious* possesses a strangeness that calls for close investigation.
ANT. **Even.**

OFFENCE, CRIME, MISDEED, MISDEMEANOUR, SIN, VICE. *Offence* is the general term, implying the breaking of any law whether human or divine; a *misdeed* is a breach of private duty; a *misdemeanour* a relatively unimportant breach of the civil law. A *crime* is a serious breach of that law; a *sin*, a breach of divine law; a *vice* is commonly a *sin* that chiefly affects the person indulging in it.

OFFEND, AFFRONT, INSULT, OUTRAGE. One can *offend* with or without intention; but *affront*, *insult* and *outrage* represent an ascending scale of deliberate offence: *insult* is perhaps the strongest term from the point of view of the aggressor; *outrage*, from the point of view of his victim.

OFFER *v.*, PRESENT, PROFFER, TENDER. *Proffer* is to *offer* somewhat formally, and implies a certain diffidence in the offerer; *tender* is to *offer* still more delicately; *present* either makes a ceremonious *offer* or else is used in a specialized sense, as when we say, 'The play was *presented* by so-and-so'.

OFTEN, FREQUENTLY. *Frequently* suggests a closer interval between repeated events than *often* does: 'He visited me *frequently*' implies greater intimacy than 'He *often* visited me'.

OLD, ANCIENT, ANTEDILUVIAN, ANTIQUATED, ANTIQUE, ARCHAIC, OBSOLETE, OLD-FASHIONED, VENERABLE. *Old*, the general term, is opposed to the *new*, the *young*; the *ancient* is opposed to the *modern*. *Antique* applies generally to what has come down to us from former times, such as articles of furniture; *antiquated* implies such things in this class as are of an *old fashion* or unserviceable. *Antediluvian* (that which existed before the Flood) means excessively *old*; *obsolete*, out of date, though it is used with less of a sense of derision than *antiquated*; *archaic*, that it belongs to a former time and is now used only in exceptional

circumstances. *Venerable* is applied to that which is revered for its antiquity.
ANT. **New.**

ONLY, ALONE. 'Man shall not live by bread *alone*' is far more emphatic than 'Man shall not live *only* by bread'.

ONWARD, FORTH, FORWARD. *Forward* is opposed to *backward*; but *onward* presupposes a goal in front: '*Onward*, Christian soldiers'. *Forth* is equivalent to *forward* ('The Son of God goes *forth* to war'), but implies greater vigour of movement.

OPINION, BELIEF, CONVICTION, NOTION, PERSUASION, SENTIMENT, VIEW. An *opinion* is a more or less carefully formed conclusion; a *belief* is usually an *opinion* based upon external authority; a *conviction*, a *belief* or *opinion* held with certitude. A *view* is an *opinion* coloured by the temperament of the person who forms it; a *persuasion*, one coloured by his own wishes; a *sentiment*, one coloured by his own feelings. A *notion* is an immature or not-very-well-considered *opinion*.

OPPORTUNE, SEASONABLE, TIMELY, WELL-TIMED. The *opportune* is that which comes by chance, to further one's projects; the *seasonable* is that which is suited to the season of the year, and so, by extension, is fitted to the needs of the moment. The *timely* is that which is so *seasonable* that it is of real use; the *well-timed* is so *timely* as to suggest deliberate care and forethought.
ANT. **Inopportune.**

OPPOSE, COMBAT, RESIST, THWART, WITHSTAND. *Oppose* implies simple opposition, but *combat* contains the idea of actual conflict with that which one *opposes*. *Resist* suggests that the opposite side has already attacked; *withstand*, that such attack has been, at least temporarily, resisted successfully. *Thwart* (across, athwart) carries a definite suggestion of crossing, or working against, and is a more positive term than any of the others, implying a successful *opposing*.

ORDER *v.*, ARRANGE, MARSHAL, METHODIZE, ORGANIZE. *Arrange* is now the commonest term for setting in order a number of objects; *order*, as in the phrase 'to *order* one's affairs', has a slightly archaic ring. *Marshal*, originally a military term, still carries in its figurative use the idea of an arrangement made under some pressure; *organize* suggests an arrangement in which the organic relationship of the parts to the whole is recognized; to *methodize* is to impose an orderly procedure upon one's arrangements.

ORIGIN, INCEPTION, ORIGINAL, ROOT, SOURCE. The *original* is the first thing of its kind from which all others like it arise: the *original* painting is the *origin* of its copies. *Source* indicates the place whence the *original* has arisen, and so does *root*, which is stronger than *source*, for the reason that a *root* is commonly deeper than a *source* ('The love of money is the *root* of all evil'). *Inception* carries a weaker reference to the underlying cause of the thing concerned, and so is nearer to *beginning*.

ORNATE, ADORNED, DECORATED, EMBELLISHED, FLORID. The *adorned* makes the best of what it already possesses; the *decorated*, to improve its appearance, adds something; *embellished* implies a lavish degree of decoration. The *ornate* is decorated so heavily as to be almost pretentious; the *florid* possesses such richness of embellishment as to be ostentatious.
ANT. **Chaste; Austere.**

OUTLIVE, OUTLAST, SURVIVE. To *survive* is simply to live longer than another thing, person or event; to *outlive* implies greater tenacity in survival as compared with some other thing; to *outlast* implies greater comparative durability.

OVERTURN, CAPSIZE, OVERTHROW, SUBVERT, UPSET. *Upset* is now the common term; but one *capsizes* a boat; *overthrows* by superior force an institution or a person in high place; and *subverts* – by the process of undermining – similar things. *To overturn* in contrast to *to upset* implies the sudden throwing over of a material object in such a way that it either lies on its side or has its base where its top should be.

P

PAIN, ACHE, PANG, THROE, TWINGE. *Pain* is the undifferentiated term; an *ache* is a dull steady *pain*; a *pang*, a sharp and sudden one; a *twinge*, one slight, momentary and darting; a *throe*, one recurrent and convulsive.

PAINT *v.*, **COLOUR, DEPICT.** One *paints* or *colours* with pigments; *depicts* with words. If *paint* is used in the place of *depict* in the latter and figurative sense, it implies greater activity of the imagination: the poet *paints*; the historian *depicts*. The distinction between to *colour* and to *paint* depends upon the medium employed: to *paint* usually suggests the use of oil paints, to *colour*, any other colouring matter. *Colour* can also, however, be applied to such activities as filling in an outline.

PALE, ASHEN, LIVID, PALLID, WAN. *Pale* is the common term implying absence of intensity; *pallid* suggests a high degree of paleness usually arising from some deprivation; *ashen* suggests the pallor of ashes; *wan*, a diseased and sickly paleness; and *livid* (which means leaden-hued) is applied to countenances or colours which exhibit the opaque pallor of lead.

PALLIATE, EXTENUATE, GLOSS, GLOZE, WHITEWASH. To *palliate* is to conceal or cloak the gravity of someone's offence; to *extenuate* is to attempt to lessen by excuses the magnitude of an offence or one's own guilt. To *gloss* or *gloze* over is to represent the offence as less heinous than it really is; *gloze* being the stronger term. To *whitewash* is to endeavour to cover up an offence by a partial and corrupt investigation which results in an acquittal.

PART, DIVISION, FRAGMENT, PIECE, PORTION, SECTION, SHARE. *Part* is the comprehensive term for that which is less than the *whole*; *portion* means the same, except that it does not necessarily presuppose a complete whole: you can divide half a pie into six equal *portions*; if they come as by prescribed right to the participants, they are *shares*. A *piece* is a separated *part* of the whole; so is a *division*, with the difference that the latter implies greater exactitude in arriving at the size of the *piece*. A *section* is similar to a *division*, though it applies customarily to a small *division*; a *fragment* is smaller still – a *piece* broken off the whole.
ANT. **Whole.**

PARTICULAR, INDIVIDUAL, RESPECTIVE, SPECIAL, SPECIFIC. The *particular* is opposed to the *general*; the *individual* implies a reference to one object as distinct from any other in its class; the *special* implies the unusual or uncommon object in its class; and the *specific* is opposed to the *generic*, *i.e.* it stresses the qualities pertaining to the species rather than those of any larger category to which that species belongs. *Respective*, without being a true synonym for the preceding words, comes close to their meaning in such phases as 'the *respective* members of the team', meaning each individual member of it as distinguished from the others.

ANT. **General; Universal.**

PATIENCE, ENDURANCE, FORBEARANCE, LONG-SUFFERING, RESIGNATION. The *patient* man persists through many difficulties; the *long-suffering* one is *patient* through many trials; the *resigned* one is *patient* because he expects nothing better. *Endurance* implies a capacity for putting up with trials, and may arise from mere vitality; *forbearance* is *long-suffering* plus restraint both in word and deed.

ANT. **Impatience.**

PAY, COMPENSATE, INDEMNIFY, RECOMPENSE, REIMBURSE, REMUNERATE. *Pay* is the common term for discharging an obligation; *remunerate* carries some suggestion of reward and so is used in cases where the word *pay* is deemed indelicate. To *reimburse* is to pay back what has already been expended on one's behalf; to *compensate* is to make a payment which is nicely adjusted to the value of the thing paid for; to *indemnify* is to pay for damage suffered; to *recompense* is a more figurative version of to *compensate* and often implies payment otherwise than in cash.

PEACEABLE, PACIFIC, PACIFIST, PEACEFUL. *Peaceable* people are peace-loving; a *peaceful* place is one where there is peace; a *pacific* person is one who by his actions and example tries to promote peace; *pacifist* is a recent coinage characterizing the activities of those who are militantly *pacific*.

ANT. **Bellicose.**

PENITENCE, COMPUNCTION, CONTRITION, REMORSE, REPENTANCE. *Penitence* is the state of being sorry for one's sin; *repentance* implies further an attempt at amendment; *contrition* is *penitence* that exhibits itself in outward, though genuine, manifestations of regret. *Compunction* and *remorse* both relate to the sting of conscience, but *compunction* is, etymologically, to *remorse* as a pin-prick is to a bite.

PILLAR, COLUMN, PILASTER. A *pillar* is a shaft that extends upwards; a *column* is a more elaborate *pillar* with a cap and a base; a *pilaster* is a *pillar* attached to a wall, and is usually square. Both *pillar* and *column* have numerous metaphorical uses, as 'a *pillar* of society', 'a *column* of smoke'; but these uses are seldom likely to be confused.

PITEOUS, PITIABLE, PITIFUL. The *pitiful* is that which excites compassion because of its pathos; *piteous* describes that which excites pity: 'a *piteous* look, a *piteous* cry'. *Pitiable* now suggests a shade of patronage or contempt on the part of the user.

PITY, COMMISERATION, COMPASSION, CONDOLENCE, RUTH, SYMPATHY. *Pity* is pure feeling; *compassion* adds to it the desire to help and alleviate; *commiseration* is strongly expressed *pity* in a case where help is often impracticable; *condolence* is little more than a formal expression of regret; *sympathy* is a capacity to enter into the sorrows (or joys) of other people; and *ruth* (now archaic) adds to *compassion* the suggestion that the emotion has sprung up suddenly out of a soil of indifference or even hostility.

PLACE, BERTH, BILLET, JOB, OFFICE, POSITION, POST, SITUATION, STATION. A man's *place* or *position* refers to his employment; the latter implies a higher social status than the former. *Job, berth* and *billet* are colloquial renderings of the same idea, but *job* stresses the work involved; *berth*, the place one holds in an organization; and *billet*, the fact that the job is by appointment (in the 'every bullet has its *billet*' sense). An *office* is a position of trust or authority; a *post* implies responsibility, as of a soldier at his *post*; a *station* is a specifically assigned *place*; a *situation* is much the same as a *position*, but carries a stronger sense of filling up a vacancy.

PLAN, DESIGN, PLOT, PROJECT, SCHEME. A *design* relates to ends; a *plan*, to the means to those ends: the *plan* is a practical working-out; the *design* incorporates the ultimate intention of the planner. A *scheme* is a careful and elaborate *plan*; a *project*, a *scheme* of considerable magnitude. *Plot*, in this grouping, is generally technical and applies to the *plans* of land-surveyors or of persons composing imaginative works of literature.

PLAY *v.*, FROLIC, GAMBOL, GAME, ROMP, SPORT. *Play* is the general term; *sport* implies an absence of seriousness; *frolic* adds a suggestion of levity; *gambol* implies *frolicking* with an excess of movement; and *romp* is rougher and more boisterous. A *game*, on the other hand, is organized *play*, with rules and restrictions.

PLEASE, DELIGHT, GLADDEN, GRATIFY, REGALE, REJOICE. To *please* suggests satisfaction; to *gratify*, a higher degree of satisfaction. *Delight* is emotional rather than rational, and suggests happiness; *rejoice*, a high degree of happiness. *Gladden* implies progression from a less to a more happy state; and *regale*, a kind of feasting upon the thing (sometimes actual food) that gives pleasure to the person concerned.
ANT. **Displease; Vex.**

PLEASURE, DELECTATION, DELIGHT, ENJOYMENT, JOY. *Pleasure* implies satisfaction and gratification, and is opposed to *pain*; but *delight*, which is keener, is also more transient. *Joy* is an altogether more spiritual thing, ecstatic and deeply rooted. *Enjoyment* is the savouring of that which one enjoys and is not a particularly lofty condition; it can be applied to such pleasures as those of the table. Among the unthinking, *delectation* has nowadays sunk to be roughly equivalent to diversion or amusement.
ANT. **Displeasure.**

PLEDGE, DEPOSIT, EARNEST, HOSTAGE, TOKEN. A *pledge* is something temporarily given as security for a debt or an obligation; if the *pledge* is a person, that person is a *hostage*. An *earnest* or a *deposit* is a partial payment made to the seller to clinch a bargain: the former is the older, more literary, expression; the latter, the one in current use. A *token* is an object, other than money, that represents money paid or a promise to pay it. Bank notes, in this sense, are *tokens*.

PLENTIFUL, ABUNDANT, AMPLE, COPIOUS, PLENTEOUS. *Plenteous* is archaic; *plentiful* is the current use; *abundant* implies great plenty; *ample* is more than sufficient for the purpose; *copious* implies a plenty that is almost excessive.
ANT. **Scanty.**

PLOT, CONSPIRACY, INTRIGUE, MACHINATION. A *plot* is a plan calculated to damage some person or persons; an *intrigue* is an attempt to gain one's ends by elaborate and clandestine scheming; *machinations* are crafty devices conducing to the furtherance of a *plot*; a *conspiracy* is a combination of persons for the purpose of committing unlawful acts often involving treachery.

POINT *v.*, AIM, DIRECT, LAY, LEVEL, TRAIN. These words are synonymous when they refer to directing an object towards a goal. One *points* a stick; *aims* a gun; *levels* a lance; *lays* or *trains* a field-gun; *directs* a searchlight. *Aim* suggests a superior degree of care and exactitude.

POISE, BALANCE, EQUILIBRIUM, EQUIPOISE. *Balance* implies that condition in an object which exists when each of its component parts is in such due proportion that it maintains a normal position. *Equilibrium* means the same, but is in practice restricted to physical and scientific usages. *Equipoise* implies a stable *equilibrium*; and so does *poise*, except that, whereas the latter resembles *balance* in the wideness and figurativeness of its applications, the former resembles *equilibrium* in its restriction to technical usages. *Poise* is, in fact, a shortened form of *equipoise.*

POISON, BANE, TOXIN, VENOM. *Poison* is the general term; *venom* is either literally or figuratively the sort of *poison* that is secreted by a snake or similar creature. A *toxin* is a *poison* manufactured in the body of the poisoned creature; *bane* is archaic and is now only used figuratively in such phrases as 'the *bane* of my existence'.

POLITICIAN, STATESMAN. *Politician*, since Shakespeare's day, has been very nearly a term of abuse; but *politicians* of whom we approve we call *statesmen*. Strictly, a *politician* is merely one who engages in politics, whereas a *statesman's* concern is 'to ruin or to rule the state': the latter being the role he supposes himself to fill, though his critics think it is the former.

POOR, IMPECUNIOUS, INDIGENT, NEEDY, POVERTY-STRICKEN. *Poor* is the general term; the *impecunious* have no money; the *needy* lack necessities; the *indigent* are *needy* in the rather loftier way of those who have 'seen better days'; the *poverty-stricken* have been poor so long that, even when money comes their way, they persist in their cheese-paring.
ANT. **Rich.**

POSITION, ATTITUDE, POSE, POSTURE, all here relate to the human body. *Position* has the widest and most general application; *posture* implies a *position* of the body fitted to the exigencies of the moment, *e.g.*

a standing, a sitting *posture*. An *attitude* is a *posture* assumed either consciously or unconsciously to express a state of mind; a *pose* is the same thing, consciously assumed, as when one *poses* for a portrait.

POSSIBLE, FEASIBLE, PRACTICABLE, PRACTICAL. Anything is *possible* that is not inherently *impossible*; but a thing is *practicable* only if it can be readily done under normal conditions by ordinary people; the *feasible* is that which is highly *practicable*. *Practical* is not truly a synonym for any of the foregoing, since it means that which is opposed to the *theoretical*; by extension, however, it has come to mean that which is useful: we speak of 'a *practical* knowledge of Spanish'.
ANT. **Impossible.**

POVERTY, DESTITUTION, INDIGENCE, NEED, PENURY, WANT. *Poverty*, the most general of these terms, can include the state of voluntary *poverty*; *indigence* is a shabby-genteel *poverty*; *penury* introduces the idea of hunger, though sometimes because of niggardliness. *Need* implies a lack of necessities which may or may not be temporary; *want* and *destitution* are the strongest terms in this group, but *destitution* suggests a more complete absence of all resources than *want*.
ANT. **Riches.**

POWER, AUTHORITY, DOMINION, ENERGY, FORCE, MIGHT, STRENGTH. *Power* is the general term; and when *power* over other persons is implied, *authority* and *dominion* come into close comparison: but *authority* is *power* exercised by an outside source, and *dominion* is sovereign *power* exercised over a subject. *Force* is *power* in action, engaged, usually, in overcoming resistance; *energy* is also *power* in action, but contrasted with latent *power*; *strength* is the *power* inherent in a specific person or object; and *might* is great or even superhuman *power*, and is thus peculiarly appropriate to the *power* of gods, heroes and so forth.
ANT. **Impotence.**

PRAISE *v.*, ACCLAIM, APPLAUD, COMMEND, EULOGIZE, EXTOL, LAUD. *Commend* is the weakest of these terms; to *praise* is to *commend* highly; *laud* suggests high, even excessive, *praise*. To *applaud* is to *praise* publicly and noisily; to *acclaim*, to do so vociferously; to *extol*, to do so in a fashion which exalts and magnifies the subject of it; to *eulogize*, to do the same more formally by such means as a setoration or panegyric.
ANT. **Blame.**

PRAYER, APPEAL, ENTREATY, PETITION, PLEA, SUIT. A *prayer* is a request to authority, whether human or divine; a *suit* is a humble and somewhat formal request addressed to an individual; an *entreaty* is an urgent request from one person to another. A *plea* implies pleading on the part of him who advances it, and therefore contains some suspicion of self-justification; an *appeal* is a strongly reiterated *plea*; a *petition* is a more formal and specific request, often written, made to such authority as is competent to grant it.

PREVAILING, CURRENT, PREVALENT, RIFE. The *prevailing* is that which is the most common, as a *prevailing* wind; but *prevalent* suggests a commonness that is not necessarily superlative: 'Though the *prevailing* wind is west, north winds are also *prevalent*'. *Rife* adds to *prevalent* a sense of rapid increase in the commonness of the thing concerned; *current* means that which is *prevailing* at the present moment, as when we speak of '*current* fashions; *current* prices'.

PREVENT, AVERT, OBVIATE, PRECLUDE. *Prevent* in current English no longer means (as it did once) to go before to help, but only to go before to hinder. *Preclude* differs from this use of *prevent* by suggesting that all possible steps have been taken to aid the prevention; *obviate* has the same meaning, but with the difference that the human will has been deliberately engaged in the process: circumstances may *prevent* or *preclude*, but human actions *obviate*. *Avert* differs from the preceding terms in that it always carries the suggestion that the thing to be prevented is unpleasant.
ANT. **Permit.**

PRIDE, CONCEIT, VANITY are actually quite different things, though they are often confused. *Conceit* consists in having a high opinion of oneself and showing it; *vanity*, in having a rather low opinion of oneself and trying to hide it; *pride*, in having a high degree of self-esteem which may or may not be justified: this may manifest itself in self-respect and the maintenance of a high standard of conduct, or, alternatively, in arrogance and pomposity. Though the latter manifestations are commoner than the former, *pride* itself, in its basic meaning, is not responsible; human nature is.
ANT. **Humility.**

PRIMARY, PRIMAL, PRIME, PRIMEVAL, PRIMITIVE, PRIMORDIAL, PRISTINE. *Primary* is the generic term meaning that which comes first in order of succession; *primal* is a more poetic version of the word, implying *initial, elemental*. The *primordial* is that which acts as the starting point in a process of growth (the *primordial* slime). *Primitive*, on the other hand, means little more than *early*, and so barbarous and unsophisticated. *Pristine* suggests the newness and freshness of something that has just come into existence; *primeval*, strictly, something that pertains to the first age of the earth, though in practice it generally means 'very old'. *Prime*, as in '*Prime* Minister' and '*prime* cuts', means first in the sense that nothing comes before it.

PRIORITY, PRECEDENCE. *Priority* simply implies an order of succession, in which that which comes first (usually in point of time) has the *priority*. *Precedence* is a more formal term, and relates to that which comes first because of its rank or status.

PROBABLE, LIKELY, POSSIBLE. Though not synonyms, these words are sometimes confused. The *possible* is anything that is not in its own nature impossible; the *probable* is that which, on weighing up the evidence, is the most *likely* of two or more alternatives. *Likely* resembles *probable*, but is looser and suggests a slightly higher degree of uncertainty.
ANT. **Improbable.**

PROFANE *adj.*, BLASPHEMOUS, IMPIOUS, SACRILEGIOUS. *Impious* implies a disrespect for sacred things; and *profane* is applied to people, words or actions which exhibit such disrespect. *Blasphemous* adds to *profane* the sense of deliberate and conscious insult to what is sacred, and *sacrilegious* implies the physical or figurative defilement of such things. In a secondary sense, *profane* means no more than *lay* or *secular*, as opposed to *sacred*.

PROGRESS, ADVANCEMENT, PROGRESSION. *Progress* implies a movement forward considered as a whole; *progression*, the movement in itself: we speak of the *progress* of a schoolboy; the *progression* of a sound-wave. *Advancement*, not a strict synonym of the other two, suggests that the *progress* in question is made towards a definite and considered goal.

PROMISE *v.*, CONTRACT, COVENANT ENGAGE, PLEDGE, PLIGHT. To *promise* is to give one's word that one will perform some defined action; to *pledge* is to make a solemn *promise*; to *engage* is to make one not lightly to be broken; to *plight* is similar, but is now archaic and idiomatic, as in such an expression as 'to *plight* one's troth'. To *covenant* implies a *promise* made by two or more parties and backed by a quasi-legal agreement; to *contract*, the same but backed by a fully legal one.

PROPORTIONAL, COMMENSURABLE, COMMENSURATE, PROPORTIONATE. *Proportional* refers only to the proportions that exist between two or more closely related things; *proportionate* is used when the stress lies on the point that the relations between the things in question should be in keeping: we speak of *proportional* representation, but of making *proportionate* the punishment to the crime. *Commensurate* and *commensurable* differ from *proportionate* in the sense that they carry a stronger implication of equality between the related things, *e.g.* 'His exertions are not *commensurate* with his output'.

PROPOSAL, PROPOSITION. A *proposal* is an offer; a *proposition* is, strictly, a statement advanced for consideration. In loose usage, *proposition* may, but should not, take the place of *proposal*, as when one says, 'The *proposition* seems an attractive one', with reference to an offer.

PROUD, ARROGANT, HAUGHTY, INSOLENT, OVERBEARING, SUPERCILIOUS. *Proud* does not always have a bad significance (see **PRIDE**), though in this grouping it has, suggesting an undue awareness of one's own supposed superiority and a scorn for one's supposed inferiors. The *arrogant* claim aggressively more consideration than is their right; the *haughty* are *proud* because of their birth and social position; the *insolent* are both *haughty* and rude; the *overbearing* are bullies; the *supercilious* have a sort of bloodless contempt for those they deem their inferiors and can hardly be bothered to notice them.
ANT. **Humble.**

PROVE, DEMONSTRATE, TEST. To *prove* is to establish a fact by reasoning or argument; to *test* is to establish it by experiment; to *demonstrate* is similar to *to test* but implies the presence of an audience.
ANT. **Disprove.**

PROVISIONAL, TENTATIVE. The *provisional* is anything adopted for the time being, to be discarded when no longer needed; the *tentative* is something adopted for the sake of seeing how it works. The *provisional* is

always replaced by something definitive; the *tentative* may prove its worth and be retained.
ANT. **Definitive.**

PULL, DRAG, DRAW, HAUL, PLUCK, TOW, TUG. *Pull* is the general term; to *draw* is to *pull* towards the person or thing exerting the force; to *drag* is to *draw* with difficulty something weighty; to *haul* is to *pull* with concerted and concentrated effort; to *tug* is to *pull* with sudden violence; to *pluck*, with a sudden twitch, as when one plucks a hen; to *tow* is to *pull* with a rope or other tackle an object that is temporarily incapable of movement on its own account.

PUNISH, CASTIGATE, CHASTEN, CHASTISE, CORRECT, DISCIPLINE. *Punish*, the most general of these terms, implies the infliction of a penalty for actual or supposed misdeeds; *chastise*, that the punishment is of a corporal kind; *castigate*, which once meant much the same as *chastise*, is now chiefly used to distinguish a verbal lashing from an actual one. To *chasten* implies that improvement rather than retribution is the aim of the punishment ('Whom the Lord loveth He *chasteneth*'); to *discipline* is to subject to discipline, which may or may not involve punishment; to *correct* is to *discipline* with a view to effecting the reformation of the offender.
ANT. **Excuse; Pardon.**

PURPOSE *v.*, DESIGN, INTEND, MEAN, PROPOSE. *Mean* is the weakest of these terms, signifying little more than a vague intention to do the thing one day; *intend* suggests a greater degree of determination than *mean*; and *design* implies a degree of both deliberation and forethought. *Propose* is stronger still and embodies the idea of both defining and of stating one's intention; and *purpose* is stronger even than *propose* and usually suggests a higher degree of clarity in the mind of the person proclaiming the intention.

PUSH, PRÒPEL, RAM, SHOVE, THRUST. To *push* and to *shove* imply that the bodies concerned are in actual contact, but *shove* suggests greater expenditure of energy than *push*. To *thrust* and to *ram*, on the other hand, suggest the use of an instrument, as when one *thrusts* a poker into the fire, or *rams* a square peg into a round hole; in this case, *ram* carries the sense of greater violence. To *propel* is to *push* by some force or power—wind, steam, or human strength—usually from behind.

PUT, LAY, PLACE, SET. *Put* is the most general of these terms; to *place* is to *put* in a suitable or specified place; to *lay* is to *put* a thing in a horizontal position, just as to *set* is to *put* it in an upright one: we *lay* a book on the table, but *set* a jug upon it.

Q

QUALITY, ACCIDENT, ATTRIBUTE, CHARACTER, PROPERTY. *Quality* is the widest, most general, of these terms which have reference to the inherent nature of a thing; but whereas *quality* may apply to any of its distinguishing factors, a *property* is a *quality* which is inseparable from the species to which the thing belongs. A *character* is the distinctive *quality* of a class of things and is usually confined to scientific usage, and an *attribute* is a *quality* ascribed by us to something of which we have no very certain knowledge: we speak, for instance, of the *attributes* of Deity. An *accident*, in this grouping, is the same as a *quality*, and can be used in a philosophical sense to mean one of the *qualities* by which a thing manifests itself. It is, however, more often used to mean that the *quality* specified is not in itself of essential or superior value.

QUARREL *n.*, AFFRAY (or FRAY), ALTERCATION, SQUABBLE, WRANGLE. *Quarrel* is the most common of these words which suggest a noisy and heated dispute. A *squabble* is a childish and undignified *quarrel*; a *wrangle* is a noisy and futile one; an *altercation* is a *wrangle* conducted on what one hopes is a slightly more dignified plane. An *affray* (or *fray*) suggests an exchange of blows; so may a *quarrel*, which however can also remain verbal. *Quarrel* may also suggest a much more protracted period of discord than any of the other expressions.

QUESTION *n.*, QUERY. The distinction here is that a *question* may be foolish, but a *query* is usually taken to be a reasonable *question* asked to elicit information.

QUICK, EXPEDITIOUS, FAST, FLEET, HASTY, RAPID, SPEEDY, SWIFT. Whereas *fast* usually applies to the moving object, *rapid* more often qualifies the movement itself: we say a *fast* train, but *rapid* progress. *Swift* suggests a high degree of rapidity; *fleet* adds the idea of lightness and skimming along; *quick*, a liveliness in action rather than mere velocity of motion; and *speedy* carries a suggestion of willing alacrity. *Hasty*, on the other hand, suggests an excessive and bustling speed that defeats its own object; and *expeditious*, a calm and efficient quickness, the very reverse of *hasty*.
ANT. **Slow.**

R

RACE, NATION, PEOPLE. A *nation* is a political aggregation of people under a single government; but *race* refers to anthropological and ethnological divisions as illustrated by physical characteristics. *People* is looser than *nation* and embodies the idea of a common culture rather than of a common government, *e.g.* 'The English-speaking *peoples*'.

RANGE, COMPASS, KEN, PURVIEW, REACH, SCOPE. All these words suggest a capacity for mastering by one or other of the senses; but *range* implies that which is within *reach* of the eye, and *reach*, that which, either literally or figuratively, is within grasp of the hand. *Ken* is that which lies within the *reach* of the understanding; and *purview*, though in strict use applicable chiefly to written or printed matter, is in fact used in much the same way as *ken*. *Compass* resembles *range* and *reach* but with the added suggestion of a circumscribing limit; and *scope*, in one of its uses is similar, as when we say, 'It is not possible within the *scope* of this book to do so and so'. In another use, however, *scope* rejects the idea of circumscription, as when we say, 'Here you will find *scope* for all your energies'.

RARE, INFREQUENT, OCCASIONAL, SCARCE, UNCOMMON. The *infrequent* occurs seldom; the *occasional*, now and then, but with no predictability; the *uncommon* is that which is not ordinarily found and is therefore exceptional; the *scarce* is that which at any one place and time cannot be found without difficulty; the *rare* is that of which there is an absolute scarcity, and the word usually applies to that which is in itself choice and of intrinsic value.

RATIFY, CONFIRM. Though similar in meaning, *ratify* has commonly more formal connotations: we *ratify* a treaty, *confirm* the receipt of a letter.

RAVAGE, DESPOIL, DEVASTATE, PILLAGE, SACK, WASTE. One *despoils* a building; *sacks* a city; *devastates* or *wastes* (or *lays waste*) a whole countryside. *Pillage* carries an implication of stealing and plundering with more method and less senseless damage than when one *sacks*. To *ravage*, on the other hand, suggests a long succession of acts of violence: we speak of the *ravages* of time.

RAY, BEAM. A *ray* of light is thin; a *beam* is wider than a *ray*.

REACH *v*., ACHIEVE, ATTAIN, COMPASS, GAIN. *Reach* is the general, unemphatic term: one *reaches* one's destination; *gain* suggests more difficulty and struggle; *compass*, that either skill or guile has been employed. To *achieve* emphasizes endurance and effort; to *attain*, that the goal reached is a difficult one set by ambition or aspiration.

READY, APT, PROMPT. *Prompt* implies a quick response to an order or other stimulus, because of training rather than natural aptitude; *ready* adds a suggestion of skill and ease in the response; *apt*, that the response arises from natural intelligence and ability.

REAL, ACTUAL, TRUE. We say a thing is *actual* when its existence is demonstrable by our senses; that it is *real* when its existence can be proved either by the senses or by the reason. What is *true* can be either *actual* or *real* but adds to these words the suggestion that there is a standard by which its truth can be measured. Thus we speak of *actual* happenings (which we have observed); *real* pearls (which our senses alone cannot distinguish from artificial ones); and *true* doctrines (the truth of which we can only vouch for by comparison with the standards in which we have been accustomed to believe).
ANT. **Unreal; Imaginary.**

REASON *n.* (1), ARGUMENT, GROUND, PROOF, all apply to the point or points advanced by one party in a dispute in his endeavour to convince the other party to it. A *reason*, in this grouping, is often personal and self-justificatory; an *argument*, more dispassionate; a *proof*, a clinching *argument*. *Ground* or *grounds* is often used in the place of *reason* or *reasons*, particularly when the emphasis is upon concrete evidence rather than abstractions.

REASON *n.* (2), INTUITION, UNDERSTANDING, all refer to those powers of the intellect by which we obtain knowledge; but whereas *understanding* implies a strict use of the logical and reasoning faculty, *intuition* suggests a kind of knowing that is direct and outside or beyond the scope of reasoning. The *reason*, on the other hand, is, in present usage, a kind of midway term between *understanding* and *intuition*; it is, so to speak, the *understanding* coloured by the intuitive process.

REBEL, ICONOCLAST, INSURGENT. A *rebel* is one who sets himself up against authority; authority is apt to describe political rebels as *insurgents*; an *iconoclast* (a breaker of images) is one who attacks established institutions.

REBELLION, INSURRECTION, MUTINY, REVOLT, REVOLUTION, UPRISING. A *revolution* is a successful *rebellion* against constituted authority; a *revolt* or *insurrection* is one that has not yet succeeded, though *revolt* is the stronger word of the two. An *uprising* is still less effective than an *insurrection*; a *mutiny* is a *rebellion* against naval or military authority.

REBOUND, RECOIL, REVERBERATE, all mean to spring back; but *rebound* is a springing back after an impact, and *reverberate* suggests the springing back of a wave, usually one of sound. To *recoil* is to spring back after being stretched or depressed, and involves a return to the original position of the thing in question.

RECEDE, BACK, RETRACT, RETREAT, RETROGRADE. To *recede* is the reverse to proceeding or advancing; to *retreat* implies a receding from a point already gained, by reason of opposition; *retrograde* implies a movement contrary to that which is natural and normal; *retract*

in the biological sense is the reverse of *protract*, the thrusting forward of such things as claws. To *back* is applied chiefly to driving a vehicle backwards.
ANT. **Proceed; Advance.**

RECEIPT, PRESCRIPTION, RECIPE. Formerly *receipt* meant a set of directions for making a medicine or a cooked dish; now *prescription* is mostly used for the former, and *recipe* for the latter.

RECIPROCAL, COMMON, MUTUAL. *Reciprocal*, in this grouping, suggests a fair each-way traffic between two parties, as when we speak of *reciprocal* civilities. *Mutual* can be similar in meaning, but is, in effect, the equivalent of *each other*: a *mutual* relationship means that *a* is to *b* as *b* is to *a*, and the point to remember is that only two parties are involved. If more than two come into consideration, *common* is the right term. That is, *mutual* friends are friends to *each other*; two people who each possess the same friend have a *common* friend. Unfortunately the connotations of the word *common* make many people fight shy of this usage, so that (aided and abetted by Dickens's title *Our Mutual Friend*) it seems probable that *mutual* will eventually take over this function of *common*. But it has not done so yet.

RECOVER, RECOUP, RECRUIT, REGAIN, RETRIEVE. *Recover* is the general term for getting back that which has been lost. *Recoup* is used when the loss is financial; *regain*, when the thing lost has been taken forcibly or when a special exertion has been called for. *Retrieve* is similar to *regain*, but stronger; and *recruit*, which implies growth through addition, is used in senses where the loss is made good by replenishments from the original source, *e.g.* one *recruits* one's strength.

REFER, ADVERT, ALLUDE. We *refer* to something directly; we *allude* to it indirectly. To *advert* is properly to turn from the point under discussion to take up another, so that the use of the word as a synonym for *refer* is loose and incorrect.

REFORM, REFORMATION. *Reform* has general application; *reformation*, particular application. A *reform* is any attempt to make changes for the better; a *reformation* is the definite eradication of defects whether from characters or institutions, and is consequently the more precise word of the two.

REFUSE, DECLINE, REBUFF, REJECT, REPEL, REPUDIATE, SPURN. To *decline* is the most courteous of these terms; to *refuse* implies a more decided negative; to *reject*, which is a throwing away, is stronger still. To *repel* is to *reject* with violence; to *rebuff*, to *refuse* with contempt; to *repudiate* is to cast off or *reject* with disdain and contumely. To *spurn* is literally to kick against, and so is stronger even than *repudiate*.
ANT. **Accept.**

RELATE, DESCRIBE, NARRATE, RECOUNT, REHEARSE, REPORT, STATE. To *relate* is to give an account of something; to *rehearse* is to give a repetitive account of it; to *recount* is to run over a series of events; to *narrate* is to *relate* in a quasi-literary manner; to *describe* involves some elaboration of descriptive detail. To *state* is to *relate* clearly and baldly; to *report* suggests a certain formality of narration.

RELIEVE, ALLAY, ALLEVIATE, ASSUAGE, LIGHTEN, MITIGATE, all mean to lessen. *Relieve* is the strongest; *alleviate* suggests a temporary relief; *lighten*, a transitory lifting of the burden; *assuage* applies to the relieving of emotion rather than of physical suffering; *mitigate* also suggests partial relief, but differs from *alleviate* in implying that some of the suffering remains. To *allay* is to calm or quieten, and is applied both to emotional and physical discomforts.
ANT. **Intensify.**

RELIGION, CHURCH, CREED, CULT, DENOMINATION, FAITH, PERSUASION, SECT. *Religion* is the comprehensive term; *church* implies membership of a specific organization; so does *denomination*, though the latter is a vaguer and more formal use. *Faith* and *creed* apply to any clearly formulated system of doctrine; and *sect* and *persuasion* (which do not necessarily refer solely to religious beliefs) are usually employed in a somewhat derogatory sense, the first suggesting a narrow and insignificant sector of belief, the other a certain jocularity in the user. *Cult* resembles *sect* in being customarily applied to a relatively small and narrow set of doctrines, but is more properly applied to non-theistic *sects*.

REMARK, ANNOTATION, COMMENT, COMMENTARY, NOTE, OBSERVATION. A *remark* is a more or less casual utterance; an *observation*, a weightier one; a *comment* is one made in criticism or elucidation. A *note* is a written *comment*; a *commentary* is a collection of notes; an *annotation* is simply a more grandiose form of the word *note*.

REMEMBER, RECALL, RECOLLECT. We *remember* what is already in our minds; we *recollect* by an effort what we have forgotten. *Recall* is similar to *recollect* except that it may properly be used on occasions when the memory is stimulated by something outside itself: a *scent* will unconsciously *recall* an experience; once *recalled*, we *recollect* it.
ANT. **Forget.**

REPEAT, ITERATE, RECAPITULATE, REITERATE. *Repeat* is the general term; *iterate* implies continual repetition; *reiterate* is stronger still. To *recapitulate* is to go over the general heads of an argument, and is not strictly synonymous with to *repeat*.

RESPONSIBLE, ACCOUNTABLE, AMENABLE, ANSWERABLE, LIABLE. *Responsible*, *answerable* and *accountable* are very similar in meaning, but *accountable* is the strongest, *e.g.* 'Man is *accountable* to God for his sins'. *Answerable* suggests legal responsibility; *responsible*, moral answerability. *Liable* and *amenable* suggest a contingent rather than a certain accountability: one is *amenable* to the law of the land; *liable* to military service; but in neither case may the power involved adopt a positive course.

REST, COMFORT, EASE, LEISURE, RELAXATION, REPOSE. *Rest* is the general term; *repose* implies freedom from all movement; *relaxation*, release of tension; *leisure*, a freedom from task-work; *ease*, a freedom from both mental and physical activity. *Comfort*, on the other hand, relates to one's material surroundings: a man may be hard at work, but be working in *comfort*.

RESTRAIN, CHECK, CURB, INHIBIT, RESTRICT. *Restrain* is the general term; to *check* implies an abrupt restraint; to *curb*, a similar but more stringent one. To *inhibit* comes from the jargon of psychiatry and implies a self-curbing because of one's conscience or beliefs. To *restrict*, on the other hand, implies a limiting by outside force: we learn to *restrain* ourselves; the Chancellor *restricts* our spending.
ANT. **Impel; Incite.**

RETALIATION, REPRISAL, RETRIBUTION, REVENGE. *Retaliation* is returning a blow for a blow; a *reprisal* is a calculated act of *retaliation* based on the belief that such act will restrain the other party to the quarrel. *Revenge* is personal and often vindictive *retaliation*: 'a kind of wild justice'. *Retribution*, on the other hand, is a *retaliation* which is generally considered salutary and deserved.

RETURN, RECUR, RECRUDESCE, REVERT. *Return* is the simple term; to *revert* is to *return* to a previous and usually more primitive state of affairs; to *recur* is to return to something that has previously happened; to *recrudesce* is to *return* to former activity, and is usually applied to the breaking out of something previously repressed, such as an epidemic.

RICH, AFFLUENT, OPULENT, WEALTHY. *Rich*, the general term, simply implies possessing more than the average, not necessarily of money only, *e.g.* 'a *rich* cake'; but *wealthy*, which refers almost wholly to worldly possessions, suggests a higher degree of wealth than *rich*. *Affluent*, which means that riches are still flowing in, applies properly to persons or institutions that are steadily growing richer; *opulent* characterizes those that are ostentatiously or overwhelmingly rich.
ANT. **Poor.**

RIDICULE, DERIDE, MOCK, RALLY, TAUNT. To *ridicule* implies a greater or lesser degree of belittlement; to *deride*, of bitterness; to *mock*, of contempt. To *taunt* is to mix mockery with reproach; to *rally* is to *ridicule* with reasonable good-humour.

RIGHT, BIRTHRIGHT, PERQUISITE, PREROGATIVE, PRIVILEGE. *Right* is the general and inclusive term meaning something to which one is inherently entitled; a *birthright* is a *right* to which one is entitled because of the circumstances of one's birth; a *prerogative* is a right which belongs to a person because of his rank or other special quality; a *privilege* is a right granted to him for special reasons; a *perquisite* is something of value to which he is entitled by custom because of his employment or office.

RISE, ARISE, ASCEND, MOUNT, SOAR, SURGE, TOWER. *Rise* is the general expression; *arise*, the poetical or rhetorical form of it. To *ascend* and to *mount* have a stronger sense of progressive upward movement: one *rises* from one's bed, but *ascends* the stairs, or *mounts* a horse. *Soar* suggests the upward flight of a bird; *surge*, a heaving upwards, as of a wave; *tower*, a rapid shooting upward: flames *tower*. In a secondary sense, a thing *towers* above a lesser object which, by comparison, it dwarfs.

ANT. **Decline.**

RIVAL *v.*, COMPETE WITH, EMULATE. To *rival* is to attempt to outdo; to *compete with* suggests a struggle with others for an object or a reward; to *emulate* is to attempt to surpass another by imitating what he does, or modelling yourself upon him.

ROB, LOOT, PLUNDER, RIFLE, THIEVE. *Rob* is the common term; to *plunder* is to engage in organized robbery on a large scale; to *rifle* is to ransack for plunder such obvious depositories as treasure-chests or strong-rooms; to *loot* is to *plunder* under specially reprehensible circumstances as when, for example, a disaster has preceded the looting; to *thieve* is to *rob* squalidly and by stealth.

ROOM, APARTMENT, CHAMBER. *Room* is the general term; *chamber* the grandiose or poetic one; *apartment* is now pretentious except when applied to a very large *room*, such as a state *apartment*.

ROUGH, HARSH, RUGGED, UNEVEN. *Rough*, the general term, is all that is opposed to *smooth*; *harsh* is stronger than *rough*, for it implies a higher degree of unpleasantness to the senses whether of touch, sight or sound. *Uneven* merely stresses the absence of evenness, without relation to general texture; and *rugged* suggests unevenness of the highest degree, as when we speak of a *rugged* hillside.

ANT. **Smooth.**

ROUND, ANNULAR, CIRCULAR, GLOBULAR, ORBICULAR, SPHERICAL. *Round* is the comprehensive term; *annular* adds to *round* the idea of being hollow in the middle, and therefore ring-shaped. *Circular* is applied to *round* flat bodies in two dimensions; *spherical*, to truly *round* or ball-shaped ones in three dimensions; and *globular*, to those that are approximately *spherical*. *Orbicular* can be applied to bodies either approximately *circular* or *spherical*.

RUDE, CALLOW, CRUDE, GREEN, RAW, ROUGH. The *rude* is inexpertly made and finished; the *rough*, in this grouping, is made without much care, *e.g.* 'a *rough* sketch'; the *crude* is unprocessed; the *callow*, unfledged; the *green*, unripe; the *raw*, literally, uncooked. Each of these terms signifies, therefore, an imperfectly finished article: *crude* oil; a *callow* youth; a *green* girl; a *raw* recruit.

RURAL, BUCOLIC, PASTORAL, RUSTIC. *Rural* is the most general, uncoloured, term; *rustic* (except for such uses as '*rustic* seat') now generally carries a sneer at 'the country bumpkin'; *pastoral* is poetical and relates to the allegedly idyllic life of the countryman; *bucolic*, once more or less equivalent to *pastoral*, has now become, even more than *rustic*, a synonym for oafish.

S

SAD, DEJECTED, DEPRESSED, DISMAL, GLOOMY, MELANCHOLY, MOURNFUL, SORROWFUL. *Sad* is the most general term and describes the chastened manner in which the man of experience regards life; *dejected* suggests the mood of one who is downcast by his misfortunes; *depressed,* a similar mood induced, as a rule, by physical causes. *Melancholy* implies a more settled depression which may be constitutional; *mournful,* a generally lachrymose state. *Gloomy* suggests the absence of brightness; *dismal* adds to it the sense of positive as well as negative discomfort; *sorrowful* resembles *sad,* but is so much stronger that it is not a true synonym.
ANT. **Glad.**

SAFE, SECURE. Both mean free from danger. Crabb amusingly illustrates the difference between them by saying: 'A person may be very *safe* on top of a coach in the daytime; but if he wishes to *secure* himself, at night, from falling off, he must be fastened'. In other words, to be *secure* is to be free not only from danger but also from the apprehension of it.
ANT. **Dangerous.**

SAVE, CONSERVE, PRESERVE, all mean to keep free from injury. *Save* is the common term; *preserve* stresses the idea of keeping the object concerned away from harmful agents, by taking proper precautions. *Conserve* implies the necessity of taking steps to prevent loss or change, as when one tells an invalid he must *conserve* his strength.
ANT. **Spend; Consume.**

SCHOLAR, DISCIPLE, PUPIL, STUDENT. *Scholar* is the general term for one who studies in a school; *pupil* stresses the fact that one does so under supervision, and implies a teacher. A *student* is literally one who studies anywhere, but it now in practice suggests that one is undergoing higher education. A *disciple,* though semantically the same as a *pupil,* is now either used with Scriptural connotations or to imply a particularly zealous adherence to the doctrines of one's master.

SCHOOL, ACADEMY. Boswell's father, old Auchinleck, sneered at Dr Johnson as one who 'keepit a *school,* and ca'd it an *Academy*'. An *academy* is, properly, a place of association for those who have already had some schoolіng.

SCOFF, GIBE, GIRD, JEER, SNEER. To *scoff* is to ridicule that which should be treated seriously; to *jeer* is to deride vulgarly; to *gibe* is to taunt, usually sarcastically; to *gird* (archaic) is to rail and revile; to *sneer* is to deride with ill-natured and low-bred contempt, and is the strongest and nastiest of these expressions.

SECRET, CLANDESTINE, COVERT, FURTIVE, LATENT, OCCULT, STEALTHY, SURREPTITIOUS. *Secret* is the most general of these terms; *covert* implies an action done under cover, not openly; *stealthy* suggests a stealing on tip-toe as when one stalks a quarry. *Furtive* (from the Latin, *fur*, a thief) is similar to *stealthy*, but has stronger suggestions of criminality; *clandestine* implies a vigorous desire for concealment, usually for no virtuous end. *Surreptitious* also implies concealment, though it has lighter connotations than *clandestine*. The *latent* is that which lies hidden and is the secret cause of things; the *occult* is that which is hidden in the supernatural sense: we speak of *latent* power; of *occult* forces.

SECULAR, LAY, PROFANE, TEMPORAL are all words meaning not devoted to religious uses. The *profane* is opposed to the *sacred* in a purely descriptive, not derogatory, sense; *lay* is applied to persons other than the clergy; the *temporal* is opposed to the spiritual: we speak of *temporal* power. The *secular* is of the world as opposed to the Church, and is used in such phrases as *secular* authorities, *secular* music.
ANT. **Religious.**

SEE, BEHOLD, CONTEMPLATE, DISCERN, ESPY, NOTE, NOTICE, OBSERVE, PERCEIVE, REMARK, SURVEY, VIEW. *See* is the general term; *behold* is rhetorical and hortatory; *espy* implies seeing under difficulties; *view* and *survey*, seeing in detail that which is spread out for inspection: *view*, however, usually implies that one is making the inspection for a particular purpose. To *contemplate*, in this sense, is a vague way of looking; but *notice* and *observe* imply special vigilance: the latter being the stronger term. *Remark* and *note* carry even more strongly than *notice* the idea of mentally registering an impression; *perceive* suggests special insight and penetration in the seer; *discern* adds to the idea of seeing that of discriminating.

SEEK, SEARCH. To *search* is to *seek* for that which is hard to find.

SEEM, APPEAR, LOOK. When we say a person *seems* (or *looks*, or *appears*) ill, there is little difference in the meaning; but, strictly, *seems* implies that we have formed our opinion on all the evidence, and *looks*, upon visual evidence only. In the same way, *appears*, in this connection, carries with it a slight suggestion that we are judging by appearances, and appearances can deceive.

SENSE, JUDGMENT, WISDOM. *Sense*, in this grouping, is what is more often called good sense or common sense, which means practical wisdom; *judgment* adds to this good sense a suggestion of mental training and discipline; and *wisdom*, though strictly impossible to define, is, roughly, a mixture of common or good *sense* with a *judgment* that has grown mellow with years and experience. 'Common *sense* in an uncommon degree', says Coleridge, 'is what the world calls *wisdom*.'

SENTENCE, ATTAINT, CONDEMN, DAMN, DOOM. To *sentence* is to pass judgment after an adverse verdict; to *condemn*, to pass a severe judgment involving, usually, death, or, in the case of something non-human, destruction. To *doom* is similar but generally carries the additional implication that destiny or the supernatural are involved in the judgment. To *damn* is to *condemn* in a theological sense, though it can also be used colloquially, as when one '*damns* with faint praise'. To *attaint* is a historical usage, harking back to the Bill of Attainder by which the state formerly punished its enemies, with or without juridical assistance.

SENTIMENT, SENTIMENTALITY, SENTIMENTALISM. *Sentiment*, which simply means feeling, is not a term of disapproval; but *sentimentality*, which implies an excess of insincere or vamped-up *sentiment*, is. *Sentimentality* describes the quality itself; its manifestations are called *sentimentalism*. The adjective *sentimental* is consequently ambiguous, since it may refer either to *sentiment* or *sentimentalism*.

SEPARATE, DISJOIN, DIVIDE, DIVORCE, PART, SEVER, SUNDER. To *separate* is to disunite two or more things that properly belong together; to *disjoin* suggests that the separation is made at the existing and appropriate joints. To *part* implies the separation by a long distance of two (or occasionally more) things or persons that are naturally closely united; so (as regards a pair) does *divorce*. To *divide* suggests separation with some exactitude into defined parts or shares; to *sever* adds the idea of quickness and violence in the separation; to *sunder*, a rending or tearing apart.
ANT. **Combine.**

SERVITUDE, BONDAGE, SLAVERY. *Servitude* is the condition in which one is obliged to obey the will of one's master; but *slavery* is subjection to a master who actually owns one's person. *Bondage*, now chiefly used figuratively, implies a state of duress for which there is no cure but revolutionary action; it may be applied to such things as one's own bad habits.

SET, CIRCLE, CLIQUE, COTERIE. A *set* is a good-sized group bound together by common tastes, *e.g.* 'the smart *set*'; a *circle* implies a common centre or purpose in the group, *e.g.* 'a sewing *circle*'. A *coterie* is small and usually thinks well of itself; a *clique* is still more exclusive and still more self-approving.

SHADE, ADUMBRATION, PENUMBRA, SHADOW, UMBRAGE. *Shade* is that which protects from both heat and light; but *shadow* is the obscurity caused by the interception of the rays proceeding from the source of light. *Umbrage*, in this group, is the shade cast by trees and their foliage; *penumbra* is an astronomical term relating to the partial shadow that is visible during an eclipse. *Adumbration*, on the other hand, is a purely figurative word, implying a foreshadowing or sketch of something which is to be more fully developed later.

SHAKE *v.*, QUAKE, QUAVER, QUIVER, SHIVER, SHUDDER, TOTTER, TREMBLE, WOBBLE. *Shake* is the comprehensive term; *tremble*, an uncontrolled shaking of the human body; *quake*, which incorporates the idea of a violent convulsion (as in earth*quake*), is often used to describe violent trembling; and *totter* suggests the shakiness of the very old or the very young. To *quiver* is to vibrate like the string of a musical instrument, but is a less violent motion than trembling; to *shiver* and *shudder* both imply a temporary quivering of the human flesh, *shivering* being caused by cold, and *shuddering*, by horror. *Quaver* is usually applied to the voice to denote tremulousness; and *wobble* describes a quivering motion like that of jelly.

SHAMELESS, BAREFACED, BRAZEN, IMMODEST, IMPUDENT. To be *shameless* is to be literally without shame; to be *brazen* is to have a conscience as hard as brass: it thus adds to shamelessness the idea of defiance. *Barefaced* implies a contempt for appearances amounting to extreme effrontery; *immodest* implies an absence of shame in respect of modesty alone; *impudent*, in this grouping, adds to the idea of shamelessness that of boldness and inveteracy.

SHARP, ACUTE, KEEN. All these words have relation to the properties of the knife: a blade is *sharp*, it has a *keen* edge, and an *acute* point. But, figuratively, *sharp* often suggests a certain over-cleverness, *keen* carries the suggestion of shrewdness and clear-headedness, and *acute*, of penetrative and discriminatory powers.
ANT. **Dull; Blunt.**

SHINE, GLARE, GLITTER, RADIATE, SPARKLE are all words that suggest the emission of light. *Shine* expresses the general idea; *glitter*, that of an intermittent and irregular shining; *glare*, a shining of the brightest, most disagreeable, kind. To *radiate* is to emit in rays; to *sparkle*, in what appear to be sparks.

SHOCK, COLLISION, CONCUSSION, IMPACT, IMPINGEMENT, PERCUSSION. *Shock* denotes the effect produced by an *impact*, which is caused by the more or less violent contact of two objects; a *collision* is a more violent *impact* between two moving objects, just as an *impingement* is a less violent one that carries, however, a suggestion of encroachment or overlapping. *Concussion* is usually applied to the physical shock produced by an *impact*; *percussion*, to the deliberate striking together of two things for such purposes as producing a noise or an explosion.

SHOOT, DART, FLOAT, FLY, SAIL, SCUD, SKIM. In their extended senses, these terms are synonymous when they mean to pass very quickly over or above a surface. *Shoot* suggests the speed of a bullet; *dart*, that of a lance or javelin; *float*, that of a floating object; *fly*, that of a winged creature; *sail* or *scud*, that of a swift boat; *skim*, that of a bird or pebble gliding over the surface of the water. It is, therefore, a matter of appropriateness which word to use in a particular context: to *dart*, for instance, suggests a less vigorous and protracted movement than to *shoot*: a cat may *dart* on a mouse, but an aeroplane *shoots* across the sky. *Sail*, also, implies a greater majesty of movement than *float* or *scud*.

SHORT, BRIEF, CONCISE, SUCCINCT, SUMMARY. *Short* is the comprehensive word; *brief* refers to duration alone, save for jocular allusions to *short* garments, etc. The other three terms, which refer exclusively to brevity in statement or expression, are not strict synonyms of the two earlier: a thing is *concise* because of the removal of superfluities;

succinct, because it is compressed; *summary*, because it presents the main outlines without going into details.
ANT. **Long.**

SHOW *v.* (1), DEMONSTRATE, EVIDENCE, EVINCE, MANIFEST, all, in this grouping, mean to reveal. *Show* is the common term; *manifest* implies a completer revelation; and *evidence*, a high degree of positiveness in the matter of the revelation, *e.g.* 'His manner *evidenced* hostility'. *Evince* is the weakest of these terms, implying only outward manifestations of the thing revealed; *demonstrate*, on the other hand, suggests a strong and even emotional manifestation, *e.g.* 'He *demonstrated* his affection'.

SHOW *v.* (2), DISPLAY, EXHIBIT, EXPOSE, FLAUNT, PARADE, all, in this grouping, mean to present in a way to invite notice. *Show* is again the common term; to *exhibit* is to *show* prominently and openly; to *display* is to *show* to the best advantage; to *expose* is to *show* what has been concealed; to *parade* is to *show* ostentatiously; to *flaunt* is to *parade* offensively.
ANT. **Disguise.**

SHREWD, ASTUTE, PERSPICACIOUS, SAGACIOUS. *Shrewdness* is cleverness of a worldly kind; *sagacious* suggests wisdom and far-sightedness; *perspicacious*, penetration; and the *astute* man is one who will not easily be deceived.

SICK, ILL, INDISPOSED. Setting aside the common equating of *sick* with *vomiting*, the difference between *illness* and *sickness* is that the first presupposes an actual disease or disorder, the other any malaise whether of the body, the mind, or the spirit. To be *indisposed* is to be slightly *ill.*
ANT. **Healthy.**

SIGN, SIGNAL. A *sign* is the general term; a *signal* is an arbitrary, agreed and recognizable *sign.*

SILENT, RESERVED, RETICENT, SECRETIVE, TACITURN, UNCOMMUNICATIVE. *Silent* is the comprehensive term; *uncommunicative* implies habitual parsimony of speech; *taciturn* is still stronger and adds the idea of congenital unsociability; *reticent* suggests a disposition to be silent in certain circumstances rather than as a matter of habit; *reserved*, a psychological inability to let oneself go. *Secretive* implies keeping silent for the sake of keeping silent, even when speech is desirable.
ANT. **Talkative.**

SIMILAR, AKIN, ALIKE, ANALOGOUS, COMPARABLE, HOMOGENEOUS, IDENTICAL, LIKE, PARALLEL. Things are *similar* which, though not the same, are easily mistaken for one another; they are *like* or *alike* when, though not identical, they appear to be the same. They are *identical* when they are exactly the same; *akin*, when, though different, they possess essential characteristics in common. Things are *analogous* to one another when, though differing, they may properly be compared with one another; and they are *comparable* when they are sufficiently alike for comparison between them to be reasonable; they are *parallel* when they resemble one another by proceeding, like parallel lines, upon the same course; they are *homogeneous* when they are composed of identical elements.

ANT. **Dissimilar.**

SIMPLE, ASININE, FATUOUS, FOOLISH, SILLY. The *simple* person has a childlike mentality; the *foolish* one lacks elementary judgment; the *silly* one is giddy as well as *foolish*. *Fatuous* is a term of contempt, suggesting a bustling and self-important fool; and *asinine*, rather unfairly to the ass, suggests crass irrationality.

ANT. **Wise.**

SIMULATION, DISSIMULATION. *Simulation* implies the pretence that one is something one is not; *dissimulation*, the concealing of what one really is.

SINCERE, HEARTFELT, HONEST, UNFEIGNED, WHOLEHEARTED. *Sincerity* implies complete straightforwardness and truthfulness; of which *honesty* is a part. *Wholehearted* adds to *sincerity* the idea of zeal and devotion; *heartfelt*, of emotion; and *unfeigned*, of willingness and spontaneity.

ANT. **Insincere.**

SIZE, AREA, BULK, DIMENSIONS, EXTENT, MAGNITUDE, VOLUME. *Size* is the general term; a *dimension* is a measurement in one direction, so that the word *dimensions* is a close synonym of *size*. *Area* relates to the measurements of plane figures; *volume*, to those of three-dimensional ones; and *extent*, to extension in either one or two dimensions. *Magnitude* relates to specific measurements, usually of large or very large objects; *bulk* is less specific and refers to large, but not very large, three-dimensional bodies.

SKETCH, DELINEATION, DIAGRAM, DRAFT, OUTLINE. A *sketch* exhibits the main lines of its subject; an *outline* is a simplified *sketch*; a *delineation* (though semantically equivalent to *sketch*) now simply means a drawing. A *draft* is an expendable rough *sketch* made in preparation of the more finished article; a *diagram* is a graphic arrangement which explains in skeleton form and without full representational intent such things as mechanisms, statistical facts and so on.

SKIN *n.*, BARK, HIDE, PEEL, PELT, RIND. *Skin* is the general term; *hide* is the undressed *skin* of such large beasts as are tanned and converted into leather; a *pelt* is the undressed *skin* of a furred animal; the *rind* is the hard outer *skin* of a fruit; *bark* is the outer *skin* of a tree. *Peel* is *rind* after it has been stripped from the fruit.

SKIN *v.*, FLAY, PARE, PEEL. *Skin* is the most general of these terms; we *peel* an orange, but *pare* an apple, the difference being that in the first case we strip and in the other we cut or scrape off the skin. *Flay* means to *skin* any creature, including man, and because of its former use as a torture it has now become figuratively equivalent to almost any sort of attack, *e.g.* 'T.U.C. *flays* Minister'.

SLANT, ACCLIVITY, DECLIVITY, GRADIENT, INCLINE, SLOPE. A *slant* diverges, usually sharply, from both the horizontal and the vertical; a *slope* is a rather gradually slanting surface; an ascending *slope* of ground is an *acclivity*; a descending one, a *declivity*. An *incline* is a *slope* connecting one level with another; the word *gradient* describes the steepness of a *slope*: '*gradient* 1 in 10' means a rise of one foot in every ten feet measured horizontally.

SLEEP *n.*, DOZE, DROWSE, NAP, SLUMBER, SOMNOLENCE. *Sleep* is the comprehensive expression; *slumber* is light refreshing *sleep*. A *doze* is a short sleep, closely resembling a *nap*. *Somnolence* is a more grandiloquent version of *drowsiness*, which stresses heaviness, lethargy, a propensity to sleep at unseasonable times: one may become *drowsy* or *somnolent* after a heavy meal; one becomes *sleepy* at bedtime.

SLOW, DELIBERATE, DILATORY, LAGGARD, LEISURELY, TARDY, TEDIOUS. *Slow*, the general term, is opposed to *fast*; but *dilatory* is a term of reproach applied to persons who procrastinate; *laggard* (also a noun) is worse than *dilatory* and is used in the same way as a term of reprehension. *Deliberate* means only that one takes one's time about what one is doing; *leisurely*, that one does so because there is no reason to do otherwise. To be *tardy* is to be so slow that one is always late; to be *tedious* is to bore others by one's slowness.
ANT. **Fast.**

SMELL, AROMA, BOUQUET, FRAGRANCE, ODOUR, ODOR (*Amer.*), PERFUME, SCENT. *Smell* is the most general, most neutral, of these terms; *scent* is largely a laudatory word used for *smells* that give pleasure: the *scent* of a rose, or (to a hound) the *scent* of a fox; *fragrance* is a still stronger expression of the same idea. *Odour* is a much less approving term: there are good and bad *odours*; it is a more precise word than *smell*, a more forthright one than *scent*. *Perfume* is highly laudatory and is applied to the pervasive and pungent compounds that are supplied by perfumers; an *aroma* is a peculiarly volatile *fragrance*; *bouquet* is the *aroma* of a good wine.

SOAK, DRENCH, IMPREGNATE, SATURATE, STEEP. To *soak* is to immerse an object in liquid; to *saturate* it is to do so to the extent that it can absorb no more. To *drench* is similar to *to soak* with the difference that the liquid is visualized as being poured down upon the object: one is *drenched* by rain, which *soaks* one to the skin. To *steep* is to soak a thing so as to extract its essence: the process of making tea involves *steeping*; to *impregnate* is fairly lightly to interpenetrate one substance with another, not necessarily with fluid: a cloth, for instance, can be *impregnated* with metal polish.

SOBER, CONTINENT, TEMPERATE, UNIMPASSIONED. *Sober* is the direct opposite of *drunken*; *temperate* implies an ability to control one's appetites while indulging them rationally; *continent* suggests a strong capacity for deliberate self-restraint. *Unimpassioned*, on the other hand, stresses the absence of impassioned feelings of every kind, and suggests either a phlegmatic temperament or an extreme ability to obey the dictates of reason.
ANT. **Drunk.**

SOCIAL, COMPANIONABLE, CONVIVIAL, GREGARIOUS, HOSPITABLE, SOCIABLE. *Social* refers to one's dealings with society; if one enjoys such dealings, one is *sociable*; if one enjoys them to the extent of inviting society to one's own house, one is *hospitable*; if one is impelled by a rather indiscriminate desire to mix with one's fellows, one is *gregarious*; if one has a special aptitude for friendly association, one is *companionable*; if one likes social joviality and eating and drinking, one is *convivial.*
ANT. **Unsocial; Antisocial.**

SOCIETY, ASSOCIATION, CLUB, COMPANY, ORDER are all terms denoting a union of persons for a common object. *Association* is the wide general term; the members of a *company* associate for business purposes; those of a *society* or an *order*, for specifically learned or charitable or other purposes; those of a *club*, for enjoyment or recreation. With a *club*, however, some process of election is usually involved; with an *order*, such things as ritual, a uniform and other formalities.

SOFT, BALMY, BLAND, GENTLE, LENIENT, MEEK, MILD. *Soft* implies the absence of all harshness and roughness; *bland* suggests smoothness and suavity; *mild* and *gentle*, moderation, with the difference that *mildness* is innate but *gentleness* can be acquired. We speak of *mild* weather; *gentle* heat; a *soft* breeze. The *lenient* is soothing and, by extension, unsevere, as when we speak of a *lenient* sentence; the *balmy*, at once soothing and refreshing; the *meek* resembles the *mild* but carries stronger moral overtones: ale can be *mild*, but it takes a human being to be *meek*.
ANT. **Hard.**

SORROW, AFFLICTION, ANGUISH, GRIEF, REGRET, WOE. *Sorrow* is the general term; *grief* is deep *sorrow*; *affliction* is a stronger term than *grief. Anguish* is *grief* raised to the height of physical torment; *woe* is deep and inconsolable *grief. Regret* implies a brooding on the past and a futile desire that it might be altered.
ANT. **Joy.**

SOUL, MIND, SPIRIT are all words that refer to the immaterial part of a human creature. *Mind* defines his intellectual faculties; *soul*, what is presumed to be left after these intellectual faculties have perished with the material brain. *Spirit*, in this sense, is equivalent with *soul*, but the words are employed in different contexts: one prays for the *souls* of others; lifts up one's own *spirit* in prayer.
ANT. **Body.**

SOUR, ACID, DRY, TART. *Sour* is opposed to *sweet* where *sweet* means in good condition, *e.g. sour* milk; *acid* is applied to that which has an acid taste; *tart* implies a sharp but not necessarily disagreeable acidity; and *dry*, as applied to wines, means that they are neither sweet nor, in any disagreeable sense, acid.

SPEAK, CONVERSE, DISCOURSE, TALK, all mean to express oneself in articulate words, but *speak* is the simplest of these terms: one learns to *speak*, but *talk* implies an audience. To *converse* is to interchange *talk*;

to *discourse* is to *talk* instructively and fairly consecutively: a sermon is a *discourse*.

SPEECH, ADDRESS, HARANGUE, HOMILY, LECTURE, ORATION, SERMON, TALK. A *speech* is any public utterance; an *address* is a more or less carefully prepared *speech*; an *oration* is an eloquent and impassioned one; a *harangue* is a derogatory term for what one considers a tiresome *oration*; a *lecture* is a carefully prepared dissertation on a special subject, often, as its etymology suggests, read; and a *talk* is an informal *address*. *Sermon* and *homily* imply religious or ethical instruction, the former being the preferred term for a doctrinal pulpit address, the latter for any generalized moral dissertation.

SPEED *n.*, **IMPETUS, MOMENTUM, PACE, VELOCITY.** *Speed* here refers to the rate of motion; *velocity*, to the *speed* of an object directed along a given path: we speak of the *speed* of a car, the *velocity* of a bullet. *Momentum* is, strictly, the product of the mass of a moving body and its velocity: falling objects gather *momentum*; *impetus* means driving-force; and *pace*, a much looser word than *speed*, is used in such contexts as, 'He set off at a steady *pace*'.

SPEED *v.*, **ACCELERATE, HASTEN, HURRY, PRECIPITATE, QUICKEN.** *Speed* emphasizes swiftness and rapidity; *accelerate*, a mere increase in the rate of motion; *quicken*, a reduction in the time consumed. *Hasten* suggests bringing a thing to pass before its appointed time; *hurry*, a sort of confused and indisciplined quickness; *precipitate*, a rash and impetuous hurrying.

SPEND, CONSUME, DISBURSE, DISSIPATE, EXPEND, SQUANDER, WASTE. To *spend* is the common term, meaning to make use of, for example, one's money; to *disburse* is a more grandiose term for the same activity. To *expend*, however, implies to some extent the exhausting of one's resources, whereas to *consume* is to exhaust them completely. If they are expended to no good purpose, they are *wasted*; if exhausted foolishly, *squandered*. To *dissipate* is to *squander* piecemeal and fecklessly. ANT. **Save.**

SPREAD, DIFFUSE, DISPERSE, SCATTER. We *spread* both the indivisible and the divisible, *e.g.* butter, hay; but we *scatter* only the divisible, *e.g.* seed. A gas *diffuses* when it spreads out in all directions; a crowd *disperses* when it is charged by the police: we can *diffuse* useful knowledge, or *disperse* tracts among those we think have need of them.

SPRING *v.*, **ARISE, DERIVE, EMANATE, FLOW, ISSUE, ORIGINATE, PROCEED, RISE.** The idea of one object coming out of another is expressed by any of these terms. *Spring* suggests a sudden emergence; *rise*, an ascent; *arise*, a coming into being without much reference to antecedent circumstances: 'rumours *arise* whence we know not'. *Originate* supposes a definite starting point; *derive*, less strongly, a defined source; and *flow* and *issue* carry a suggestion of fluid movement: 'Praise God from whom all blessings *flow*'; 'water *issues* from the rocks, or rather from a small opening between them'. *Emanate*, on the other hand, implies an invisible connection between the source and that to which it gives rise, and applies usually to abstract matters; *proceed,* in this grouping, stresses emergence from a definite point of origin.

SPRINKLE, ASPERSE, BEDEW, SPATTER, SPLASH. To *sprinkle* is to scatter a fluid or powder in drops or small particles; to *spatter* is to *sprinkle* a fluid by accident; to *splash* is to do so largely and violently. To *asperse* is to *sprinkle* as in the act of baptism; to *bedew,* which is literally to cover with dew, is sometimes used as a poetical equivalent for *sprinkle.*

STATE, CONDITION, ESTATE, SITUATION, STATUS. *State,* in this grouping, refers to the circumstances under which a thing exists, and is used in such phrases as a *state* of siege, a *state* of nature. It is the general and comprehensive term. *Condition* is a close synonym; we speak of the human *condition,* the *condition* of the patient. *Situation* relates to those external circumstances which effect one's *state* or *condition,* as in such phrases as a difficult *situation*; *status,* strictly a legal term, refers to one's *situation* in society as based upon such things as age, sex, wealth, capacity and so on. *Estate,* which is now largely archaic, is confined to a few idiomatic expressions such as 'man's *estate*', meaning grown-up.

STAY, ABIDE, LINGER, REMAIN, TARRY, WAIT. *Stay* is the general term; *remain* means to *stay* behind after the others have gone. To *wait* is to stay in preparedness; to *abide* is to stay for a long time; to *tarry* is to stay inopportunely; and to *linger* implies much the same, though it is less archaic than *tarry.*

STERILE, BARREN, INFERTILE, UNFRUITFUL, UNPRODUCTIVE. The *sterile* is totally unable to reproduce its kind; the *barren* bears little or no fruit. So, though perhaps to a slightly less degree, does the *unfruitful.* The *infertile* is the opposite of the *fertile*; the *unproductive,* of the *productive*; both terms are less strong than those preceding them.
ANT. **Fertile; Exuberant.**

STICK, ADHERE, CLEAVE, CLING, COHERE. *Stick* is the general, informal expression; *adhere* now has specialized medical uses, and when employed figuratively with reference to persons usually implies deliberation, as when we speak of *adhering* to certain beliefs or tenets. *Cohere* implies a sticking together to produce a homogeneous whole; *cling* suggests dependence: ivy *clings,* one *clings* to one's money. *Cleave,* now mostly literary, implies a strong and devoted attachment: one *cleaves* to one's wife or husband.

STIFF, INFLEXIBLE, RIGID, STARK, TENSE are all words meaning hard to bend, of which *stiff* is the commonest. *Rigid* implies so great a degree of stiffness that the thing concerned cannot be bent without breaking it; *inflexible,* on the other hand, suggests an inability to bend at all. *Tense,* in this grouping, implies a thing stretched so tightly as to be therefore *inflexible*; and *stark* is now chiefly archaic, as in the phrase '*stiff* and *stark*': the rigidity in this case being that which is associated with death.
ANT. **Relaxed; Supple.**

STIR *n.,* ADO, BUSTLE, FLURRY, FUSS. *Stir* suggests movement as of a crowd; *bustle,* noise and a display of energy; *flurry,* agitation and

haste; *fuss*, futile and fidgety agitation. *Ado*, in one use, suggests bustle and waste of energy; in another, trouble and difficulty.
ANT. **Tranquillity.**

STIR *v.*, AROUSE, AWAKEN, RALLY, ROUSE, WAKEN. One is *stirred* to action by emotion; *roused* by activity or commotion; *wakened* (or *awakened*) by a suitable stimulus. *Arouse* is a little weaker than *rouse*; and *rally* implies a gathering together of that which *stirs* or *rouses*.

STOP, CEASE, DESIST, DISCONTINUE, QUIT. *Stop* applies to that which is already in motion; *cease*, to states and conditions: a bus *stops*, but a pain *ceases*; a noise can both *stop* and *cease*. *Discontinue* is a rather pompous way of saying that something that once existed has ceased to exist; *desist* is a forcible way of saying *stop*, though it can also sometimes mean that one *stops* because it is useless to go on; *quit* is an Americanism which can mean either *stop* or *cease* according to the context.

STORY, ANECDOTE, NARRATIVE, TALE, YARN. *Story* is the general term; *narrative* implies that some pains have been taken in the manner of its narration; *tale* is at once a more poetic and a looser word than *story*: one tells a *tale*, but reads a *story*. An *anecdote* is a brief account of a single incident, often illustrating a truth or a principle; a *yarn* is a rambling, inexpert *narrative*, usually of adventure.

STRAIN, SPRAIN. *Strain* is the general term and implies injury to a muscle; *sprain* is properly an injury to a joint: one *strains* one's back, but *sprains* one's ankle.

STRAIT, CHANNEL, PASSAGE, SOUND, STRAITS are all geographical terms: a *strait* (or *straits*) is short and narrow: *e.g.* the *Strait* (or *Straits*) of Gibraltar. A *sound* is longer than a *strait*; a *channel* is larger than a *sound*; a *passage* is a connecting body of water wider than a *strait*.

STRANGER, ALIEN, FOREIGNER, IMMIGRANT. *Stranger* is the general term, but *foreigner* implies that the *stranger* is of a different nationality. An *alien* is the opposite of a citizen; a man after naturalization cannot be an *alien*, but he can still be a *foreigner*. An *immigrant* is a *foreigner* who is no longer an *alien* but has settled in his adopted country.

STRESS, PRESSURE, SHEAR, STRAIN, TENSION, THRUST, TORSION, all relate to the effects of forces upon a rigid structure. *Stress* is the force exerted by one member of the structure upon another and tending to distort it; *strain* is the alteration caused by this *stress*. *Pressure* is *stress* directed against a surface; *tension* is the *stress* exerted, and the *strain* effected, by two forces pulling in opposite directions; *shear* is the *stress* or *strain* that occurs when one member of a structure tends to slide off an adjacent parallel member; *thrust* is the pressure of one part of a structure against another; and *torsion* is the *strain* produced by twisting, or the *stress* displayed by a non-rigid body to resist such twisting. Except for *shear*, *thrust* and *torsion*, all these terms are also used figuratively.

STRIFE, CONFLICT, CONTENTION, DISCORD, DISSENSION, VARIANCE. *Discord* implies a want of harmony; *strife*, a struggle for mastery; *conflict*, a clashing uncertain in its outcome. *Contention* is *strife*

that manifests itself in quarrelling and dispute; *dissension* implies a number of discordant factions; *variance* suggests such clash of opinion or character as makes for disharmony.
ANT. **Peace; Accord.**

STRIKE, CLOUT, CUFF, HIT, KNOCK, PUNCH, RAP, SLAP, SMITE. *Strike* is the most general term; *hit* has greater relation to the thing struck at, and implies that the blow has landed. *Smite* is largely archaic, but if used implies a very heavy blow. A *slap* is a blow with the open hand; a *clout*, in colloquial usage, is a clumsy blow; a *punch* is a blow with the closed fist; a *cuff* is, usually, a box on the ear; a *rap* is a slight *knock*; and a *knock* is properly a blow that produces a noise, as when one *knocks* on a door.

STRONG, STALWART, STOUT, STURDY, TENACIOUS, TOUGH. *Strong* is the comprehensive term; *stout* implies superior resolution: one may have a *strong* body but lack a *stout* heart. *Sturdy* suggests rude, vigorous health; *stalwart*, great strength and stature; *tough*, wiriness and a high capacity for resistance; *tenacious*, doggedness.
ANT. **Weak.**

STUPID, CRASS, DENSE, DULL. *Stupid* implies a congenital lack of intelligence; *dull*, a slowness that may be congenital or may be caused by external factors, such as fatigue. *Dense* suggests thickheadedness, an imperviousness to ideas; and *crass*, perhaps the strongest term in this grouping, a gross fatheadedness which renders the mind incapable of any delicacy of perception.
ANT. **Intelligent.**

SUAVE, BLAND, SMOOTH, URBANE. To be *suave* (literally *sweet*) is to be easy and well bred, perhaps to an excessive degree; to be *urbane* is to adopt a civilized, man-of-the-world attitude. *Bland* suggests a mildness that is positively benign; *smooth*, a suavity that is insincere and assumed for purposes of deception.
ANT. **Bluff.**

SUCCESSION, CHAIN, PROGRESSION, SEQUENCE, SERIES, SET, SUITE, TRAIN, all apply to things that have a certain definite relationship to one another. *Succession* implies that the things follow one another in order without interruption, *e.g.* a *succession* of misfortunes. A *progression* is a *succession*, usually orderly, which is also a building up, *e.g.* an arithmetical *progression*. A *series* relates to a number of similar things in which the idea of order is of secondary importance; a *sequence* is a *series* in which the later items have causal connection with the earlier ones, *e.g.* a logical *sequence*. A *set* denotes a number of related things which together make up a recognized whole, *e.g.* a tea *set*; *suite* is used instead of *set* in certain cases: a *suite* of rooms, a king's *suite*, meaning his retinue. *Chain* and *train* apply to a *series* in which things are logically related to one another, *e.g.* a *chain* of reasoning, a *train* of thought.

SUPPOSED, CONJECTURAL, HYPOTHETICAL, PUTATIVE, REPUTED, SUPPOSITIOUS, SUPPOSITITIOUS. The *supposed* is what one believes, without certainty, to be true; the *conjectural*, what one infers

from incomplete evidence; the *hypothetical* is an assumption put forward to see how it works in practice. The *reputed* and the *putative* are assumptions or suppositions based upon popular belief, the latter being reserved as a rule to certain legal usages. The *suppositious*, however, which means the assumed or the hypothetical, is quite different from the *supposititious*, which means the spurious or counterfeit.
ANT. **Certain.**

SUPREME, INCOMPARABLE, PEERLESS, PRE-EMINENT, SUPERLATIVE, SURPASSING, TRANSCENDENT are all terms meaning the highest of their kind. *Supreme* means that which has and can have no fellow; *superlative*, that which is the best in comparison with others of its sort; *transcendent*, that which attains the ideal; *surpassing*, that of which the excellence almost exceeds belief. *Pre-eminent* is a little less strong and implies the best of its day and age; *peerless* suggests the absence of equals; *incomparable*, the impossibility of there being equals.

SURE, CERTAIN, POSITIVE. To be *sure* is a subjective state of certainty; to be *certain* implies that one has objective grounds for one's assurance; to be *positive*, on the other hand, hints at dogmatic over-confidence that one is right.
ANT. **Unsure.**

SURPRISE, AMAZE, ASTONISH, ASTOUND, all mean to be impressed by the unusual or the unexpected. *Surprise*, in this grouping, is the simplest, least emphatic, term; *astonish* is stronger, implying great *surprise*. *Astound* stresses shock more than *astonish* does; *amaze* suggests a degree of astonishment which produces bewilderment.

SWEAR, AFFIRM, ASSEVERATE, DEPONE, TESTIFY. One *swears* upon a Bible or other sacred object; *affirms*, when one's conscience forbids the taking of such oaths; *asseverates*, if one pledges one's word of honour, informally. To *depone* is to make a statement in writing, on oath; to *testify* is to give evidence on oath.

SYMMETRY, BALANCE, HARMONY, PROPORTION. *Symmetry* implies a regular and formal balance in the parts of a composition, such as a picture or statue; *proportion*, a fitness in the relation between the parts and the whole; and *balance*, a fitting, though not necessarily a symmetrical, relationship between the various portions of such a composition. *Harmony*, in this grouping, is a general rightness produced by a combination of *symmetry*, *proportion* and *balance*.

SYMPATHY, AFFINITY, ATTRACTION. *Sympathy*, in this group, stresses the susceptibility to a common influence of two or more persons or things, *e.g*. the *sympathy* which exists between the moon and the tides. *Attraction*, on the other hand, implies the possession by one person or thing of qualities which draw or attract another. *Affinity* is the name given to this attraction: a magnet *attracts* iron; iron has an *affinity* for the magnet.
ANT. **Antipathy.**

SYSTEM, COMPLEX, NETWORK, ORGANISM, SCHEME. A *system* is an organized whole made up of inter-related parts, *e.g*. the solar *system*; an *organism* is a *system* which possesses life, such as the human body; a *scheme* is a *system* which has been planned by a directing intelligence, *e.g.* 'This sorry *scheme* of things entire'. A *network* is a *system* all the components of which come under a central control, *e.g.* 'The B.B.C. *network*'; a *complex* is an integrated whole having diversity of parts; it is chiefly used where such words as *system*, *organism* and so forth are self-evidently inappropriate: we speak, for example, of a *complex* of emotions. ANT. **Chaos.**

T

TACT, ADDRESS, POISE, SAVOIR-FAIRE. *Tact* consists in saying and doing the right, kindly and graceful thing at the right time; *address*, in so conducting oneself that one emerges with flying colours from the most difficult situations; *poise* stresses self-possession and equanimity; and *savoir-faire*, a wide knowledge of the way of the world.
ANT. **Awkwardness.**

TACTICS, STRATEGY. *Tactics* is the art of handling troops in battle; *strategy* is the art of planning a battle or a war: in other words, *strategy* is theoretical, and *tactics* practical. Both words are also used figuratively.

TAKE, CLUTCH, GRAB, GRASP, SEIZE, SNATCH. *Take* is the general unemphatic word; to *seize* is to *take* forcibly; to *grasp* is to *take* firmly; to *clutch* is to *grasp* greedily, though not always with success. *Snatch* implies taking very hastily; *grab*, uncouthly and unscrupulously.

TALKATIVE, GARRULOUS, LOQUACIOUS, VOLUBLE. *Talkative* means merely given to talking; *loquacious* implies a horrid fluency of utterance; *garrulous*, a drivelling fluency; and *voluble*, a gay, carefree and rather innocent loquacity—'a flow of words so violent as to give an impression of a lack of balance' (*Anthony Powell*).
ANT. **Silent.**

TAME, SUBDUED, SUBMISSIVE. *Tame* is the reverse of wild, as when we speak of *tame* animals; but *subdued* implies a certain neutralism, as when we speak of *subdued* voices, *subdued* tints. *Submissive* implies total acceptance of control, and introduces the idea of meekness and subservience.
ANT. **Fierce.**

TASTE, FLAVOUR, RELISH, SAVOUR, SMACK. *Taste* is the general term in this group; *flavour* is determined by both *taste* and *smell*; *savour* relates more particularly to smell; *relish* implies tasting with enjoyment; *smack* applies to a single prominent ingredient in a multiple flavour: 'I have a *smack* of Hamlet in myself, if I may say so', as Coleridge observes.

TAX, ASSESSMENT, DUTY, IMPOST, LEVY, RATE, TARIFF, TOLL, TRIBUTE, all relate to compulsory contributions levied by authority. *Tax* is the comprehensive term; a *levy* is a special or emergency *tax*; an *assessment* is an estimate of the amount of *tax* due; a *rate* is a *tax* on property usually levied by a local authority; an *impost* (or *duty*) is a *tax* on imports; a *tariff* is the specific *duty* on an import; a *toll* is a *tax* paid for a privilege or service; a *tribute*, now only used figuratively, was formerly a *tax* levied upon subject peoples for the benefit of those who had conquered them.

TEACH, DISCIPLINE, EDUCATE, INSTRUCT, SCHOOL, TRAIN. To *teach* is to impart knowledge; to *instruct*, literally to build up, is to furnish with orders and behests, which may or may not imply teaching: we speak of '*instructing* our solicitor'. To *educate* is to bring out, by teaching, the potentialities of the person taught. To *train* implies a measure of subjection: one *trains* animals, also soldiers; to *discipline* carries the idea of rigorous training still further; to *school* adds to *to discipline* the idea of a discipline somewhat hard to bear: one *schools* oneself to endure hardships.

TEAR, CLEAVE, REND, RIP, RIVE, SPLIT. To *tear* is to pull asunder by force; to *rip* is to *tear* violently, often along the line of a seam or junction; to *rend* is usually rhetorical: '*Rend* your heart, and not your garments'. To *split* is to break or separate completely in two; to *cleave* is to *split* violently; to *rive* is a poetical equivalent of *cleave*.

TEMPORARY, TEMPORAL. The *temporary* is that which is not permanent; we speak of a *temporary* expedient. The *temporal* is that which is not eternal or spiritual: we speak of *temporal* matters, meaning those concerned with this life, and *temporal* power, meaning that which is opposed to ecclesiastical power.
ANT. **Permanent.**

TENDENCY, CURRENT, DRIFT, TENOR, TREND, all imply a leaning towards a certain course of action. *Tendency* suggests that such leaning exists provided it does not meet much opposition; *trend*, that the leaning is subject to change should any sufficiently strong force intervene. *Drift*, *current* and *tenor* embody the same idea, but *drift*, in the nature of things, is weaker than *current*, and *tenor* suggests a superior awareness of the way one is going, *e.g.* 'the noiseless *tenor* of their way', which implies a far greater deliberation than if the operative word had been *drift*.

THEREFORE, ACCORDINGLY, CONSEQUENTLY, HENCE, THEREFOR (except for the last) indicate a causal sequence. *Therefore* belongs to strict reasoning; *hence* stresses slightly more strongly the importance of the earlier part of the logical proposition; *consequently* implies a greater uncertainty in the logical sequence than *therefore*, and is more suited to the colloquial style. *Accordingly* is even less formal than *consequently*, and implies that the idea of causality springs more from use and wont than from logical necessity. The adverb corresponding to the conjunction *therefore* is *therefor*, meaning 'for that, or this, or it': it is of course not a synonym of the foregoing.

THICK, CLOSE, COMPACT, DENSE, all suggest a tight packing together of the particles composing something. We speak of troops in *close* order; of a *close* atmosphere. *Dense* is applied more usually to gaseous bodies: a *dense* fog, *dense* cloud; and by extension we speak also of *dense* persons. *Compact* adds a suggestion of neatness and efficiency because of careful packing; *thick*, in this grouping, suggests concentration: a *thick* soup.

THIN, RARE, SLENDER, SLIGHT, SLIM, TENUOUS. *Thin* is the general comprehensive term meaning the opposite of *thick*; *slender* suggests a lightness of frame both graceful and becoming; *slight*, a certain puniness. *Slim* resembles *slender* except that it stresses a little more strongly the absence of fat; *tenuous* implies extreme thinness or rarefaction, and is applied to things, not persons; *rare*, in this grouping, is confined to gases and is the opposite of *dense*.

ANT. **Thick.**

THINK, COGITATE, DELIBERATE, REASON, REFLECT, SPECULATE. *Think* is the common term; *cogitate* sets more store on the process of thought than on the results of it; *reflect* implies quiet and serious thought. To *reason* is to *think* logically; to *speculate* is to *reason* from indeterminate premises; to *deliberate* is to *think* slowly and carefully.

THOUGHTFUL, ATTENTIVE, CONSIDERATE. The *thoughtful* person is concerned for others; the *considerate* one puts the feelings of others before his own; the *attentive* one indulges in repeated acts of thoughtfulness, though sometimes they may minister to his own advantage.

ANT. **Thoughtless.**

THREAT, MENACE. *Menace* is the more elevated term; we are *threatened* by a small evil, *menaced* by a great one. *Threat*, however, carries a stronger suggestion of the desire to dominate than *menace* does: overt *threats* are more alarming than *menacing* attitudes.

THROW, CAST, FLING, HURL, PITCH, TOSS. *Throw* is the general term; to *cast* implies a certain lightness in the object thrown (*e.g.* dice): it is also the commoner in figurative contexts as 'to *cast* off care'. To *fling* is stronger than to *throw*; to *hurl* implies extreme and excessive vigour. To *pitch* suggests a more or less definite aim at a mark; to *toss*, to *throw* aimlessly and at random, or to *throw* fairly high into the air.

TIDY, NEAT, SHIPSHAPE, TRIM. *Neat* implies cleanliness and order; *tidy* emphasizes order; *trim* adds to both the preceding the idea of good appearance and just proportion. *Shipshape* suggests the trimness and tidiness associated with a well-ordered ship, and is applied chiefly to the affairs of people who can at once lay their hands upon whatever is wanted.

ANT. **Untidy.**

TIME, SEASON. *Time* is the general term; *season* is a special portion of *time*, *e.g.* 'Youth's the *season* made for joy'. Consequently, the *seasonable* is that which is appropriate to its particular *season*, the *timely* is that which is appropriate to the actual *time* at which one comes upon it.

TOUCH *n.*, DASH, SHADE, SPICE, SUGGESTION, SUSPICION, TINCTURE, TINGE, VEIN, all, in their extended senses, refer to a small trace of an extraneous quality which, as it were, flavours something else. We speak of a *touch* of frost, meaning a little frost; a *suggestion* is the merest *touch*; a *suspicion*, one even fainter. *Tincture*, *tinge* and *shade* all come from the vocabulary of colour; *spice* and *dash* from that of cookery. It is a matter of literary discretion which to use in a certain context. *Vein*, on the other hand, refers to that which runs through something like a submerged *vein* of ore, now visible, now concealed.

TRADE, BUSINESS, BUSYNESS, COMMERCE, DEALING, INDUSTRY, TRAFFIC. *Business*, properly, is that at which a man busies himself; this, nowadays, is frequently *trade*, which consists of buying and selling for profit. *Traffic* is also *trade*, considered from the point of view of despatching commodities from one place to another, *e.g.* the drug *traffic*. *Commerce* is simply a more grandiose word for *trade*. *Dealing* is a restricted sort of trading in which one only buys and sells certain commodities. *Industry*, like *business*, originally that in which one was industrious, is now a word embracing any kind of trading, especially that which involves the marketing of manufactured goods. *Busyness*, the state of being busy, is not of course a synonym for *business*.

TRADITIONAL, LEGENDARY. The *traditional* is based upon verbal tradition which may often be accurate; the *legendary*, upon written legends which are frequently fictitious. The *traditional* is thus more likely to be true than the *legendary*.

TRANSFER, ALIENATE, CONVEY. To *transfer* is to make over property from one owner to another; to *convey* emphasizes that the *transfer* is legally executed. To *alienate* is to transfer property by a deliberate act away from a natural heir: entailed property, for example, cannot be *alienated*.

TREACHEROUS, DISLOYAL, FAITHLESS, FALSE, PERFIDIOUS, TRAITOROUS. *Faithless* is the general term; *false*, in this grouping, is stronger than *faithless*; *disloyal* implies lack of faithfulness to that to which one owes allegiance, as a king, country or regiment. *Traitorous*, still worse, carries a suggestion of actual treason; *treacherous*, on the other hand, can imply either private or public treachery. *Perfidious* is an even stronger term than *treacherous*, adding to the idea of faithlessness that of a fundamentally base motive for it.

TRICK, ARTIFICE, FEINT, MANŒUVRE, RUSE, STRATAGEM, WILE, all relate to acts calculated to mislead. A *trick*, originally, implied cheating, though it may now mean only an innocent practical joke. A *ruse*, on the other hand, is always an attempt to create a false impression; and a *stratagem* is a more or less elaborate *ruse*. *Manœuvre*, like *stratagem*, is primarily a naval and military term, but in the present grouping can imply any adroit machination that is directed towards the gaining of one's ends; *artifice* suggests the employment of some ingenious device for the same purpose; a *wile* is an attempt to ensnare by deception; a *feint*, an attempt to distract attention from one's real purpose so as the more effectually to accomplish it.

TRITE, HACKNEYED, STEREOTYPED, THREADBARE. The *trite* (literally that which has been worn by rubbing) is that which has been said so often that it has lost all originality; the *hackneyed* is that which has been used as a cliché so often that all freshness has gone out of it; the *stereotyped* is that which is so unoriginal as to give the impression of having been mechanically produced; the *threadbare* is that which has been

employed so frequently that no virtue is left in it. It is largely a matter of judgment which word is used in a particular connection.
ANT. **Original; Fresh.**

TROUBLE *v.*, AIL, DISTRESS are all words meaning to cause unease. *Trouble*, in this grouping, implies the loss of tranquillity; *distress*, subjection to strain; *ail*, little more than that something is amiss, *e.g.* 'What *ails* you?' There is also a secondary use of the word *trouble*, for which see **INCONVENIENCE.** *Trouble*, in this use, may mean almost anything from a trifling inconvenience to a serious disturbance.

TRUCE, ARMISTICE. An *armistice* is an agreed suspension of warlike activity; a *truce* has wider applications and can be applied to any kind of conflict or dispute.

TRUST *n.*, CONFIDENCE, DEPENDENCE, FAITH, RELIANCE. *Trust* implies a strong and instinctive belief in the thing or person concerned; *confidence* is such a belief based upon good evidence; *faith* implies a stronger belief than *trust*, upon less evidence than in the case of *confidence*. *Reliance*, on the other hand, adds the suggestion of so strong a *trust* that one can base one's actions upon it: *dependence* is *reliance* in which self is subordinated to the thing relied on.
ANT. **Mistrust.**

TRUTH, VERACITY, VERISIMILITUDE, VERITY. *Truth* is abstract and impersonal; *veracity* is a quality pertaining to truthful persons. *Verity* is that quality in anything which attests its truthfulness; *verisimilitude* is that quality in a representation of anything which causes it to seem true.
ANT. **Untruth.**

TURN *v.* (1), EDDY, GYRATE, REVOLVE, ROTATE, SPIN, WHEEL are all words carrying the idea of movement in a circle. *Turn* is the most general, and may imply a partial or a complete revolution. *Revolve* implies turning round upon a centre; *rotate*, upon an axis; *gyrate* is used when the visible and sensible effect of the rotation is to be stressed; *spin* implies rapid and continuing gyration; *eddy* is a rapid gyratory motion in water or in air: *wheel* is either a whole or a partial revolution, as when troops *wheel* to left or right.

TURN *v.* (2), AVERT, DEFLECT, DIVERT, all imply change in direction. *Turn* is the most general; *divert* suggests that the turn involves a change from the natural or original direction; and *deflect*, a deliberate bending away from the normal direction. To *avert* is to turn away with the definite purpose of avoidance.

U

UNBELIEF, DISBELIEF, INCREDULITY. *Unbelief* is simply the opposite of *belief*; *disbelief* is a more positive rejection of the thing propounded; *incredulity* implies a more generally unbelieving or sceptical frame of mind.
ANT. **Belief.**

UNCERTAINTY, DOUBT, DUBIETY, MISTRUST, SCEPTICISM, SUSPICION. *Uncertainty* stresses the absence of certainty; *doubt* is more positive and adds to *uncertainty* the sense of inability to decide. *Dubiety* is a kind of wavering uncertainty, now hot, now cold. *Scepticism* is the fruit of an habitually incredulous and doubting type of mind; *suspicion* is a compound of apprehension and doubt; *mistrust* is *suspicion* so strong as to preclude trust. The two last terms are therefore only in certain cases comparable with the earlier ones.
ANT. **Certainty.**

UNDERSTAND, APPRECIATE, COMPREHEND are synonyms when they mean to have full and exact knowledge of something, but to *understand* is wider than to *comprehend*: we can, that is, *comprehend* perfectly the individual details of a transaction without fully *understanding* the transaction as a whole. To *appreciate*, in this grouping, implies little more than arriving at a just judgment. We say, 'I *appreciate* your motives', meaning that we have not misjudged them.

UNRULY, HEADSTRONG, INTRACTABLE, RECALCITRANT, REFRACTORY, UNGOVERNABLE, WILFUL, all mean, in varying degrees, insusceptible to control. *Unruly* stresses incapacity to be disciplined, *e.g*. 'The tongue is an *unruly* member'; *ungovernable* implies complete incapacity to be ruled or controlled. *Intractable* and *refractory* both suggest resistance to control, but *intractable* implies that the quality springs from an inability to be guided, and *refractory*, that it derives from a rebellious temper. *Recalcitrant*, literally 'kicking back', is still stronger than *refractory*; and *wilful* stresses the desire to have one's own way at all costs. *Headstrong* resembles *wilful*, but is stronger and implies obstinacy.
ANT. **Tractable; Docile.**

USE *n*., ACCOUNT, ADVANTAGE, AVAIL, PROFIT, SERVICE, UTILITY, all stress employment for some definite purpose, *use* being the most comprehensive. *Service* applies generally to persons (or animals), as when Othello says, 'I have done the state some *service*'; *advantage* suggests *use* for purposes of improvement; and *profit*, *use* for reward, *e.g*.

'What shall it *profit* a man, etc.?' *Account* occurs chiefly in idiomatic phrases, such as 'turn to *account*' or 'of no *account*'; and *avail* strongly suggests effective *use*. *Utility*, on the other hand, is not strictly synonymous with *use* but with *usefulness*, of which it is the more formal equivalent.

USE *v.*, APPLY, EMPLOY, UTILIZE, all mean to make a thing serviceable to oneself. *Use* is the common and comprehensive term; *employ* implies choice, selection and discrimination: one *uses* tools, but *employs* a special one for a special purpose. To *utilize*, on the other hand, stresses finding a *use* for that which, at first glance, is not eminently usable; and to *apply* is to use a thing for a special and selected purpose, *e.g.* one *applies* a test to a substance to ascertain its nature, or one *applies* one's knowledge to the unravelling of a problem.

V

VAIN, EMPTY, HOLLOW, IDLE, NUGATORY, OTIOSE. The *vain*, in this grouping, is valueless; the *nugatory*, insignificant; the *otiose*, superfluous; the *idle*, without basis or reality; the *hollow*, empty and delusive; the *empty*, without substance.

VARIATION, ADAPTATION, MODIFICATION, MUTATION are all terms employed in biology. A *variation* is a divergence from the species; *adaptation* is the cause from which such divergence arises; a *mutation* is a sudden variation; a *modification* is an individual and non-heritable divergence caused by environment.

VENIAL, PARDONABLE are both applied to sins and shortcomings that are not very serious. The difference is that *venial* sins are in their very nature trifling, while *pardonable* ones may be in themselves of some weight, though there may be more or less valid justification for them.
ANT. **Heinous.**

VICIOUS, CORRUPT, DEGENERATE, FLAGITIOUS, INFAMOUS, INIQUITOUS, NEFARIOUS, VILLAINOUS are all terms that refer to reprehensible behaviour. *Vicious*, the opposite of *virtuous*, implies moral depravity; *villainous* is stronger still, suggesting deliberate and extreme depravity. *Iniquitous* emphasizes complete indifference to civilized standards; *nefarious*, a contempt for them; and *flagitious* and *infamous* both contain the idea of deliberate wickedness, though the latter is looser than the former which, strictly, refers to disgraceful acts done in the heat of passion. *Corrupt*, suggesting internal rottenness and complete lack of integrity, is often applied to venal officials; and *degenerate* suggests deterioration to a low and primitive type of humanity.
ANT. **Virtuous.**

VICTORY, CONQUEST, TRIUMPH. *Victory* implies the winning of a contest; *conquest*, the subjugation of one's enemy or rival. A *triumph* is a brilliant and decisive *victory*.
ANT. **Defeat.**

VOCATION, AVOCATION, CALLING, EMPLOYMENT, OCCUPATION, PROFESSION. A man's *vocation* is his regular business or trade, to which he has been led by his natural aptitudes; his *avocation* is a subsidiary occupation in which he employs his leisure. *Calling* is the Germanic equivalent of the Latin *vocation*; *employment* suggests a more temporary state of affairs than *occupation*, which, essentially, means no more than that in which one occupies one's time. *Profession* is a more elevated term than *occupation*, and implies special training for such things as the Law, Medicine or the Church.

WANDER, MEANDER, PROWL, RAMBLE, RANGE, ROAM, ROVE, STRAY, all suggest movement without definite plan. To *wander* suggests indifference to one's destination; to *stray* is stronger and is almost equivalent to being lost. *Roam*, on the other hand, stresses the agreeableness of such wanderings; *ramble*, the indisciplined quality of them, as when one *rambles* in one's speech. To *rove* is to *roam* largely and comprehensively; to *range* is to *rove* to the widest extent and is often used figuratively. To *prowl* is to *rove* furtively and with purpose; to *meander* is to *wander* in a winding course like that of the classical river, Meander.

WANT *v.*, LACK, NEED, REQUIRE, all mean to be without something that one desires. *Lack* simply implies the absence of that which is desired; but *want* adds to *lack* the idea that one desires it urgently. *Need* is stronger still, implying that one cannot well do without the thing in question; *require*, in this grouping, is also strong and is practically equivalent to *demand*, as in such a phrase as 'juvenile delinquents *require* very firm handling'.

WARN, CAUTION, FOREWARN. *Warn* is the general term; *forewarn*, as well as stressing the idea of advance notification, carries a still stronger suggestion of impending danger. *Caution*, on the other hand, is less strong than *warn*, and suggests advice rather than admonition or exhortation.

WAVE, BILLOW, BREAKER, RIPPLE, ROLLER, SURGE, UNDULATION. *Wave* is the general term; a *ripple* is a small *wave*; a *billow*, a high, large one; a *roller* is a long one; a *breaker*, one that breaks into foam. *Surge*, in this grouping, is usually poetical and suggests a high roller or billow; *undulation* applies to wavelike formation wherever found, and suggests the pattern of the wave, not the wave itself.

WAY, COURSE, PASSAGE, ROUTE, all denote the road from one place to another; but *way* is general, and *route* suggests something more elaborate, covering a multiplicity of *ways*. *Course*, on the other hand, carries the suggestion of running straight on, so that we speak of the *course* of a planet, or, figuratively, of a *course* of study. *Passage* implies that the *way* traversed is open and thus capable of being passed along; it also emphasizes crossing or transit, *e.g.* 'The Middle *Passage*', by which slaves were transported to the Americas.

WEAK, DECREPIT, FEEBLE, FRAGILE, FRAIL, INFIRM. *Weak*, the general term, is simply the opposite of *strong*, *e.g.* '*weak* tea'.

Feeble introduces a moral note, implying inadequacy and pitifulness, *e.g.* 'a *feeble* light; *feeble*-minded'. *Frail* does not suggest any specific reason for weakness other than natural delicacy of constitution; and *fragile* carries this idea still further, with the added suggestion that the thing so described is easy to break: we speak of a *frail* flower, but of a *fragile* glass. *Infirm* usually suggests the weakness that arises from ill-health or old age; *decrepit*, that old age alone is the cause.
ANT. **Strong.**

WET, DAMP, DANK, HUMID, MOIST. *Wet* is the strongest, most uncompromising, of these terms; *moist* suggests a slight degree of wetness; *damp*, a less slight degree. *Dank* implies an unpleasant degree of dampness, often associated with coldness; *humid* suggests a superabundance of moisture in the atmosphere.
ANT. **Dry.**

WHITEN, BLANCH, BLEACH, ETIOLATE. *Whiten* is the common term; to *blanch* is to *whiten* by removal of the original colour; to *bleach* is similar but is usually effected by exposure to sun and air or to chemical agents. To *etiolate* is to *whiten* a plant by excluding the sunlight: celery is *blanched* by *etiolation*.
ANT. **Blacken.**

WHOLE, ALL, COMPLETE, ENTIRE, GROSS, TOTAL. The *whole* is that from which nothing has been subtracted; the *entire* is that which has not been divided; the *complete* is the perfect and finished thing. *Total* means much the same as *whole* but is limited in its application since it emphasizes more strongly the idea that it is in opposition to *partial*, *e.g.* '*total* darkness'. *Gross* is used in specialized financial connections as the equivalent of *total*, indicating that no deductions whatever have been made. *All*, in this grouping, may mean the *whole*, the *entire* or the *total*, according to the context.
ANT. **Partial.**

WILL, VOLITION. *Will* is the comprehensive, all-embracing term; *volition* is simply the act of making a decision.

WISE, JUDICIOUS, PRUDENT, SAGE, SANE, SAPIENT, SENSIBLE. To be *wise*, experience and a knowledge of men and affairs are necessary; *sage* suggests the wisdom of age and is not invariably used in a complimentary sense; *sapient*, though it can mean *wise*, is now more often used ironically. *Judicious* suggests wisdom in judgment; *prudent*, a strong reasonableness; *sensible*, circumspection and intelligence rather than actual wisdom; *sane*, mental health and level-headedness.
ANT. **Simple.**

WIT, HUMOUR, IRONY, REPARTEE, SARCASM, SATIRE. *Humour* is *wit* leavened by kindliness and human sympathy; *irony* is a form of *wit* in which one appears to say the opposite of what one really means; *sarcasm* (literally, tearing flesh as a dog tears it) is a bitter kind of *wit* which often employs *irony* and is always intended to mortify its victim. *Satire* is a species of *wit* that ridicules the vices and follies of the age. *Repartee* is the art of making barbed and witty rejoinders.

WITTY, FACETIOUS, HUMOROUS, JOCOSE, JOCULAR. The difference between the *witty* and the *humorous* is described under the last heading, though *humorous* has now sunk to mean almost anything that excites merriment. The *facetious* is a laboured humorousness; the *jocular* suggests jollity without much depth; the *jocose*, the desire to get a laugh at almost any cost.

WONDER, ADMIRATION, AMAZE, AMAZEMENT, WONDERMENT. *Wonder* suggests the emotion aroused by that which is strange and inexplicable; *amazement* stresses the bewilderment produced by such things. *Wonderment* and *amaze* are more poetical or rhetorical forms of the preceding. *Admiration*, in this grouping, adds to *wonder* the idea of absorption and veneration, *e.g.* one is 'lost in *admiration*'.

WORD, TERM, VOCABLE. *Word* is the generic and comprehensive expression; but *term* implies a *word* or group of words with a specific meaning: we must, we say, 'define our *terms*'. *Vocable* also means a *word*, but here the emphasis comes upon the sound and pronunciation rather than upon the meaning: one speaks of 'barbarous *vocables*', meaning sounds.

WORK, DRUDGERY, LABOUR, TOIL, TRAVAIL. *Work* is the common term; *labour* is hard *work*, often manual; *toil* is *work* so hard that it wearies; *drudgery* is dull, hard and irksome *labour*: *cf.* Dr Johnson's definition of a lexicographer as 'a harmless *drudge*'. *Travail*, in this grouping, stresses the painfulness of hard work.
ANT. **Play.**

WORRY, ANNOY, HARASS, HARRY, PESTER, PLAGUE, TANTALIZE, TEASE. *Worry* embodies the idea of repeated attacks, as when a dog *worries* a sheep; *annoy* resembles it, but is less strong; *harass* implies petty persecution; *harry*, definite oppression and maltreatment. To *plague* is to torment; to *pester* implies repeated trivial assaults; to *tease* is to *annoy* by a series of pinpricks, the idea coming from that of scratching cloth with a *teasle* to raise the nap. To *tantalize* is to treat someone after the fashion of *Tantalus*, who was always having a good dinner put in front of him only to see it whisked away untasted.

WORTH, VALUE. Though *value* is the Latin equivalent of the Germanic *worth*, the latter has much stronger moral connotations than the former. *Value* is money's *worth*, which is dependent upon circumstances and fashion; but *worth* relates to a more permanent scale of values: '*Worth* makes the man', says Pope.

WRITER, AUTHOR, COMPOSER. A *writer* is anyone who writes; an *author*, literally an originator, is a professional and more or less recognized *writer*: the word can also imply other kinds of creation, as when we use such a phrase as 'the *author* of his being'. A *composer* is anyone who composes a work; but in practice it is now chiefly confined to those who compose music.

WRITHE, AGONIZE, SQUIRM, all mean to twist about in physical or mental distress. *Writhe* is the most usual expression; *agonize* suggests a loftier mode and a much more painful manner of writhing; *squirm*, a less dignified kind: a worm *squirms*; a sufferer *writhes*; a hero *agonizes*.

WRONG *v.*, AGGRIEVE, OPPRESS, PERSECUTE, all mean to injure someone without just cause; but to *aggrieve* is to inflict a slight *wrong*, and to *oppress* and to *persecute* are very much stronger. To *oppress* contains the idea of laying heavy burdens on another; to *persecute*, that of pursuing one's victim with a succession of plagues and torments.

Y

YIELD, BOW, CAPITULATE, DEFER, RELENT, SUBMIT, SUCCUMB. To *yield* implies one's being overcome, either by force or by argument; to *submit* is to surrender after resistance; to *capitulate* means literally to surrender upon terms, though it is now often used as the equivalent of *submit*. To *succumb* is to *yield* completely, by sudden collapse; to *relent* emphasizes that the yielding is done by him who has the upper hand; to *defer* is to yield because of respect. To *bow* is to *yield* gracefully, as when one '*bows* to the inevitable'.

YOUTH, ADOLESCENCE, PUBERTY. *Youth* is the general term; *puberty* relates to that stage of youth when the boy or girl is changing into man or woman; *adolescence*, to the period between *puberty* and full maturity.

YOUTHFUL, BOYISH, JUVENILE, MAIDEN, PUERILE, VIRGINAL are related words but not full synonyms. *Youthful* simply implies the possession or appearance of youth; *juvenile* stresses the immaturity of the condition. *Boyish* is used in a good sense to characterize boys and boy-like qualities; but *puerile* only in a bad one, as when we speak of '*puerile* antics'. *Virginal* underlines innocence and purity in either sex, but especially in the female; *maiden*, the quality of beginning, as in '*maiden* voyage, *maiden* speech'.

INDEX

Note: In this Index the words in bolder type are parent-words listed in the text in alphabetical sequence. All other words are to be found under the parent-word or words that follow them, *e.g.* 'address, *n.* – speech; tact' means that the last two words should be turned up in the alphabetical sequence to obtain definitions of the first. Where the parent-word is capable of being read ambiguously, it is followed by an explanatory word in parentheses, *e.g.* '**Attention** (application)'; but this does *not* mean that the word in parentheses is to be consulted.

adolescence – youth
Adorn
adorned – ornate
adroit – clever
adumbration – shade
Advance, *v.*
advancement – progress
advantage – use, ***n.***
adventitious – accidental
Adventurous
Adverse
adversity – misfortune
advert – refer
advertise – declare
Advice (counsel)
advice – news
advisable – expedient
advise – confer
Affair
Affect (influence)
affect – assume
affecting – moving
affection – disease; love
affinity – likeness; sympathy
affirm – assert; swear
Afflict
affliction – sorrow
affluent – rich
affray – quarrel, ***n.***
affront – offend
afraid – fearful (1)
After
aftermath – effect
age – generation
aggrieve – wrong, ***v.***
agitate – discuss
agonize – writhe
agony – distress
agree – assent, ***v.***
aid – help
ail – trouble
ailment – disease
aim – point, ***v.***
air – melody
akin – similar
alarm – fear, ***n.***
alarm, ***v.*** – frighten
alien – stranger
alienate – transfer
alike – similar
aliment – food (2)
alive – aware
All (each)
all – whole
allay – relieve
allegiance – fidelity
allegory – fable
alleviate – relieve
Alliance
allocate – allot
Allot
allow – let
allude – refer
allure – attract
Alone (solitary)
alone – only
Also
alter – change
altercation – quarrel, ***n.***
alternative – choice, ***n.***
amalgamate – mix
amaze, ***n.*** – wonder
amaze, ***v.*** – surprise
amazement – wonder
Ambassador
ambiguous – obscure
amenable – obedient; responsible
amend – mend
amenity – courtesy
Amiable
ample – plentiful
Amuse
analogous – similar
analogy – likeness
ancient – old
ancillary – auxiliary
anecdote – story
Anger, *n.*
Anger, *v.*
Angry
anguish – sorrow
Animadversion
Animal
animated – gay
animosity – enmity
annex – add (2)
anniversary – annual
annotation – remark
announce – declare
annoy – inconvenience; worry
Annual
annul – abolish
annular – round
anomalous – irregular
Answer
answerable – responsible
antagonism – enmity
antagonistic – adverse
antecedent – cause
antediluvian – old
anticipate – foresee
antipathy – enmity
antiquated – old
antique – old
antithesis – comparison
antithetical – contrary
antonymous – contrary
anxiety – care
anxious – eager
apartment – room
ape – copy, ***v.***
aphorism – maxim

apologue – fable
Apology
apophthegm – maxim
apostasy – defection
appal – dismay, *v.*
appalling – fearful (2)
Apparent (ostensible)
apparent – evident
appeal – prayer
appear – seem
Appearance
appellation – name
append – add (2)
applaud – praise, *v.*
application – attention
apply – use, *n.*
apportion – allot
Appreciate (cherish)
appreciate – understand
Apprehend (comprehend)
apprehend – foresee
apprehensive – fearful (1)
apprise – inform
Approbation
appropriate – fit, *adj.*
approval – approbation
Apt (likely)
apt – fit; ready
arbiter – judge, *n.*
arbitrary – absolute
arbitrate – judge, *v.*
arbitrator – judge, *n.*
arcane – mysterious
archaic – old
arctic – cold
ardent – hot
arduous – hard (2)
area – size
argot – dialect
argue – discuss
Argument (controversy)
argument – matter; reason, *n.* (1)
arise – rise; spring, *v.*
armistice – truce
army – multitude
aroma – smell
arouse – stir, *v.*
arraign – accuse
arrange – order, *v.*
arrive – come
arrogant – proud
Art
artifice – art; trick
ascend – rise
ascertain – discover
ashen – pale
asinine – simple
Ask (1) (request)
Ask (2) (enquire)
aspect – appearance
asperity – acrimony
asperse – sprinkle
aspersion – animadversion
assail – attack
assassinate – kill
assault – attack
assemble – gather
Assent, *v.*
Assert
assessment – tax
asseverate – swear
assign – allot
assist – help
association – society
assuage – relieve
Assume
astonish – surprise
astound – surprise
astute – shrewd
athirst – eager
attachment – love
Attack
attain – reach, *v.*
attaint – sentence
Attempt, *v.*
attend – accompany
Attention (application)
attention – courtesy
attentive – thoughtful
attitude – position
Attract
attraction – sympathy
attribute – quality
audacious – brave
augment – increase
augur – foretell
auspicious – favourable
Authentic
authenticate – confirm
author – writer
authority – influence; power
autochthonous – native
autonomous – free, *adj.*
Auxiliary
avail – benefit; use, *n.*
avaricious – covetous
Avenge
average – mean, *n.*
averse – adverse
avert – prevent; turn, *v.* (2)
avid – eager
avocation – vocation
avoid – escape, *v.*
avow – assert
awaken – stir, *v.*
Aware
awful – fearful (2)
Awkward

bacillus – germ
back, *v.* – recede
bacterium – germ

Bad (1) (evil)
Bad (2) (poor)
badge – mark
balance, *n.* – poise; symmetry
balance, *v.* – compensate
bald – bare
balk – demur
balmy – soft
ban – forbid
banal – insipid
bane – poison
Banish
barbarous – fierce
Bare
barefaced – shameless
bark – skin, *n.*
barren – sterile
Base (basis)
base – low
basis – base
battle – contend
baulk – demur
Be
beam – ray
beaming – bright
Bear, *v.* (1) (produce)
Bear, *v.* (2) (endure)
beast – animal
Beat, *v.* (belabour)
beat – conquer
beatitude – happiness
Beautiful
beautify – adorn
bedew – sprinkle
befall – happen
Beg
Begin
beguile – deceive
behave – act, *v.* (1)
Behaviour
behind – after
behold – see
belabour – beat, *v.*
Belief (credence)
belief – opinion
Below
bemoan – deplore
beneath – below
Benefit
benign – favourable; kind
benignant – kind
benumbed – numb
berth – place
beseech – beg
besides – also
betide – happen
betray – deceive
bewail – deplore
bewitch – attract
bid – command, *v.*
big – great
bigot – enthusiast
bill – account (1)
billet – place
billow – wave
birthright – right
Blame, *n.*
blame, *v.* – criticize
blanch – whiten
bland – soft; suave
blandish – coax
blank – empty
blasphemous – profane, *adj.*
bleach – whiten
Blemish
blend – mix
bliss – happiness
Bloom
blossom – bloom
blubber – cry
blunder – mistake
blunt – dull
Boat
Body
boggle – demur
bold – brave
bondage – servitude
Border
bound – limit, *n.*
boundless – infinite
bountiful – generous
bouquet – smell
bow – yield
boyish – youthful
brace – couple
brain – mind, *n.*
Brave
brazen – shameless
Breach
breaker – wave
brief – short
Bright
brilliant – bright
brim – border
Bring
brink – border
Broad
brute – animal
bucolic – rural
buffet – beat, *v.*
buffoon – fool (2)
bulk – size
burlesque – caricature
burning – hot
business – affair; trade
bustle – stir, *n.*
busyness – trade
Buy

cabal – combination
cadaver – body
cajole – coax

calamity – disaster
Calculate
calculating – cautious
Call, ***v.***
calling – vocation
callow – rude
Calm
Can, ***v.***
candid – frank
cant – dialect; hypocrisy
capability – ability
capacity – ability
capital – chief, *adj.*
capitulate – yield
Caprice
capsize – overturn
captious – critical
captivate – attract
carcase – body
Care
Careless
Caricature
carping – critical
Case
cash – money
cashier – dismiss
cast – add (1); throw
castigate – punish
casual – accidental
casuistry – fallacy
cataclysm – disaster
catalogue – list
catastrophe – disaster
catching – infectious
catechize – ask (2)
Cause, ***n.***
caution – warn
Cautious
cavilling – critical
cease – stop
celebrate – keep (1)
celebrated – famous
celebrity – fame
censorious – critical
censure – criticize
cerebral – mental
ceremonial – form
ceremony – form
Certain (inevitable)
certain – sure
chain – succession
chamber – room
Chance, ***n.***
chance, *v.* – happen
Change, ***v.***
channel – strait
chaos – confusion
character – disposition; quality
charge, *v.* – accuse; command
charm – attract
chary – cautious
chase – follow (2)
Chaste
chasten – punish
chastise – punish
cheap – contemptible
Cheat, ***v.***
check – restrain
cheerful – gay; glad
cherish – appreciate
Chief, ***adj.***
chilly – cold
chivalrous – civil, *adj.*
Choice, ***n.***
Choose
chronicle – account (2)
church – religion
circle – set
circular – round
circumscribe – limit, *v.*
circumspect – cautious
Circumstance
citation – encomium
Civil, ***adj.***
Claim, ***n.***
claim, *v.* – demand
clamorous – loud
clamour – noise
clandestine – secret
Clear (limpid)
clear – evident
cleave – stick; tear
clemency – mercy
clement – forbearing
Clever
cliché – commonplace
cling – stick
clique – set
Close, ***v.*** (1) (shut)
Close, ***v.*** (2) (finish)
Close, ***adj.*** **and** ***adv.***
close, *adj.* – thick
clout – strike
clown – fool (2)
club – society
clumsy – awkward
clutch – take
coalesce – mix
coalition – alliance
Coarse
Coax
coercion – force
cogitate – think
cognizant – aware
cognomen – name
cohere – stick
coin – money
Cold
collation – comparison
collect – gather
collected – cool
collision – shock

colossal – enormous
Colour, *n.*
colour, *v.* – paint, *v.*
column – pillar
combat – oppose
Combination
combine – combination
Come
comely – beautiful
comestibles – food (1)
Comfort, *v.*
comfort, *n.* – rest
comic – laughable
comical – laughable
comity – courtesy
Command, *v.*
commence – begin
commend – praise, *v.*
commensurable – proportional
commensurate – proportional
comment – remark
commentary – remark
commerce – trade
commiseration – pity
Commit
Common (familiar)
common – reciprocal
Commonplace
Communicate
compact – thick
companionable – social
company – society
comparable – similar
Comparison
compass, *n.* – range
compass, *v.* – reach
compassion – pity
compatible – consonant
Compensate (balance)
compensate – pay
compete with – rival
competent – enough
complaint – disease
complaisant – amiable
complete, *v.* – close, *v.* (2)
complete, *adj.* – full; whole
complex – system
Compose
composed – cool
composer – writer
comprehend – apprehend; understand
comprise – compose
compulsion – force
compunction – penitence
compute – calculate
conceal – hide
Conceit (egoism)
conceit – pride
concentration – attention
concept – idea
conception – idea
concern – affair; care; interest
concise – short
conclude – close, *v.* (2)
concluding – last
Conclusive
concussion – shock
condemn – criticize; sentence
condition – state
condolence – pity
condone – excuse
conduct, *n.* – behaviour
conduct, *v.* – accompany
confederation – alliance
Confer
confess – acknowledge
confide – commit
confidence – trust, *n.*
confine – limit, *n.*
confine – limit, *v.*
Confirm (authenticate)
confirm – ratify
conflict – strife
Confusion
congenial – consonant
congratulate – felicitate
congruous – consonant
conjectural – supposed
Conjecture
connote – denote
Conquer
conquest – victory
conscious – aware
consent – assent, *v.*
consequence – effect; importance
consequently – therefore
conserve – save
Consider (1) (study)
Consider (2) (regard)
considerate – thoughtful
consign – commit
consist of – compose
consistent – consonant
console – comfort, *v.*
Consonant
conspiracy – plot
constant – continual
consternation – fear, *n.*
constitute – compose
construe – explain
consult – confer
consume – monopolize; spend
Consummate
contagious – infectious
Contain
contemn – despise
contemplate – consider (1); see
contemporary – new
Contemptible
Contend
Content, *v.*
contention – strife

contiguous – adjacent
continent – sober
contingent – accidental
Continual
continuance – continuation
Continuation
Continue
continuity – continuation
continuous – continual
contract – promise, *v.*
contradict – deny
contradictory – contrary
Contrary
contrast – comparison
contravention – breach
contributory – auxiliary
contrition – penitence
controversy – argument
contumacious – obstinate
convene – call, *v.*
Converse, *n.* (reverse)
converse, *v.* – speak
convey – transfer
conviction – opinion
convivial – social
convoke – call, *v.*
convoy – accompany
Cool (collected)
cool – cold
cope – contend
copious – plentiful
Copy, *v.*
cordial – gracious
corpse – body
Correct, *adj.*
correct, *v.* – punish
corroborate – confirm
corrupt – vicious
cosmos – earth
Costly
coterie – set
counsel – advice
countenance – face, *n.*
counter – adverse
counterbalance – compensate
counterfeit – assume
Couple
courageous – brave
course – way
courteous – civil, *adj.*
Courtesy
courtly – civil, *adj.*
covenant – promise, *v.*
covert – secret
covet – desire, *v.*
Covetous
Cowardly
craft – art; boat
crass – stupid
crave – desire, *v.*
craven – cowardly
create – invent
credence – belief
credit – belief
creed – religion
crime – offence
Critical
Criticize
crude – rude
cruel – fierce
crumble – decay, *v.*
Cry
cryptic – obscure
cuff – strike
culpability – blame, *n.*
cult – religion
cumbrous – heavy
cunning, *n.* – art; deceit
cunning, *adj.* – clever
curb – restrain
Cure, *v.*
Curious (inquisitive)
curious – odd
currency – money
current, *n.* – tendency
current, *adj.* – prevailing
custom – habit

dainty – nice
dally – delay (2)
damage – injury
damn – sentence
damp – wet
Danger
dank – wet
daring – adventurous
Dark (dusky)
dark – obscure
dart, *v.* – shoot
dash, *n.* – touch, *n.*
dastardly – cowardly
daunt – dismay, *v.*
dauntless – brave
dawdle – delay (2)
Dead
Deadly
deal – distribute
dealing – trade
dear – costly
Death
debate – discuss
Decay, *v.*
decease – death
deceased – dead
Deceit
deceitful – dishonest
Deceive
decent – chaste; decorous
Decide
Decided
decisive – conclusive; decided
deck – adorn

Declare (announce)
declare – assert
decline – refuse
declivity – slant
decompose – decay, *v.*
decorate – adorn
decorated – ornate
Decorous
decrease – abate
decrepit – weak
Deduction
deed – action
deem – consider (2)
deep – broad
defeat – conquer
defect – blemish
Defection
defective – deficient
defend – guard, *v.*
Defer (postpone)
defer – yield
deference – honour
Deficient
definitive – conclusive
deflect – turn, *v.* (2)
defraud – cheat, *v.*
defunct – dead
degenerate – vicious
degrade – abase
dejected – sad
Delay (1) (detain)
Delay (2) (procrastinate)
delectable – delightful
delectation – pleasure
deliberate, *v.* – think
deliberate, *adj.* – slow
delicious – delightful
delight, *n.* – pleasure
delight, *v.* – please
Delightful
delineation – sketch
deliver – free, *v.*
Deliverance
delivery – deliverance
delude – deceive
Delusion
Demand, *v.*
demise – death
demolish – destroy
demonstrate – prove; show, *v.* (1)
Demur
demure – decorous
denomination – name; religion
Denote (connote)
denote – mean, *v.*
denounce – criticize
dense – stupid; thick
Deny
depart – go
departed – dead
dependence – trust, *n.*
depict – paint, *v.*
Deplore
depone – swear
deport – banish
deportment – behaviour
deposit – pledge
deprecate – disapprove
depressed – sad
derange – disorder
deride – ridicule
derive – spring, *v.*
describe – relate
desert – abandon
desertion – defection
design, *n.* – plan
design, *v.* – purpose, *v.*
designation – name
Desire, *v.*
desist – stop
desolate – alone
despairing – despondent
despatch – haste; letter
desperate – despondent
despicable – contemptible
Despise
despoil – ravage
Despondent
despotic – absolute
destiny – fate
destitution – poverty
Destroy
detached – indifferent
detain – delay (1); keep (2)
determine – decide; discover
detest – hate
devastate – ravage
devotion – fidelity
diagram – sketch
Dialect (patois)
dialect – language
Dictionary
Different
difficult – hard (2)
diffuse – spread
dilatory – slow
dim – dark
dimensions – size
diminish – abate
diminutive – little
direct – command, *v.*; point, *v.*
Dirty
disability – inability
Disapprove
disarrange – disorder
Disaster
disbelief – unbelief
disburse – spend
discern – see
Discernment
discharge – dismiss; free, *v.*
disciple – scholar

discipline – punish; teach
discomfit – embarrass
discomfort – embarrass
discommode – inconvenience
disconcert – embarrass
discontinue – stop
discord – strife
discount – deduction
discourse – speak
Discover (ascertain)
discover – invent
discrimination – discernment
Discuss
disdain – despise
Disease
disgrace, *v.* – abase
Dishonest
disintegrate – decay, *v.*
disinterested – indifferent
disjoin – separate
disloyal – treacherous
dismal – sad
Dismay, *v.*
dismay, *n.* – fear, *n.*
Dismiss
Disorder, *v.*
disorder, *n.* – confusion
disorganize – disorder
disparate – different
dispatch – kill
dispense – distribute
disperse – spread
display – show, *v.* (2)
Disposal
Disposition (character)
disposition – disposal
dispute – argument
disregard – neglect
dissension – strife
dissimulation – deceit; simulation
dissipate – spend
distemper – disease
distinct – evident
distinguished – famous
Distress, *n.*
distress, *v.* – trouble, *v.*
Distribute
Distrust
disturb – disorder
divergent – different
divers – many
diverse – different
divert – amuse; turn, *v.* (2)
divide – distribute; separate
divination – discernment
divine, *v.* – foresee
divine, *adj.* – holy
division – part
divorce – separate
docile – obedient
Doctrine
dogma – doctrine
dole – distribute
domineering – imperious
dominion – power
donation – gift
doom, *n.* – fate
doom, *v.* – sentence
doubt – uncertainty
Doubtful
doze – sleep, *n.*
draft – sketch
drag – pull
draw – pull
dread – fear, *n.*
dreadful – fearful (2)
drench – soak
drift – tendency
drive – move, *v.*
droll – laughable
drowse – sleep
drudgery – work
dry – sour
dubiety – uncertainty
dubious – doubtful
Dull (blunt)
dull – stupid
duplicity – deceit
duress – force
dusky – dark
duty – obligation; tax
dynamic – active

each – all
Eager
earnest – pledge
Earth
ease – rest
Easy
Eccentricity
Ecstasy
eddy – turn, *v.* (1)
edge – border
educate – teach
Effect
Effective
effectual – effective
effeminate – female, *adj.*
efficacious – effective
efficient – effective
effortless – easy
egoism – conceit
egotism – conceit
elect – choose
election – choice, *n.*
elevate – lift
elongate – extend
elucidate – explain
elude – escape, *v.*
emanate – spring, *v.*
emancipate – spring, *v.*
Embarrass

embellish – adorn
embellished – ornate
eminent – famous
emolument – gain, *n.*
Emphasis
employ – use, *n.*
employment – vocation
Empty (vacant)
empty – vain
emulate – rival
enchant – attract
Encomium
end – close, *v.* (2)
endeavour – attempt, *v.*
endless – everlasting
endurance – patience
endure – bear, *v.* (2); continue
Enemy
energy – power
enfranchise – free, *v.*
engage – promise, *v.*
engross – absorb; monopolize
engulf – absorb
enigmatic – obscure
enjoin – command, *v.*
enjoy – have
enjoyment – pleasure
enlarge – increase
Enmity
Enormous
Enough
enquire – ask (2)
enrage – anger, *v.*
ensue – follow (1)
Enter (1) (penetrate)
Enter (2) (admit)
entertain – amuse
Enthusiast
entire – whole
entreat – beg
entreaty – prayer
entrust – commit
envious – jealous
envoy – ambassador
epicurean – luxurious
episode – circumstance
epistle – letter
Equal
equilibrium – poise
equipoise – poise
equity – justice
equivalent – equal
equivocal – obscure
equivocate – lie, *v.*
error – mistake
erudition – knowledge
Escape, *v.*
eschew – escape, *v.*
escort – accompany
essay – attempt, *v.*
essential – necessary
establish – found
estate – condition
estimate – calculate
ethical – noble
etiolate – whiten
eulogize – praise, *v.*
eulogy – encomium
evade – escape, *v.*
event – circumstance; effect
Everlasting
every – all
evidence – show, *v.* (1)
Evident
evil – bad (1)
evince – show, *v.* (1)
exact, *adj.* – correct, *adj.*; nice
exact, *v.* – demand, *v.*
examine – ask (2)
Example (model)
example – case
Exceed
excel – exceed
Excellence
Excessive
Excite
excogitate – consider (1)
excursion – journey
Excuse, *v.*
excuse, *n.* – apology
execute – kill
exhibit – show, *v.* (2)
exigency – need
exile – banish
exist – be
exorbitant – excessive
expatriate – banish
expect – hope
Expedient
expedition – journey
expeditious – quick
expend – spend
expensive – costly
Explain
exploit – feat
expose – show, *v.* (2)
expostulate – object, *v.*
expound – explain
Extend
extent – size
extenuate – palliate
extol – praise, *v.*
extradite – banish
extravagant – excessive
extreme – excessive

Fable (myth)
fable – fiction
fabricate – make
fabrication – fiction
Face, *n.*
facetious – witty

facile – easy
faction – combination
failing – fault
fair – beautiful
faith – belief; religion; trust, *n.*
faithless – treacherous
Fallacy
False (wrong)
false – treacherous
falsehood – lie, *n.*
falter – hesitate
Fame
familiar – common
Famous
fanatic – enthusiast
fancy – imagination
fantasy – imagination
fascinate – attract
fashion – make
fast – quick
fatal – deadly
Fate
fatuous – simple
Fault (failing)
fault – blame, *n.*
faultfinding – critical
Favourable
fealty – fidelity
Fear, *n.*
Fearful (1) (afraid)
Fearful (2) (frightful)
feasible – possible
Feat
fecund – fertile
feeble – weak
feign – assume
feint – trick
Felicitate
felicitous – fit, *adj.*
felicity – happiness
Female, *adj.*
feminine – female, *adj.*
ferocious – fierce
Fertile
fetch – bring
Fiction
Fidelity
Fierce
fiery – hot
fight – contend
figment – fiction
filthy – dirty
final – last
finish – close, *v.* (2)
finished – consummate
firm – hard (1)
Fit, *adj.*
flagitious – vicious
Flagrant
flat – insipid
flaunt – show, *v.* (2)
flavour – taste
flaw – blemish
flay – skin, *v.*
fleet – quick
flightiness – lightness
fling – throw
flippancy – lightness
float – shoot
florid – ornate
flow – spring, *v.*
fluid – liquid
flurry – stir, *n.*
fly – shoot, *v.*
fodder – food (1)
foe – enemy
foible – fault
Follow (1) (succeed)
Follow (2) (pursue)
Food (1) (provisions)
Food (2) (nourishment)
Fool (1) (simpleton)
Fool (2) (clown)
foolhardy – adventurous
foolish – simple
forage – food (1)
forbearance – patience
Forbearing
Forbid
Force (coercion)
force – power
forebode – foretell
forecast – foretell
foreigner – stranger
foreknow – foresee
foremost – chief, *adj.*
Forerunner
Foresee
Foretell
forewarn – warn
forgive – excuse
forlorn – alone; despondent
Form, *n.* (ceremony)
form, *v.* – make
formality – form, *n.*
forsake – abandon
forth – onward
fortuitous – accidental
fortune – chance
forward – advance, *v.*
forward – onward
foul – dirty
Found
foundation – base
fragile – weak
fragment – part
fragrance – smell
frail – weak
frailty – fault
Frank
fray – quarrel, *n.*
freak – caprice

Free, ***v.***
Free, ***adj.***
Freedom
freezing – cold
frequently – often
fresh – new
fright – fear, ***n.***
Frighten
frightful – fearful (2)
frigid – cold
frivolity – lightness
frolic – play
frosty – cold
fruitful – fertile
Full
Fulsome
function – act, *v.* (1)
funny – laughable
further – advance, ***v.***
furthermore – also
furtive – secret
fury – anger, *n.*
fusion – alliance
fuss – stir, ***n.***

Gain, ***n.***
gain, *v.* – get; reach, ***v.***
gainsay – deny
gallant – civil, *adj.*
gallantry – courtesy
galvanize – excite
gambol – play
game – play
garrulous – talkative
Gather
gauche – awkward
gaunt – lean
Gay
gazetteer – dictionary
gelid – cold
Generation
Generous
genial – gracious
gentle – soft
genuine – authentic
Germ
Get
Ghastly
gibe – scoff
giddiness – lightness
Gift
gigantic – enormous
gird – scoff
Give
Glad
gladden – please
glance – look
glare – shine
glaring – flagrant
glee – mirth
glimpse – look
glitter – shine
globular – round
gloomy – dark; sad
glory – fame
gloss – palliate
glossary – dictionary
gloze – palliate
Go
godless – irreligious
Good
good-natured – amiable
Goodness
Goods
Govern
grab – take
grace – mercy
Gracious
gradient – slant
Grand
grandiose – grand
grasp – take
grasping – covetous
Grateful
gratify – please
gratuity – gift
Grave, ***adj.***
Great
greedy – covetous
green – rude
greet – address
gregarious – social
grief – sorrow
Grieve
grim – ghastly
grisly – ghastly
gross – coarse; flagrant; whole
ground – base; reason, *n.* (1)
groundwork – base
grow – increase
grudge – malice
gruesome – ghastly
Guard, ***v.***
guess – conjecture
Guide
guile – deceit
guilt – blame, *n.*
gyrate – turn, *v.* (1)

Habit
hackneyed – trite
hail – address
hallucination – delusion
handsome – beautiful
hanker – long
Happen
Happiness
happy – fit, *adj.*; glad
harangue – speech
harass – worry
harbinger – forerunner
Harbour

Hard (1) (firm)
Hard (2) (difficult)
harlequin – fool (2)
harm – injury
harmony – symmetry
harry – worry
harsh – rough
Haste
hasten – speed, *v.*
hasty – quick
Hate
haughty – proud
haul – pull
Have
haven – harbour
hazard – chance; danger
headstrong – unruly
heal – cure, *v.*
Healthy
Heap
Hear
heartfelt – sincere
heave – lift
Heavy
heedless – careless
Help
herald – forerunner
Heretic
heretical – heterodox
Hesitate
Heterodox
Hide, *v.*
hide, *n.* – skin, *n.*
High
hilarity – mirth
Hinder
Hint
hit – strike
hoist – lift
hold – contain
Holiness
hollow – vain
Holy
homily – speech
homogeneous – similar
honest – sincere
Honesty
Honour (respect)
honour – fame; honesty
Hope
hopeless – despondent
horrible – fearful (2)
horrify – dismay, *v.*
horror – fear, *n.*
hospitable – social
host – multitude
hostage – pledge
hostility – enmity
Hot
hue – colour, *n.*
huge – enormous
Humble, *adj.* (low)
humble, *v.* – abase
humid – wet
humiliate – abase
humorous – witty
Humour, *n.* (mood)
humour – wit
hunger, *v.* – long
hurl – throw
hurry, *n.* – haste
hurry, *v.* – speed, *v.*
hurt – injury
Hypocrisy
Hypothesis
hypothetical – supposed

iconoclast – rebel
icy – cold
Idea
ideal – example
identical – equal; similar
idiom – language
idiosyncrasy – eccentricity
idiot – fool (1)
Idle (lazy)
idle – vain
ignite – light, *v.*
ignoble – mean, *adj.*
Ignorant
ignore – neglect
ill – bad (1); sick
illimitable – infinite
illiterate – ignorant
illusion – delusion
illusory – apparent
illustration – case
illustrious – famous
Imagination
imbecile – fool (1)
imbibe – absorb
imitate – copy, *v.*
immense – enormous
immigrant – stranger
immoderate – excessive
immodest – shameless
impact – shock
impart – communicate
impartial – neutral
impeach – accuse
impecunious – poor
impede – hinder
impel – move, *v.*
Imperious
impersonate – act, *v.* (2)
Impertinent
imperturbable – cool
impetus – speed, *n.*
impingement – shock
impious – profane, *adj.*
Implant
implore – beg

imply – hint
import – mean, *v.*
Importance
importune – beg
imposing – grand
impost – tax
impregnate – soak
impress – affect
impudent – impertinent; shameless
impugn – deny
Inability
Inactive
inadvertent – careless
inanimate – dead
inaugurate – begin
incense – anger, *v.*
inception – origin
incessant – continual
incident – circumstance
incidental – accidental
Inclination
incline – slant
incommode – inconvenience
incomparable – supreme
Inconvenience
Increase
incredulity – unbelief
incriminate – accuse
inculcate – implant
indemnify – pay
independent – free, *adj.*
indict – accuse
Indifferent (unconcerned)
indifferent – neutral
indigence – poverty
indigenous – native
indigent – poor
indignant – angry
indignation – anger, *n.*
indispensable – necessary
indisposed – sick
individual – particular
individuality – disposition
indolent – idle
indulgent – forbearing
industry – trade
inept – awkward
inert – inactive
inevitable – certain
Infallible
infamous – vicious
Infectious
infertile – sterile
Infinite
infirm – weak
inflame – light, *v.*
inflexible – stiff
Influence, *n.*
influence, *v.* – affect
Inform
information – knowledge
infraction – breach
infrequent – rare
infringement – breach
infuriate – anger, *v.*
ingenious – clever
ingrained – inherent
Inherent
inhibit – forbid; restrain
inhuman – fierce
iniquitous – vicious
initiate – begin
Injury (damage)
injury – injustice
Injustice
inordinate – excessive
inquisitive – curious
inscrutable – mysterious
inseminate – implant
insight – discernment
insinuate – hint
Insipid
insolent – impertinent; proud
instance – case
instil – implant
institute, *v.* – found
instruct – command, *v.*; teach
insult – offend
insuperable – invincible
insurgent – rebel
insurrection – rebellion
integrity – honesty
intellect – mind, *n.*
intellectual – mental
intelligence – mind, *n.*; news
intelligent – mental
intend – purpose, *v.*
Intense
intercede – interpose
interdict – forbid
Interest (concern)
interfere – interpose
interminable – everlasting
intermit – defer
Interpose
interpret – explain
interrogate – ask (2)
intervene – interpose
intimate, *v.* – hint
intractable – unruly
intrepid – brave
intrigue – plot
intrinsic – inherent
introduce – enter (2)
intuition – reason, *n.* (2)
invaluable – costly
invective – abuse
Invent
Invincible
invulnerable – invincible
irate – angry
irony – wit

Irrational
Irregular
Irreligious
issue, *n.* – effect
issue, *v.* – spring, *v.*
iterate – repeat

jargon – dialect
Jealous
jeer – scoff
jejune – insipid
jeopardy – danger
Jest
jester – fool (2)
job – place
jocose – witty
jocular – witty
joke – jest
jollity – mirth
Journey
joy – pleasure
joyful – glad
joyous – glad
Judge, *n.*
Judge, *v.*
judgment – sense
judicious – wise
jumble – confusion
junto – combination
Justice
juvenile – youthful
juxtaposed – adjacent

keen – eager; sharp
Keep (1) (observe)
Keep (2) (retain)
ken – range
Kill
Kind (benign)
kind – gracious
kindle – light, *v.*
kindly – kind
knock – strike
Knowledge

labour – work
Labyrinth
lack – want, *v.*
ladylike – female, *adj.*
lag – delay (2)
laggard – slow
lambent – bright
lament, *v.* – deplore
Language
lank – lean
lapse – mistake
large – great
Last, *adj.* (final)
last, *v.* – continue
late – dead
latent – secret
latest – last
laud – praise, *v.*
Laughable
Law
Lawful
lax – loose
lay – point, *v.*; put
lay, *adj.* – secular
lazy – idle
lead – guide
leading – chief, *adj.*
league – alliance
Lean, *adj.*
leaning – inclination
learn – discover
learning – knowledge
leave – go; let
lecture – speech
legal – lawful
legate – ambassador
legendary – traditional
legion – multitude
legitimate – lawful
leisure – rest
leisurely – slow
lengthen – extend
lenient – forbearing; soft
lenity – mercy
Let
lethal – deadly
Letter
level – point, *v.*
levity – lightness
levy – tax
lexicon – dictionary
Liable (likely)
liable – apt; responsible
liberal – generous
liberate – free, *v.*
liberty – freedom
licence – freedom
license (*Amer.*) – freedom
licit – lawful
Lie, *n.*
Lie, *v.*
lifeless – dead
Lift, *v.*
Light, *v.*
light, *adj.* – easy
lighten – relieve
Lightness
like – similar
likely – apt; liable; probable
Likeness
likewise – also
Limit, *n.*
Limit, *v.*
limpid – clear
linger – stay
Liquid
List, *n.*

listen – hear
Little
liturgy – form
live, *v.* – be
live, *adj.* – active
livelihood – living, *n.*
lively – gay
livid – pale
Living, *n.*
loathe – hate
locomotion – motion
lofty – tall
loiter – delay (2)
lonely – alone
Long, *v.*
long-suffering – patience
Look, *n.* (glance)
look, *n.* – appearance
look, *v.* – seem
Loose
loot – rob
loquacious – talkative
lore – knowledge
lot – fate
Loud
Love
lovely – beautiful
Low (base)
low – humble
lowly – humble
loyalty – fidelity
lucid – clear
luck – chance
lucre – gain, *n.*
ludicrous – laughable
luminous – bright
luscious – delightful
lustrous – bright
Luxurious
ying – dishonest

machination – plot
madden – anger, *v.*
magnificent – grand
magnitude – size
maiden – youthful
main – chief, *adj.*
maintenance – living, *n.*
majestic – grand
Make
malady – disease
Male
malevolence – malice
Malice
malignity – malice
manful – male
manifest – show, *v.* (1)
manifest, *adj.* – evident
manlike – male
manly – male
mannish – male
manœuvre – trick
manufacture – make
Many
margin – border
Mark, *n.*
Marriage
marshal – order, *v.*
Martial
masculine – male
masterful – imperious
matrimony – marriage
Matter (subject)
matter – affair
Maxim
may – can
maze – labyrinth
Mean, *n.* (average)
Mean, *v.* (signify)
Mean, *adj.* (abject)
mean – purpose, *v.*
meander – wander
median – mean, *n.*
mediate – interpose
medium – mean, *n.*
meek – humble; soft
meet – fit, *adj.*
melancholy – sad
Melody
Memory
menace – threat
Mend
mendacious – dishonest
Mental
merciful – forbearing
Mercy
merge – mix
merit – excellence
methodize – order, *v.*
microbe – germ
might – power
mild – soft
military – martial
mimic – copy, *v.*
Mind, *n.* (intellect)
mind – soul
mingle – mix
miniature – little
minister – ambassador
mirage – delusion
Mirth
mischance – misfortune
mischief – injury
misdeed – offence
misdemeanour – offence
misery – distress
Misfortune
mishap – misfortune
mislead – deceive
misrepresentation – lie, *n.*
missive – letter
Mistake

mistrust – distrust; uncertainty
misuse – abuse
mitigate – relieve
Mix
mock – copy, *v.*; ridicule
model – example
Moderate
modern – new
modest – chaste
modification – variation
modify – change, *v.*
moist – wet
molest – inconvenience
moment – importance
momentum – speed, *n.*
Money
Monopolize
mood – humour, *n.*
moral – good; noble
morality – goodness
moreover – also
mortal – deadly
Motion
motive – matter
mount – rise
mourn – grieve
mournful – sad
Move, *v.*
move, *n.* – motion
movement – motion
Moving, *adj.*
muddle – confusion
mulish – obstinate
multifarious – many
Multitude
munificent – generous
murder – kill
murky – dark
muster – call, *v.*
mutation – variation
mutiny – rebellion
mutual – reciprocal
Mysterious
mystic – mysterious
myth – fable

naked – bare
Name
nap – sleep, *n.*
narrate – relate
narrative – story
Narrow
nasty – dirty
nation – race
Native
near – close, *adj. & adv.*
neat – tidy
Necessary (needful)
necessary – certain
necessity – need
Need, *n.* (exigency)
need, *n.* – poverty
need, *v.* – want, *v.*
needful – necessary
needy – poor
nefarious – vicious
negative – deny
Neglect
negotiate – confer
network – system
Neutral
never-ending – everlasting
New
News
Nice (accurate)
nice – correct, *adj.*; decorous
nigh – close, *adj. & adv.*
Nightly
Noble
nocturnal – nightly
Noise
noisy – loud
nonchalant – cool
note, *n.* – letter; mark; remark
note, *v.* – see
notice, *v.* – see
notion – idea; opinion
notoriety – fame
notorious – famous
nourishment – food (2)
novel – new
nude – bare
nugatory – vain
Numb
numerous – many
nuncio – ambassador
nuptials – marriage
nutriment – food (2)

Obedient
Object, *v.*
Obligation
obliging – amiable
obscene – coarse
obsolete – old
Obscure (ambiguous)
obscure – dark
Observance
observation – observance; remark
observe – keep (1); see
Obstinate
obstruct – hinder
obtain – get
obtuse – dull
obverse – converse, *n.*
obviate – prevent
obvious – evident
occasion – cause
occasional – rare
occult – secret
occupation – vocation
occurrence – circumstance

Odd
odor (*Amer.*) – smell
odour – smell
Offence
Offend
Offer, *v*.
office – place
offset – compensate
Often
oily – fulsome
Old
old-fashioned – old
oleaginous – fulsome
omit – neglect
Only
Onward
opaque – dark
open – frank
operate – act, *v*. (1)
operative – active
Opinion
Opportune
Oppose (resist)
oppose – object, ***v*.**
opposite – contrary
oppress – wrong, ***v*.**
opt – choose
option – choice, ***n*.**
opulent – rich
oration – speech
orbicular – round
Order, *v*. (arrange)
order – command, ***v*.**
order, *n*. – society
ordinance – law
ordinary – common
organism – system
organize – found; order, ***v*.**
Origin
original, ***n*.** – origin
original, *adj*. – new
originate – spring, ***v*.**
ornament – adorn
Ornate
ostensible – apparent
ostracize – banish
otiose – vain
outcome – effect
outdo – exceed
outlandish – odd
outlast – outlive
outline – sketch
Outlive
outrage – offend
outstrip – exceed
over – above
overbearing – imperious; proud
overcome – conquer
overlook – neglect
overreach – cheat, ***v*.**
overthrow – overturn
Overturn
own, *v*. – acknowledge; have

pace – speed, ***n*.**
pacific – peaceable
pacifist – peaceable
Pain
Paint, *v*.
pair – couple
Pale
Palliate
pallid – pale
panegyric – encomium
pang – pain
panic – fear, ***n*.**
parable – fable
parade – show, *v*. (2)
parallel, *n*. – comparison
parallel, *adj*. – similar
pardon – excuse
pardonable – venial
pare – skin, ***v*.**
parley – confer
parody – caricature
Part, *n*. (division)
part, ***v*.** – separate
Particular
party – combination
passage – strait; way
passing – death
passive – inactive
pastoral – rural
patent – evident
pathetic – moving
Patience
patois – dialect
pattern – example
Pay
Peaceable
peaceful – calm; peaceable
peculiar – odd
peel – skin, ***n*.**
peel – skin, ***v*.**
pellucid – clear
pelt – skin, ***n*.**
penetrate – enter (1)
penetration – discernment
Penitence
penumbra – shade
penury – poverty
people – race
perceive – see
perception – discernment
percussion – shock
peremptory – imperious
perennial – continual
perfection – excellence
perfidious – treacherous
perfume – smell
peril – danger
permit – let

perpetual – continual
perquisite – right
persecute – wrong, *v.*
persist – continue
personality – disposition
perspicacious – shrewd
persuasion – opinion; religion
pertinacious – obstinate
pester – worry
petition – prayer
physiognomy – face, *n.*
pick – choose
piece – part, *n.*
pierce – enter (1)
piety – fidelity
pilaster – pillar
pile – heap
pillage – ravage
Pillar
pilot – guide
pitch, *v.* – throw
Piteous
pitiable – contemptible; piteous
pitiful – piteous
Pity
Place, *n.* (station)
place, *v.* – put
placid – calm
plague – worry
plain – evident; frank
Plan, *n.*
platitude – commonplace
Play, *v.* (sport)
play – act, *v.* (2)
plea – apology; prayer
Please
Pleasure
Pledge, *n.*
pledge, *v.* – promise, *v.*
plenary – full
plenteous – plentiful
Plentiful
plight, *v.* – promise, *v.*
Plot, *n.* (conspiracy)
plot, *v.* – plan
pluck, *v.* – pull
plunder – rob
poignant – moving
Point, *v.*
Poise (balance)
poise – tact
Poison
polished – civil, *adj.*
polite – civil, *adj.*
politic – expedient
Politician
ponderous – heavy
Poor (needy)
poor – bad (2)
popular – common
port – harbour
portend – foretell
portion – fate; part
pose – position
Position (posture)
position – place
positive – sure
possess – have
possessions – goods
Possible (feasible)
possible – probable
post – place
postpone – defer
posture – position
pound – beat, *v.*
Poverty
poverty-stricken – poor
Power
practicable – possible
practical – possible
practice – habit
Praise, *v.*
Prayer
precedence – priority
precept – law
precious – costly
precipitate – speed, *v.*
precise – nice
preclude – prevent
precursor – forerunner
predict – foretell
pre-eminent – supreme
prefer – choose
preference – choice
prerogative – right
presage – foretell
prescription – receipt
present, *n.* – gift
present, *v.* – offer, *v.*
preserve – save
pressure – stress
prestige – influence
pretence – claim, *n.*
pretend – assume
pretension – claim, *n.*
pretext – apology
pretty – beautiful
Prevailing
prevalent – prevailing
prevaricate – lie, *v.*
Prevent (obviate)
prevent – hinder
priceless – costly
Pride
primal – primary
Primary
prime – primary
primeval – primary
primitive – primary
primordial – primary
principal – chief, *adj.*
Priority

pristine – primary
privilege – right
prize, *v.* – appreciate
Probable
probe – enter (1)
probity – honesty
problematical – doubtful
proceed – spring, *v.*
proclaim – declare
procrastinate – delay (2)
procure – get
produce – bear, *v.* (1)
Profane, *adj.* (impious)
profane, *adj.* – secular
profession – vocation
proffer – offer, *v.*
profit – benefit; gain, *n.*; use, *n.*
prognosticate – foretell
Progress
progression – progress; succession
prohibit – forbid
project – plan
prolific – fertile
prolong – extend
Promise, *v.*
promote – advance, *v.*
prompt – ready
promulgate – declare
prone – liable
proneness – inclination
proof – reason, *n.* (1)
propel – push
propensity – inclination
proper – decorous; fit, *adj.*
property – goods; quality
prophesy – foretell
propitious – favourable
proportion – symmetry
Proportional
proportionate – proportional
Proposal
propose – purpose, *v.*
proposition – proposal
protect – guard, *v.*
protest – assert; object, *v.*
protract – extend
Proud
Prove
provender – food (1)
proverb – maxim
Provisional
provisions – food (1)
provoke – excite
prowl – wander
prudent – wise
prying – curious
puberty – youth
publish – declare
puerile – youthful
pulchritudinous – beautiful
Pull
punch – strike
Punish
pupil – scholar
purchase – buy
pure – chaste
Purpose, *v.*
pursue – follow (2)
purview – range
Push
pusillanimous – cowardly
Put
putative – supposed
putrefy – decay, *v.*

quaint – odd
quake – shake
qualify – moderate
Quality
Quarrel, *n.*
quaver – shake
queer – odd
query – question, *n.*
Question, *n.*
question, *v.* – ask (2)
questionable – doubtful
Quick
quicken – excite; speed, *v.*
quit – go
quiver – shake

Race (nation)
radiant – bright
radiate – shine
rage – anger, *n.*
raise – lift
rally – ridicule; stir, *v.*
ram – push
ramble – wander
rancour – enmity
Range, *n.* (scope)
range, *v.* – wander
rank – flagrant
rap – strike
rapid – quick
rapture – ecstasy
Rare (infrequent)
rare – thin
rash – adventurous
rate – tax
Ratify
Ravage
raw – rude
Ray
raze – destroy
Reach, *v.* (attain)
reach, *n.* – range
react – act, *v.* (1)
Ready
Real
Reason, *n.* (1) (proof)
Reason, *n.* (2) (understanding)

reason, *n.* – cause
reason, *v.* – think
rebate – deduction
Rebel
Rebellion
Rebound
rebuff – refuse
recalcitrant – unruly
recall – remember
recant – abjure
recapitulate – repeat
Recede
Receipt
recent – new
recipe – receipt
Reciprocal
reckless – adventurous
reckon – calculate; consider (2)
recoil – rebound
recollect – remember
recollection – memory
recompense – pay
recount – relate
recoup – recover
Recover
recreant – cowardly
recreate – amuse
recrudesce – return
recruit – recover
rectitude – goodness
recur – return
reduce – conquer
Refer
referee – judge, *n.*
refined – civil, *adj.*
reflect – think
reflection – animadversion
Reform
reformation – reform
refractory – unruly
refulgent – bright
Refuse
regain – recover
regale – please
regard – consider (2)
register – list
regret – sorrow
regulation – law
rehearse – relate
reimburse – pay
reiterate – repeat
reject – refuse
rejoice – please
rejoinder – answer
Relate
relaxation – rest
relaxed – loose
release – free, *v.*
relegate – commit
relent – yield
reliance – trust, *n.*
Relieve
Religion
religious – holy
relinquish – abandon
relish – taste
remain – stay
Remark, *n.* (comment)
remark, *v.* – see
remedy – cure, *v.*
Remember
remembrance – memory
reminiscence – memory
remodel – mend
remonstrate – object, *v.*
remorse – penitence
remunerate – pay
rend – tear
renown – fame
renowned – famous
repair – mend
repartee – wit
repeal – abolish
Repeat
repel – refuse
repentance – penitence
replete – full
reply – answer
report, *n.* – account (2)
report, *v.* – relate
repose – rest
reprehend – criticize
reprisal – retaliation
reprobate *v.* – criticize
repudiate – refuse
reputed – supposed
request – ask (1)
require – demand, *v.*; want, *v.*
requisite – necessary
resemblance – likeness
reserve, *v.* – keep (2)
reserved – silent
resignation – patience
resist – oppose
resolve – decide
respect – honour
respective – particular
response – answer
Responsible
Rest
Restrain
restraint – force
restrict – limit, *v.*; restrain
result – effect
retain – keep (2)
Retaliation
retard – delay (1)
reticent – silent
retort – answer
retract – abjure; recede
retreat – recede
retribution – retaliation

retrieve – recover
retrograde – recede
Return
revenge, *n.* – retaliation
revenge, *v.* – avenge
reverberate – rebound
reverence – honour
reverse – converse, *n.*
revert – return
revoke – abjure
revolt – rebellion
revolution – rebellion
revolve – turn, *v.* (1)
ribald – coarse
Rich
Ridicule
ridiculous – laughable
rife – prevailing
rifle, *v.* – rob
Right (privilege)
right – correct, *adj.*
righteous – good
rigid – stiff
rim – border
rind – skin, *n.*
ring – combination
rip – tear
ripple – wave
Rise (ascend)
rise – spring, *v.*
risk – danger
rite – form
ritual – form
Rival, *v.*
rive – tear
roam – wander
Rob
roll – list
roller – wave
romp – play
Room
root – origin
rot – decay, *v.*
rotate – turn, *v.* (1)
Rough (harsh)
rough – rude
Round
rouse – stir, *v.*
rout – conquer
route – way
rove – wander
Rude (rough)
rude – impertinent
rugged – rough
rule – decide; govern
Rural
ruse – trick
rustic – rural
ruth – pity

sack – dismiss; ravage
sacred – holy
sacrilegious – profane, *adj.*
Sad
Safe
sagacious – shrewd
sage – wise
sail – shoot, *v.*
salubrious – healthy
salutary – healthy
salute – address
same – equal
sample – case
sanctimoniousness – hypocrisy
sanctity – holiness
sane – wise
sapient – wise
sarcasm – wit
satire – wit
satisfy – content
saturate – soak
savage – fierce
Save
savoir-faire – tact
savour – taste
saw – maxim
saying – maxim
scarce – rare
scare – frighten
scatter – spread
scent – smell
scepticism – uncertainty
schedule – list
scheme – plan; system
schismatic – heretic
Scholar
School, *n.*
school, *v.* – teach
science – knowledge
Scoff
scope – range
scorn – despise
scout – despise
scruple – demur
scud – shoot, *v.*
search – seek
season – time
seasonable – opportune
Secret
secrete – hide
secretive – silent
sect – religion
sectarian – heretic
section – part
Secular
secure, *adj.* – safe
sedate – grave, *adj.*
See
Seek
Seem
seeming – apparent
seemly – decorous

seize – take
select – choose
selection – choice, *n.*
self-esteem – conceit
semblance – appearance
Sense
sensible, *v.* – aware
sensible, *adj.* – wise
sensual – luxurious
sensuous – luxurious
Sentence, *v.*
Sentiment (feeling)
sentiment – opinion
sentimentalism – sentiment
sentimentality – sentiment
Separate, *v.*
sequel – effect
sequence – succession
serene – calm
series – succession
serious – grave, *adj.*
sermon – speech
service – use, *n.*
Servitude
Set, *n.* (clique)
set, *n.* – succession
set, *v.* – put
settle – decide
sever – separate
Shade (shadow)
shade – colour, *n.*; touch, *n.*
shadow – shade
Shake
Shameless
share – part
Sharp, *adj.*
shear, *n.* – stress
shield – guard, *v.*
Shine
ship – boat
shipshape – tidy
shiver – shake
Shock
Shoot, *v.*
Short
shove – push
Show, *v.* (1) (demonstrate)
Show, *v.* (2) (display)
Shrewd
shudder – shake
shun – escape, *v.*
shut – close, *v.* (1)
Sick
sight – look
Sign (signal)
sign – mark
signal – sign
significance – importance
signify – mean, *v.*
Silent
silly – simple
Similar
similarity – likeness
Simple (foolish)
simple – easy
simpleton – fool (1)
simulate – assume
Simulation
sin – offence
Sincere
singular – odd
situation – place; state
Size
Sketch, *n.*
skill – art
skim – shoot, *v.*
Skin, *n.*
Skin, *v.*
slack – loose
slacken – delay (1)
slang – dialect
Slant
slap – strike
slaughter – kill
slavery – servitude
slay – kill
Sleep, *n.*
slender – thin
slight, *v.* – neglect
slight, *adj.* – thin
slim – thin
slip – mistake
slothful – idle
Slow, *adj.*
slow, *v.* – delay (1)
sluggish – inactive
slumber – sleep, *n.*
smack, *n.* – taste
small – little
Smell
smite – strike
smooth – easy; suave
snatch – take
sneer – scoff
Soak
soar – rise
Sober (temperate)
sober – grave, *adj.*
sociable – social
Social
Society
Soft
solace – comfort, *v.*
solemn – grave, *adj.*
solicitude – care
solid - hard (1)
solitary – alone
somnolence – sleep, *n.*
sophism – fallacy
sophistry – fallacy
sordid – mean, *adj.*
Sorrow, *n.* (grief)

sorrow, *v.* – grieve
sorrowful – sad
sorry, *adj.* – contemptible
Soul
sound – noise; strait
Sour
source – origin
sovereign – free, *adj.*
spare – lean
sparkle – shine
spatter – sprinkle
Speak
special – particular
specie – money
specific – particular
specimen – case
speculate – think
Speech (oration)
speech – language
Speed, *n.* (velocity)
Speed, *v.*
speed, *n.* – haste
speedy – quick
Spend
spherical – round
spice – touch, *n.*
spin – turn, *v.* (1)
spirit – soul
spiritual – holy
spite – malice
splash – sprinkle
split – tear
sport – play
sprain – strain
Spread
sprightly – gay
Spring, *v.*
Sprinkle
spurn – refuse
squabble – quarrel, *n.*
squalid – dirty
squander – spend
squirm – writhe
stalwart – strong
stand – bear, *v.* (2)
standard – example
stark – stiff
start – begin
startle – frighten
State, *n.* (condition)
state, *v.* – relate
statement – account (1)
statesman – politician
station – place
status – state
statute – law
Stay (abide)
stay – defer
stealthy – secret
steep – soak
stereotyped – trite
Sterile
Stick, *v.* (adhere)
stick *v.* – demur
Stiff
stimulate – excite
Stir, *n.*
Stir, *v.*
Stop, *v.*
Story (narrative)
story – account (2)
stout – strong
Strain, *n.* (sprain)
strain, *n.* – stress
strain, *v.* – demur
Strait, *n.* (channel)
strait, *adj.* – narrow, *adj.*
straits – strait
strange – odd
Stranger
stratagem – trick
strategy – tactics
stray – wander
strength – power
Stress (tension)
stress – emphasis
stricture – animadversion
Strife
Strike, *n.* (hit)
strike, *v.* – affect
strive – attempt, *v.*
Strong
struggle – attempt, *v.*
stubborn – obstinate
student – scholar
study, *n.* – attention
study, *v.* – consider (1)
Stupid
sturdy – strong
style – name
Suave
subdue – conquer
subdued – tame
subject, *n.* – matter
subject, *adj.* – liable
subjoin – add (2)
submissive – obedient; tame
submit – yield
subscribe – assent, *v.*
subsidiary – auxiliary
subsist – be
subsistence – living, *n.*
substantiate – confirm
subvert – overturn
succeed – follow (1)
Succession
succinct – short
succour – help
succumb – yield
suffer – bear, *v.* (2); let
suffering – distress
sufficient – enough

suggest – hint
suggestion – touch, *n.*
suit – prayer
suitable – fit, *adj.*
suite – succession
sum – add (1)
summary – short
summon – call, *v.*
sunder – separate
sundry – many
supercilious – proud
superlative – supreme
supervene – follow (1)
supine – inactive
supplicate – beg
support – living, *n.*
Supposed
suppositious – supposed
supposititious – supposed
Supreme
Sure
surge, *n.* – wave
surge, *v.* – rise
surmise – conjecture
surmount – conquer
surpass – exceed
surpassing – supreme
Surprise
surreptitious – secret
survey – see
survive – outlive
susceptible – liable
suspend – defer
suspicion – touch, *n.*; uncertainty
sustenance – food (2); living, *n.*
swarm – multitude
sway – affect
Swear
swift – quick
swindle – cheat, *v.*
Symmetry
sympathetic – consonant
Sympathy (affinity)
sympathy – pity
symptom – mark
System

taciturn – silent
Tact
Tactics
Take (grasp)
take – bring
tale – story
talk, *n.* – speech
talk, *v.* – speak
Talkative
tall – high
Tame
tantalize – worry
tantamount – equal
tardy – slow
tariff – tax
tarry – stay
tart – sour
Taste
taunt – ridicule
Tax, *n.*
Teach
Tear, *v.*
tease – worry
tedious – slow
temerarious – adventurous
temper, *n.* – humour, *n.*
temper, *v.* – moderate
temperament – disposition
temperate – sober
temporal – secular; temporary
Temporary
tenacious – strong
Tendency
tender, *v.* – offer, *v.*
tenet – doctrine
tenor – tendency
tense – stiff
tension – stress
tentative – provisional
tenuous – thin
term – limit, *n.*; word
terminate – close, *v.* (2)
terrible – fearful (2)
terrific – fearful (2)
terrify – frighten
terror– fear, *n.*
terrorize – frighten
test – prove
testify – swear
text – matter
thankful – grateful
theme – matter
theory – hypothesis
therefor – therefore
Therefore
Thick
thieve – rob
Thin
thing – affair
Think
thirst, *v.* – long
thought – idea
Thoughtful
thoughtless – careless
thrash – beat, *v.*
threadbare – trite
Threat
thresh – beat, *v.*
throe – pain
Throw
thrust, *n.* – stress
thrust, *v.* – push
thwart – oppose
tidings – news
Tidy

Time
timely – opportune
tincture – touch, *n.*
tinge – colour, *n.*; touch, *n.*
tint – colour, *n.*
tiny – little
title – claim, *n.*; name
toil – work
token – mark; pledge
tolerant – forbearing
tolerate – bear, *v.* (2)
toll – tax
tongue – language
too – also
topic – matter
torment – afflict
torpid – numb
torsion – stress
tort – injustice
torture, *v.* – afflict
toss – throw
total, *n.* – whole
total, *v.* – add (1)
totter – shake
Touch, *n.* (shade)
touch, *v.* – affect
touching – moving
tough – strong
tour – journey
tow – pull
tower, *v.* – rise
toxin – poison
tractable – obedient
Trade
Traditional
traffic – trade
trail, *v.* – follow (2)
train, *n.* – succession
train, *v.* – point, *v.*; teach
traitorous – treacherous
tranquil – calm
transcend – exceed
transcendent – supreme
Transfer, *v.*
transgression – breach
translucent – clear
transparent – clear
transport, *n.* – ecstasy
transport, *v.* – banish
travail – work
travesty – caricature
Treacherous
treasure, *v.* – appreciate
treat – confer
tremble – shake
trend – tendency
trepidation – fear, *n.*
trespass – breach
tribute – encomium; tax
Trick
trim – tidy
trip – journey
Trite
triumph – victory
Trouble, *v.* (distress)
trouble, *v.* – inconvenience
Truce
truculent – fierce
true – real
truism – commonplace
Trust, *n.*
Truth
try, *v.* – afflict; attempt
tug – pull
tune – melody
Turn, *v.* (1) (revolve)
Turn, *v.* (2) (divert)
twinge – pain
tyrannical – absolute

ultimate – last
umbrage – shade
umpire – judge, *n.*
unassailable – invincible
Unbelief
unbounded – infinite
unceasing – everlasting
Uncertainty
uncommon – rare
uncommunicative – silent
unconcerned – indifferent
unconquerable – invincible
unctuous – fulsome
under – below
underneath – below
Understand
understanding – reason, *n.* (2)
undulation – wave
uneducated – ignorant
unerring – infallible
uneven – odd; rough
unfeigned – sincere
unfruitful – sterile
ungodly – irreligious
ungovernable – unruly
unimpassioned – sober
uninterested – indifferent
union – alliance
universe – earth
unlearned – ignorant
unnatural – irregular
unproductive – sterile
unreasonable – irrational
unruffled – cool
Unruly
unsettle – disorder
untruth – lie, *n.*
untruthful – dishonest
upon – above
upright – good
uprising – rebellion
upset – overturn

woe – sorrow
womanish – female, *adj.*
womanly – female, *adj.*
Wonder
wonderment – wonder
wont – habit
Word
Work, *n.* (toil)
work – act, *v.* (1)
world – earth
Worry, *v.*
worry, *n.* – care
Worth
wrangle – quarrel, *n.*
wrath – anger, *n.*
wrathful – angry
Writer
Writhe
Wrong, *v.* (oppress)
wrong, *n.* – injustice
wrong, *adj.* – bad (2); false

yarn – story
yearly – annual
yearn – long
Yield, *v.* (submit)
yield, *v.* – bear, *v.* (1)
yoke – couple
Youth (adolescence)
Youthful

zany – fool (2)
zealot – enthusiast